Tori Amos
for fingerstyle guitar with tablature

Project editor: Ed Lozano
Arrangements for publication by Marcel Robinson

This book Copyright © 1999 by Amsco Publications,
A Division of Music Sales Corporation, New York

All rights reserved. No part of this book may be
reproduced in any form or by any electronic or mechanical means,
including information storage and retrieval systems,
without permission in writing from the publisher.

Order No. AM 948618
US International Standard Book Number: 0.8256.1694.8
UK International Standard Book Number: 0.7119.7580.9

Exclusive Distributors:
Music Sales Corporation
257 Park Avenue South, New York, NY 10010 USA
Music Sales Limited
8/9 Frith Street, London W1V 5TZ England
Music Sales Pty. Limited
120 Rothschild Street, Rosebery, Sydney, NSW 2018, Australia

Printed in the United States of America by
Vicks Lithograph and Printing Corporation

Amsco Publications
New York/London/Paris/Sydney/Copenhagen/Madrid

notes about the recording

The enclosed CD is an educational tool. Each song has been recorded to demonstrate the arrangement in a concise manner. Be sure to follow the notes below as you study the music. The printed arrangements follow the original recordings.

Icicle
Start at the bottom of page 8 (𝄋), continue to page 16, and fade.

Silent All These Years
Take the second ending and continue to the end.

Pretty Good Year
There is no repeat on the Intro.

Caught a Lite Sneeze
Go to page 45 measure 3, proceed to page 48 (*Coda* ⊕), and begin fade on page 50.

China
Take the second ending, then *D.S. al Coda* ⊕ to end.

Cornflake Girl
Take the second ending on Intro and continue to end (with no repeats).

Little Earthquakes
Fade out at bottom of page 72 and fade in at bottom of page 78 (play to *D.S. al Fine* with no repeats).

In the Springtime of His Voodoo
Begin from the verse, continue to page 85, and fade.

Past the Mission
Begin on page 95, continue to *D.S.*, and fade.

Blood Roses
Play from the beginning to *D.S.* (with no repeats) and fade.

Black Swan
Fade on page 119.

Jackie's Strength
Begin fade at bottom of page 127.

Spark
Begin on page 136 (at the repeat sign), continue to page 139 (skip first and second endings), continue from the bottom of page 141 to page 143 (skip last system on 143 and skip first system on 144), continue from second system on 144 to end.

Black-Dove (January)
Play up to *D.S.* and fade.

Talula
Play up to *D.S.* and fade.

Winter
Begin at the bottom of page 170 (repeat sign), take first ending, and fade.

contents

Title	Page	CD Track
Black-Dove (January)	146	14
Black Swan	114	11
Blood Roses	102	10
Caught a Lite Sneeze	40	4
China	54	5
Cornflake Girl	60	6
Icicle	7	1
In the Springtime of His Voodoo	81	8
Jackie's Strength	122	12
Little Earthquakes	66	7
Past the Mission	92	9
Pretty Good Year	27	3
Silent All These Years	18	2
Spark	134	13
Talula	158	15
Winter	170	16

Explanation of Symbols and Techniques

Right-Hand and Left-Hand Fingers

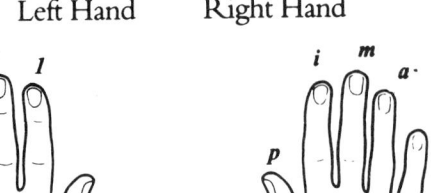

Tablature

Tablature is written on six lines. Each line represents a string of the guitar.

The 1st string (①) is the highest string; the 6th string (⑥) is the lowest.

Frets and open strings are indicated by numbers:

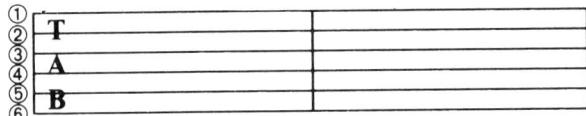

open 1st string (①)   3rd fret, 2nd string   D chord

Hammeron:

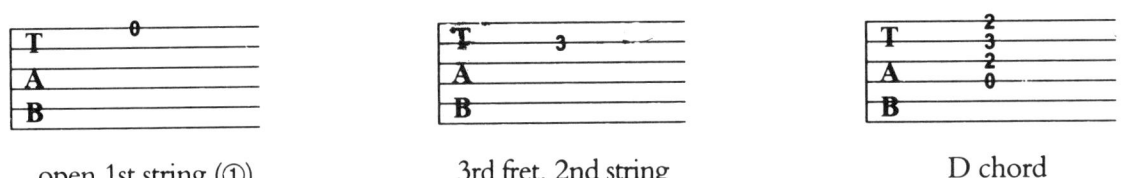

Indicates a hammeron with the left-hand finger hammering onto the second note. Only the first note is struck by the right hand.

Pulloff:

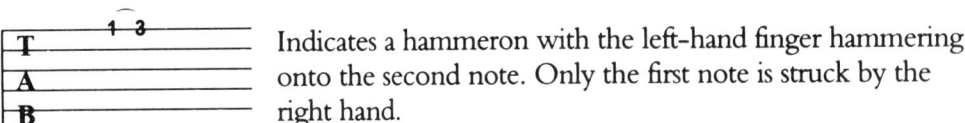

Indicates a pulloff. The right hand strikes the first note and the left-hand finger pulls away to sound the second note. Only the first note is struck by the right hand.

Rhythm

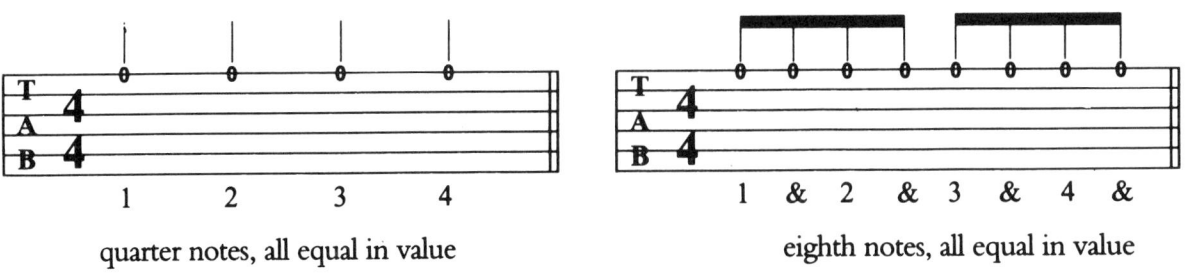

quarter notes, all equal in value   eighth notes, all equal in value

Ties:

A tie indicates that only the 1st note is played and is held for the value of the 2nd note.

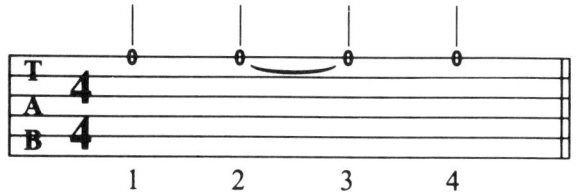

Beat 2 is played and held through the value of beat 3. Beat 3 is not played.

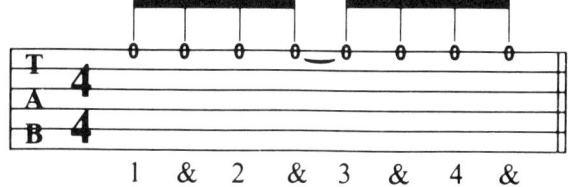

The note on beat 3 is not played.

Strumming Patterns

↑ Denotes a downstroke. A downstroke is executed by striking all of the strings indicated, from low notes to high, with the nail of the index finger.

↓ Denotes an upstroke. An upstroke is a lighter stroke executed by touching only 1, 2, or 3 strings of the chord, from high notes to low, with the nail of the index finger.

Basic Strumming Patterns

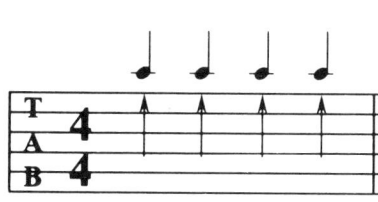

even downstrokes on a D chord

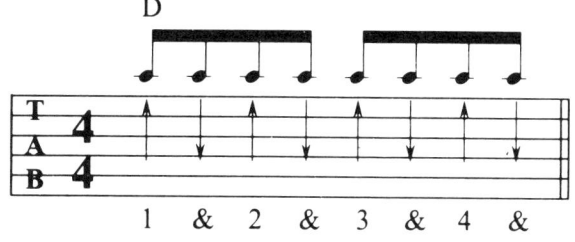

even upstrokes and downstrokes on a D chord

Rhumba or Syncopated Bass Pattern

using open strings:

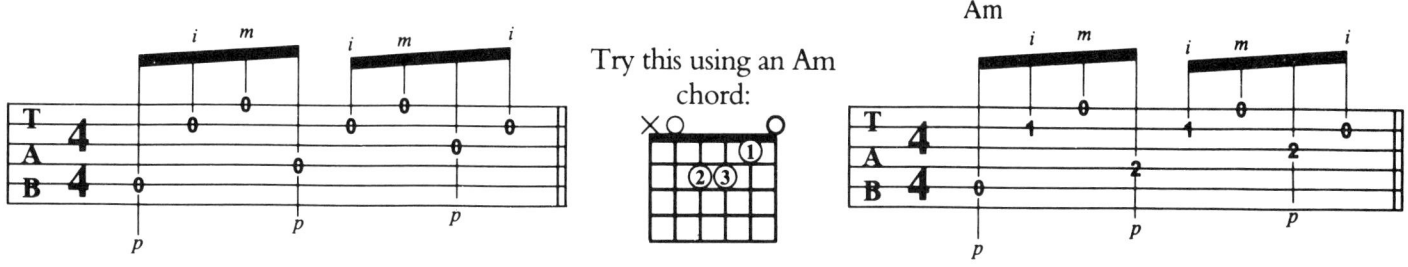

Try this using an Am chord:

Fingerpicking Patterns

As a general rule the thumb *(p)* plays the bottom three (bass) strings with an occasional move to the 3rd string. The fingers *(i, m,* and *a)* play the top three (treble) strings.

simple arpeggio using open strings:

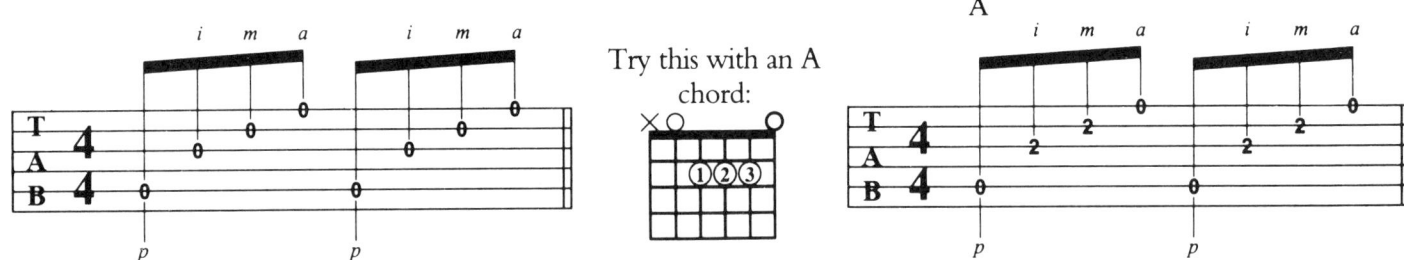

¾ time arpeggio using open strings:

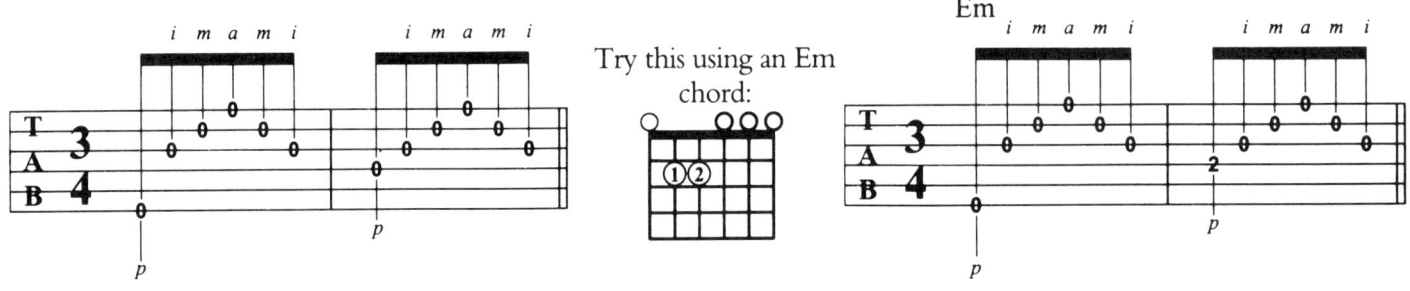

Travis Pick

In the next three examples the thumb and middle finger strike together. The remainder of the picking is exactly the same.

using open strings:

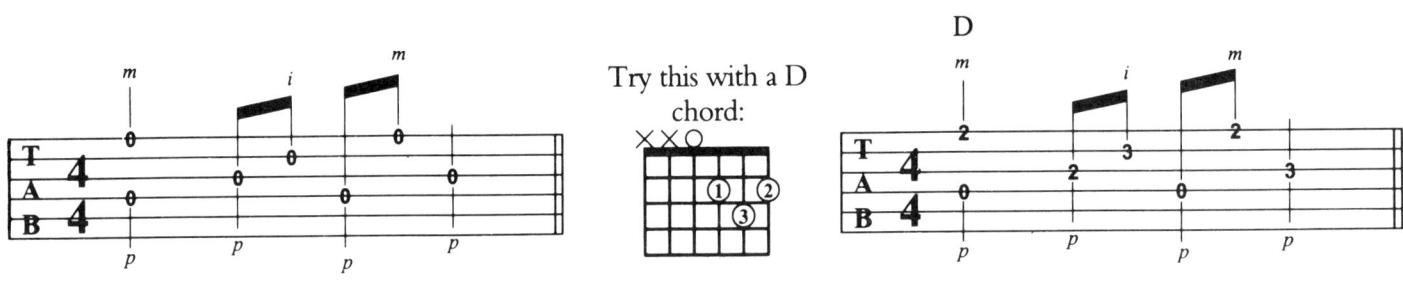

using open strings:

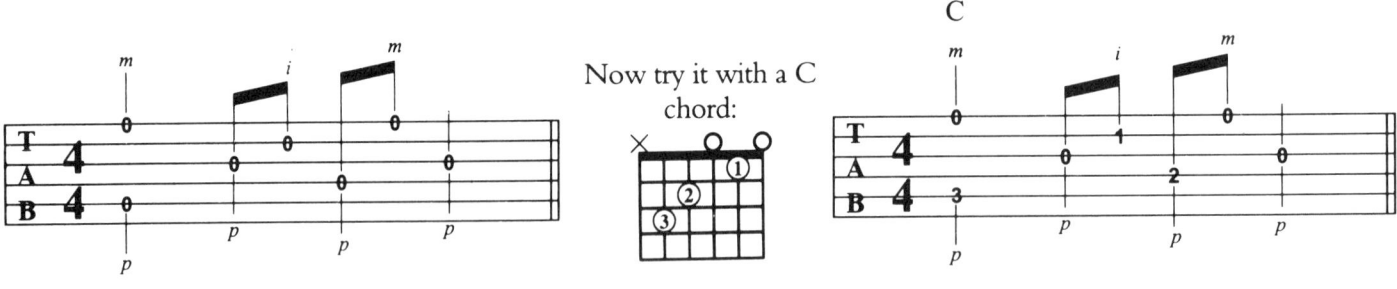

using open strings:

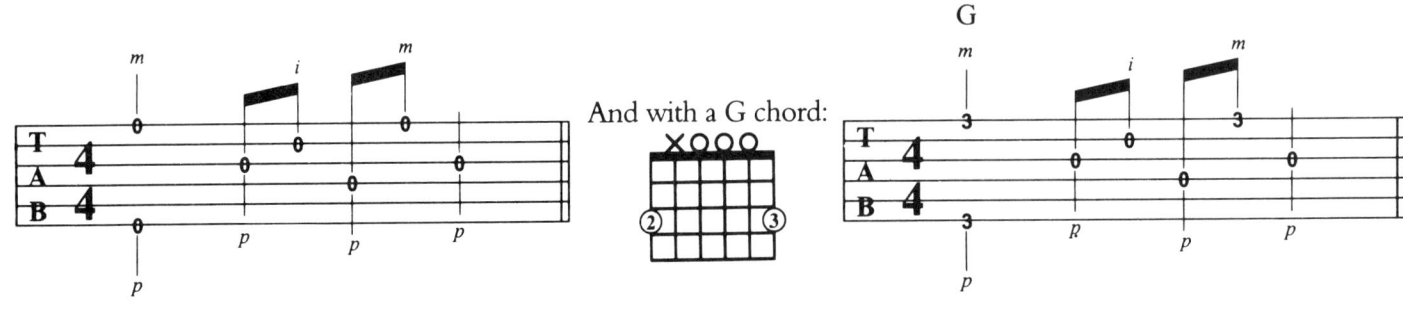

Icicle
Words and Music by Tori Amos

melody note for voice

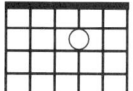

Gently flowing

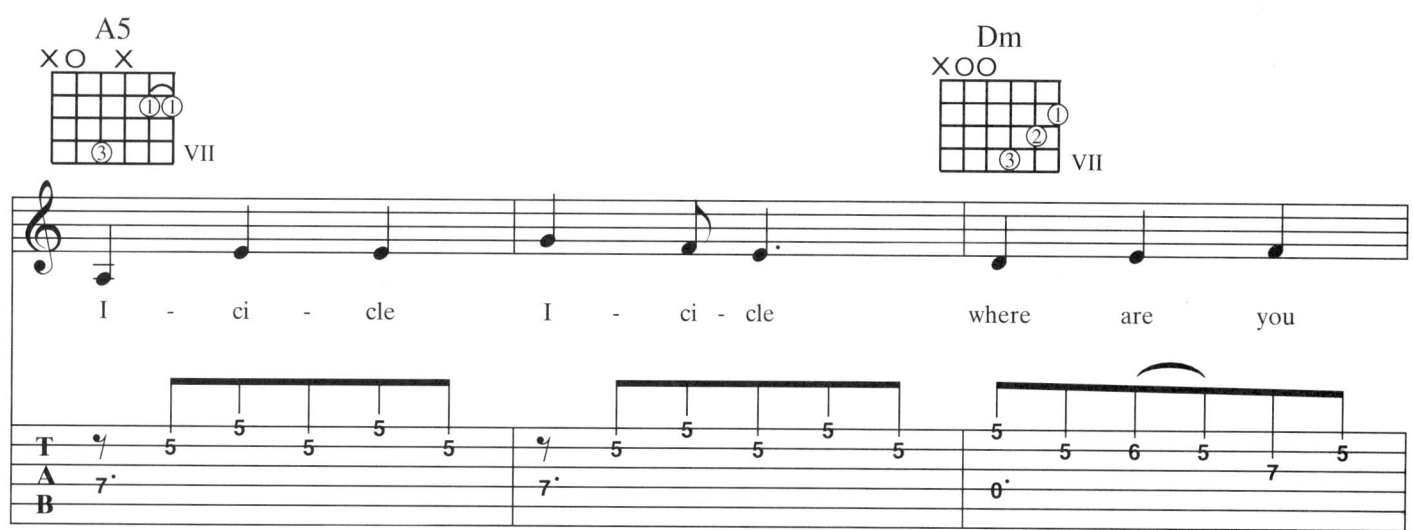

I - ci - cle   I - ci - cle   where are you

Copyright © 1993 Sword and Stone Publishing Inc. (ASCAP)
International Copyright Secured. All Rights Reserved.

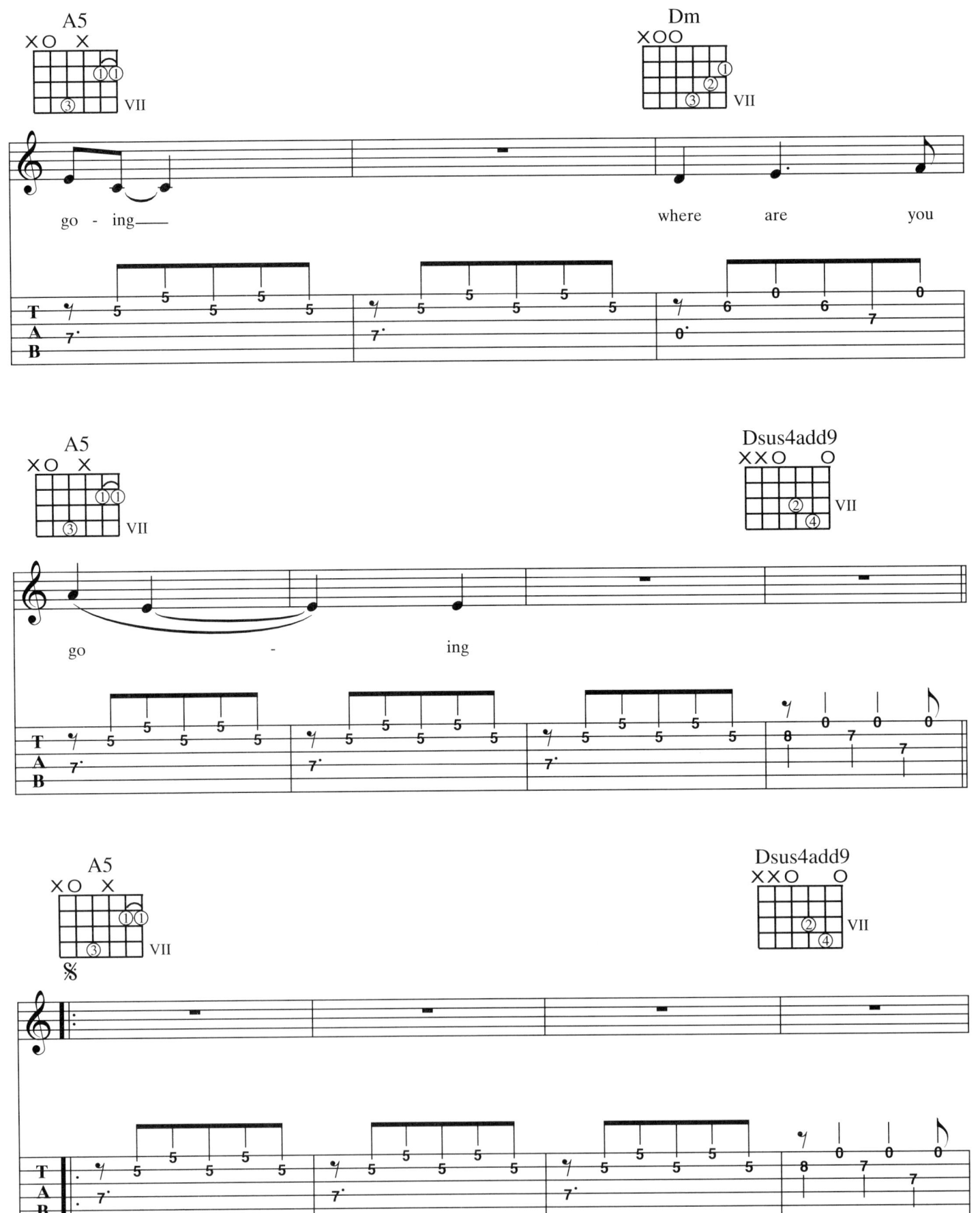

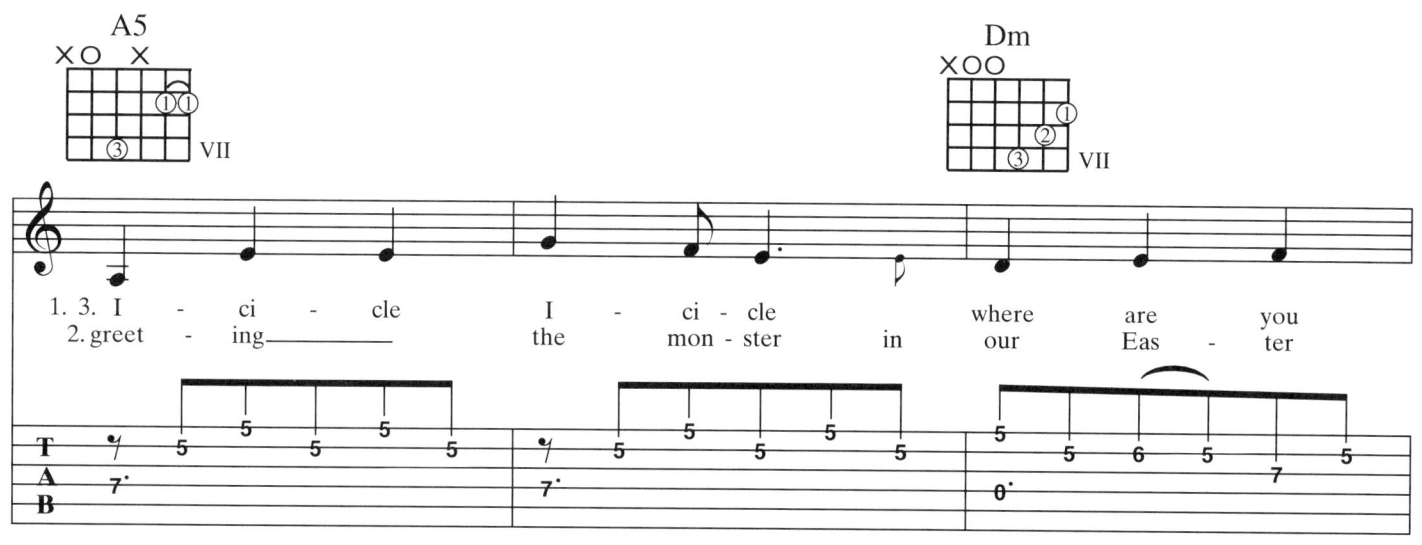
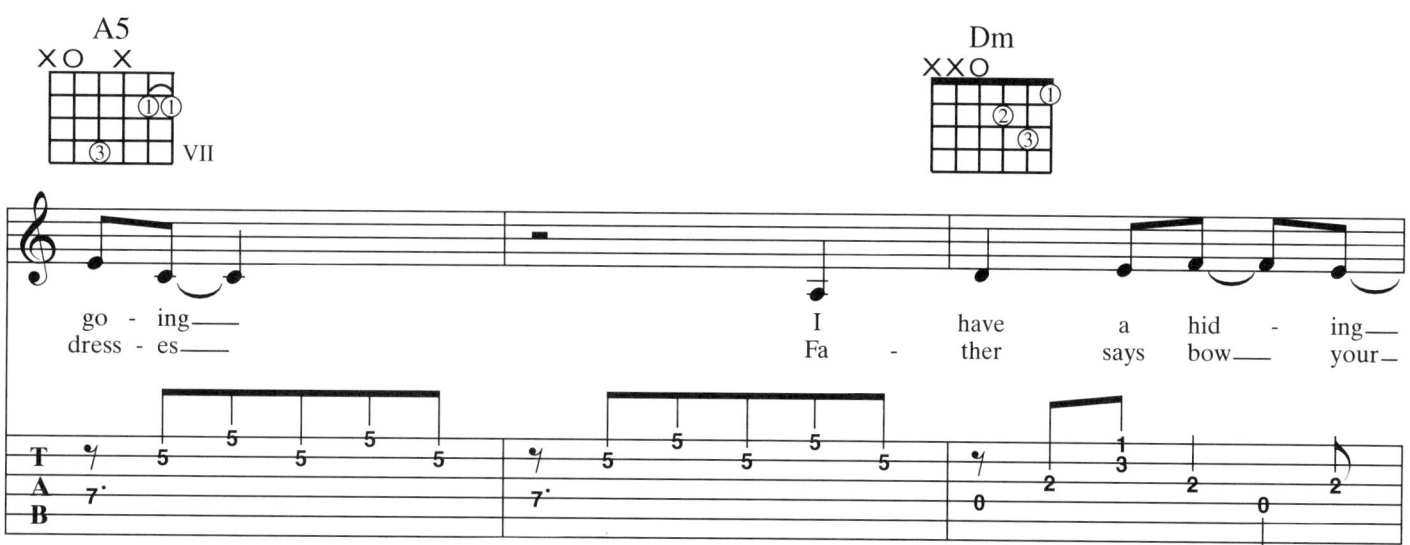
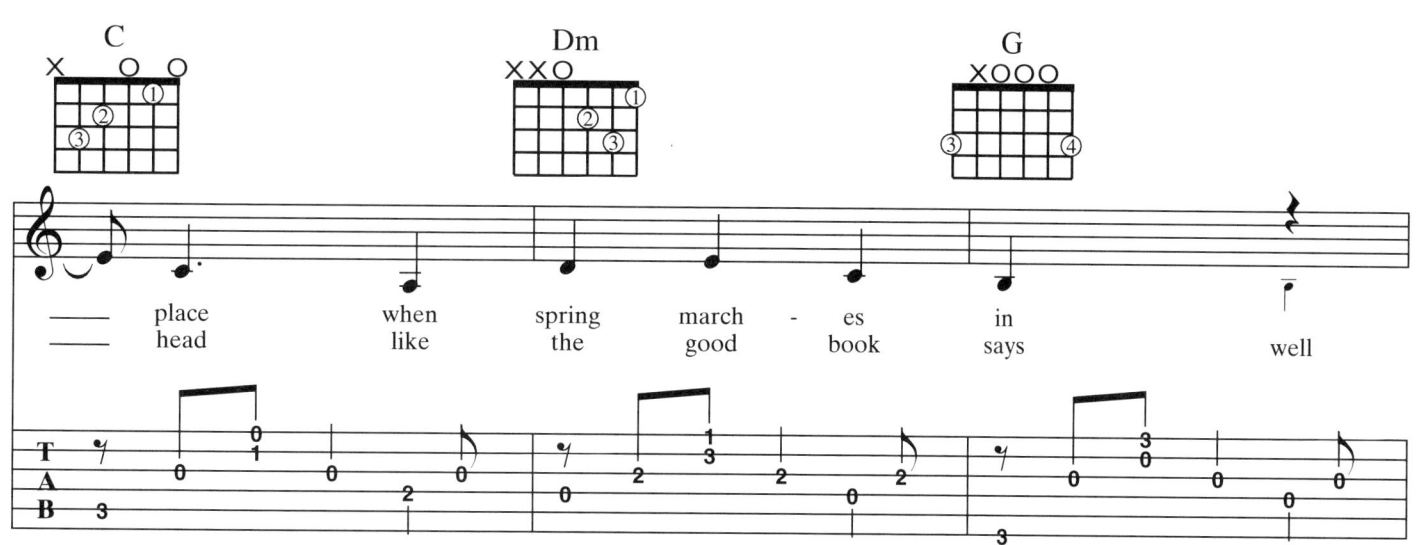

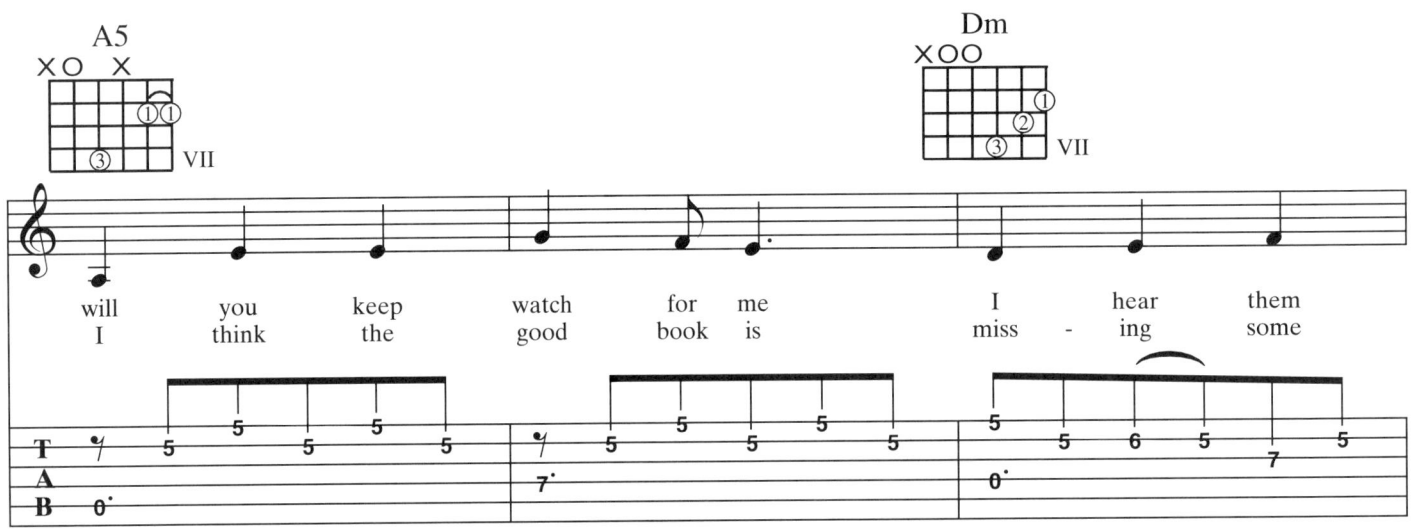
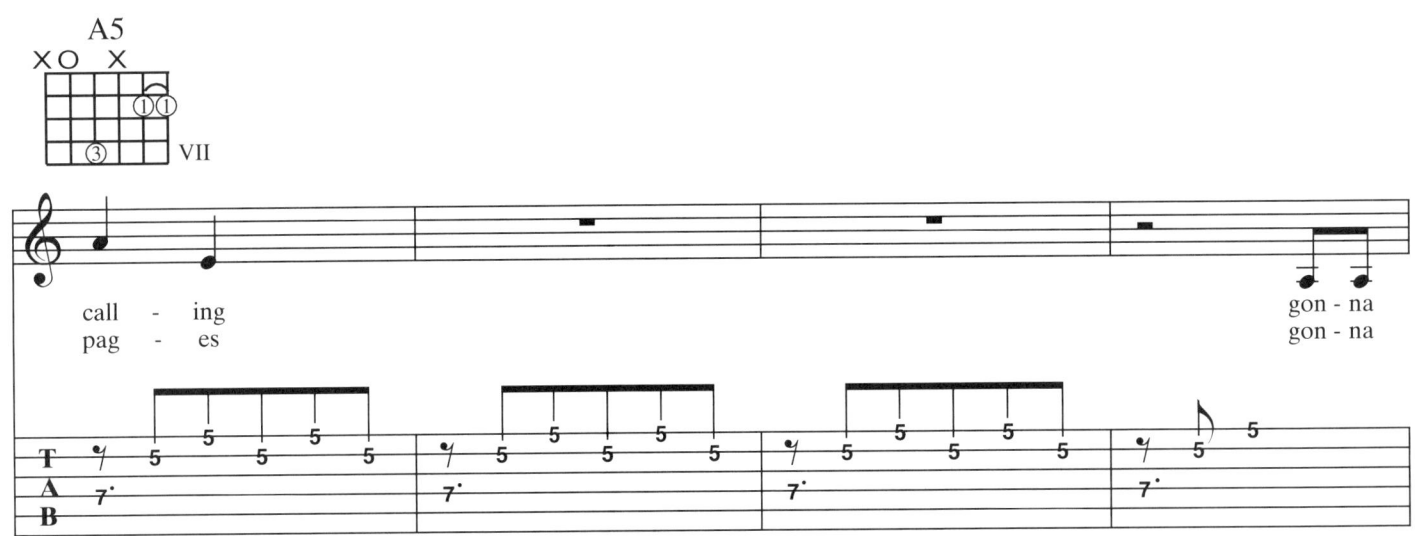
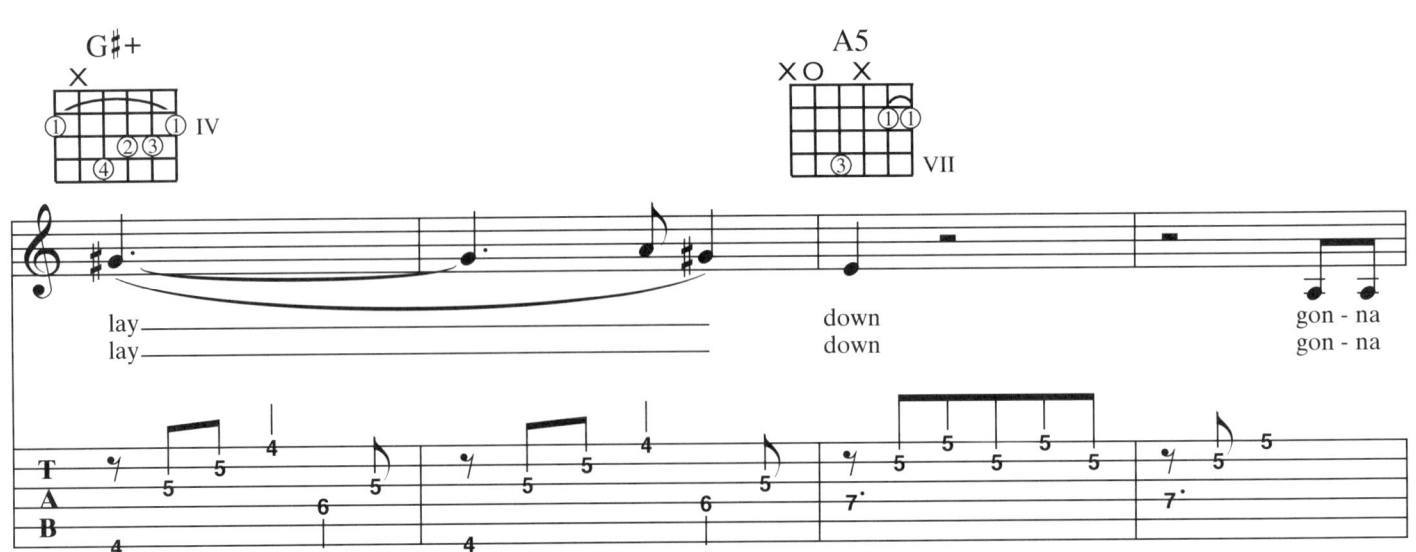

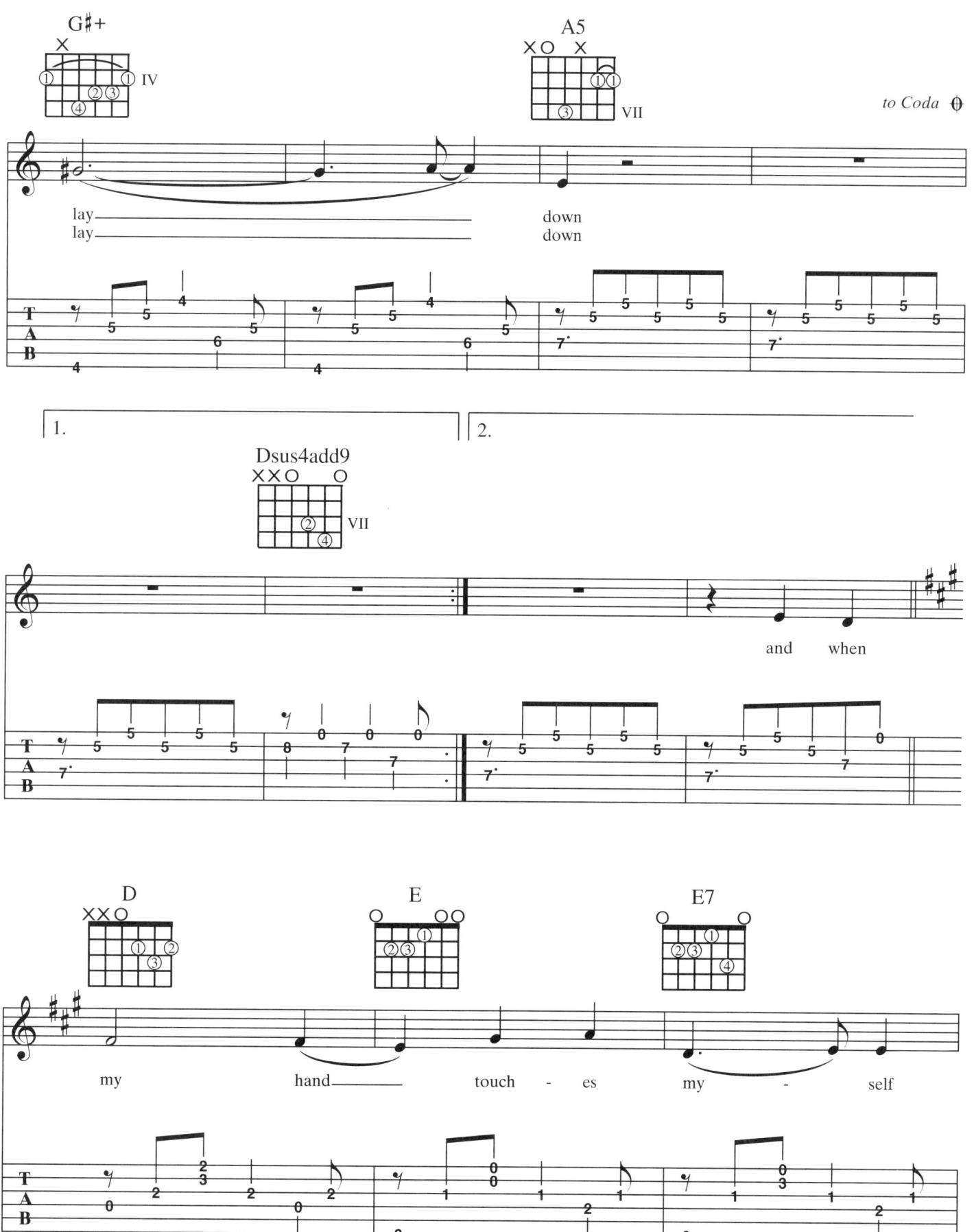

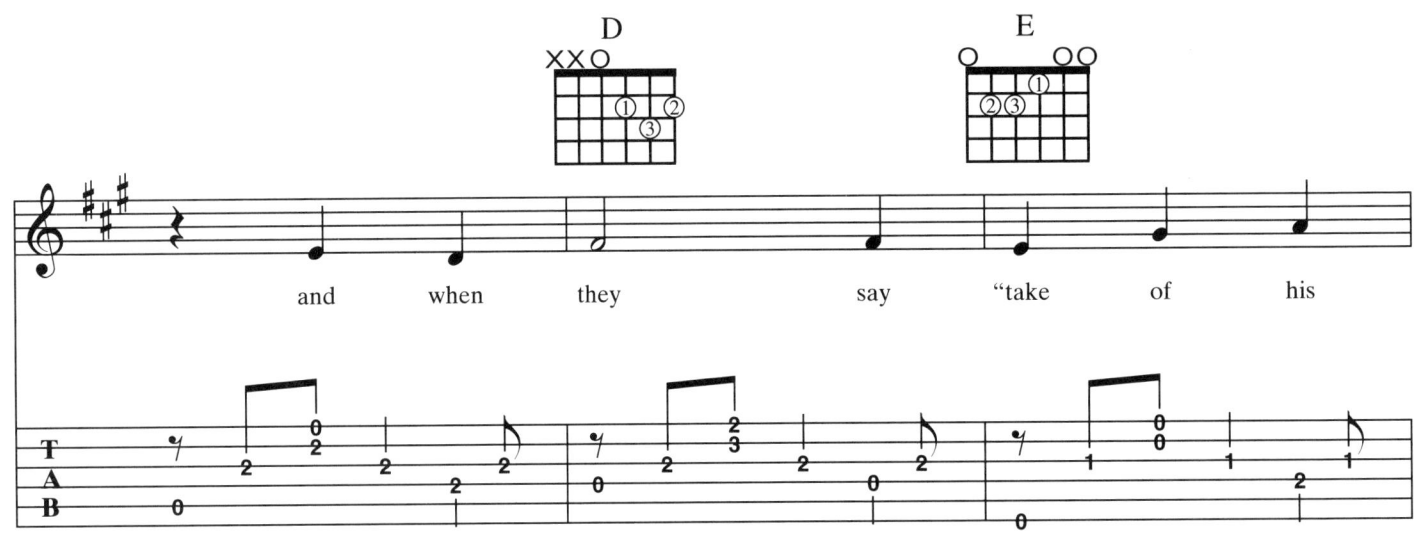

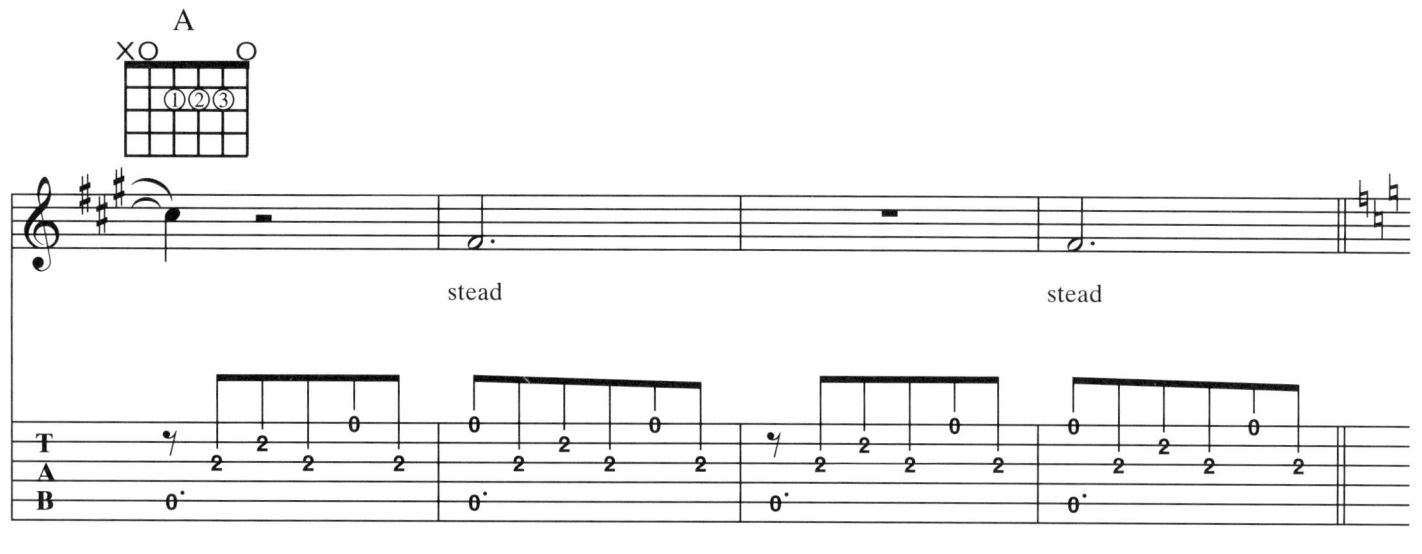
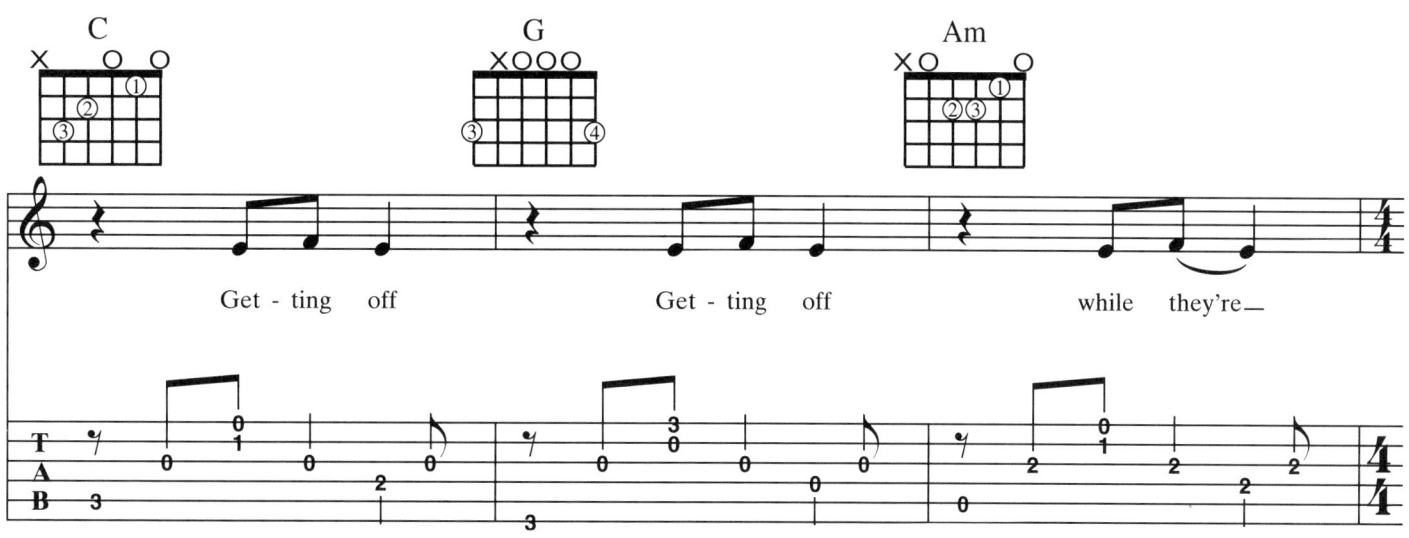
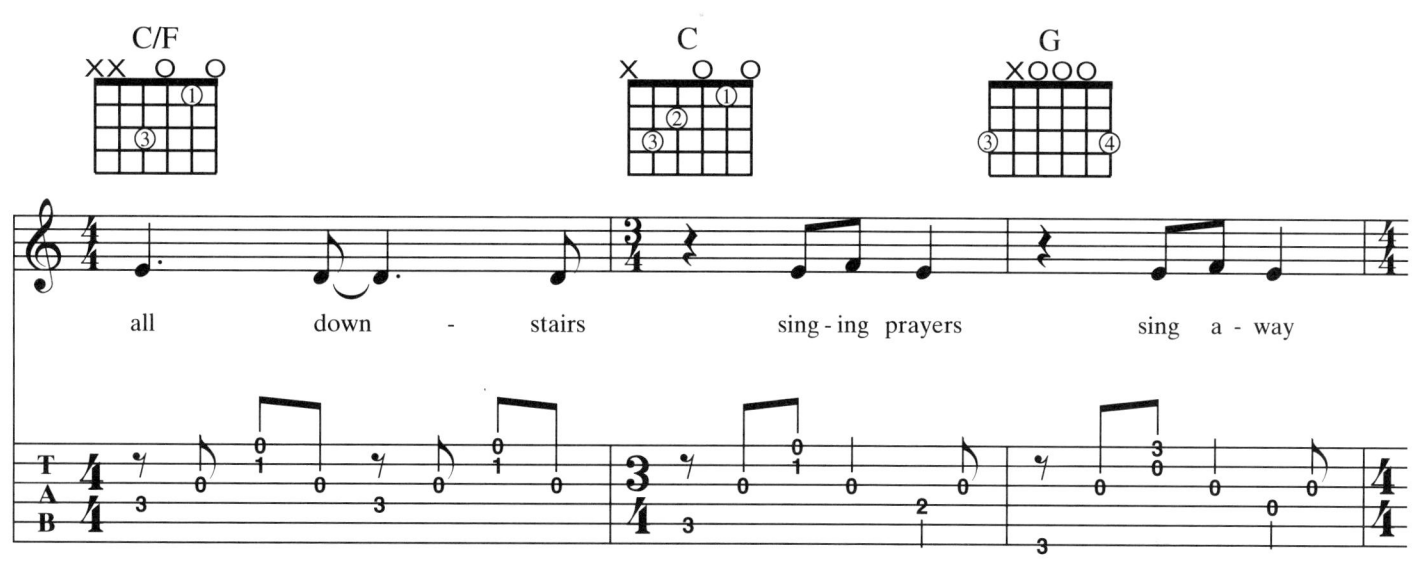

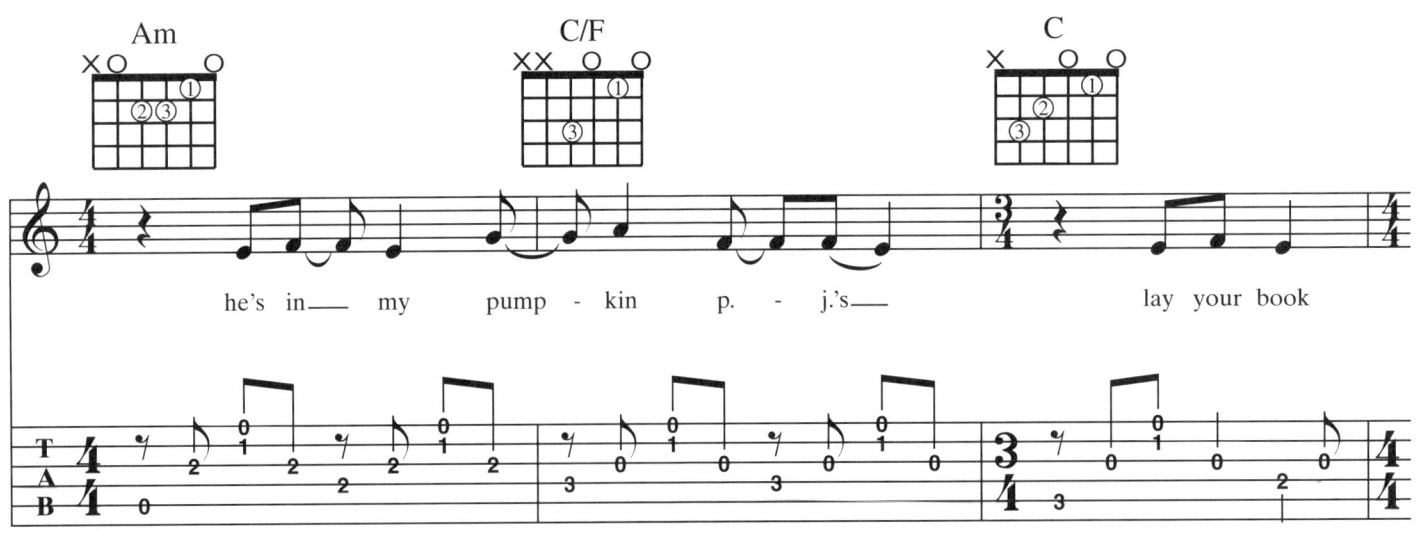
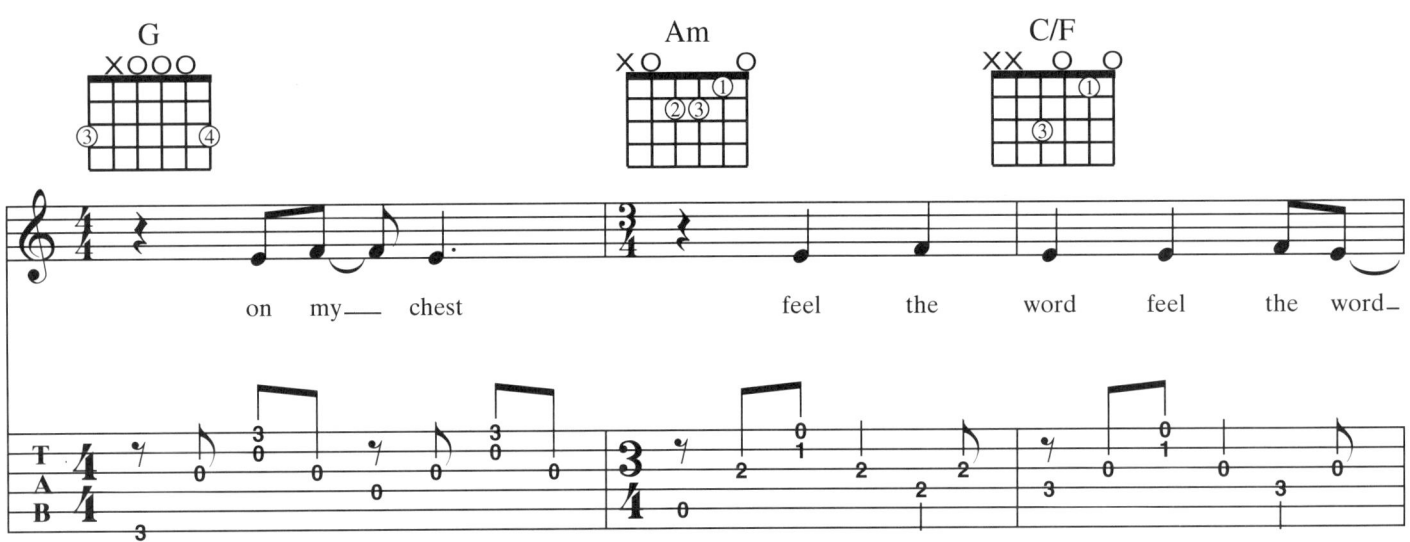
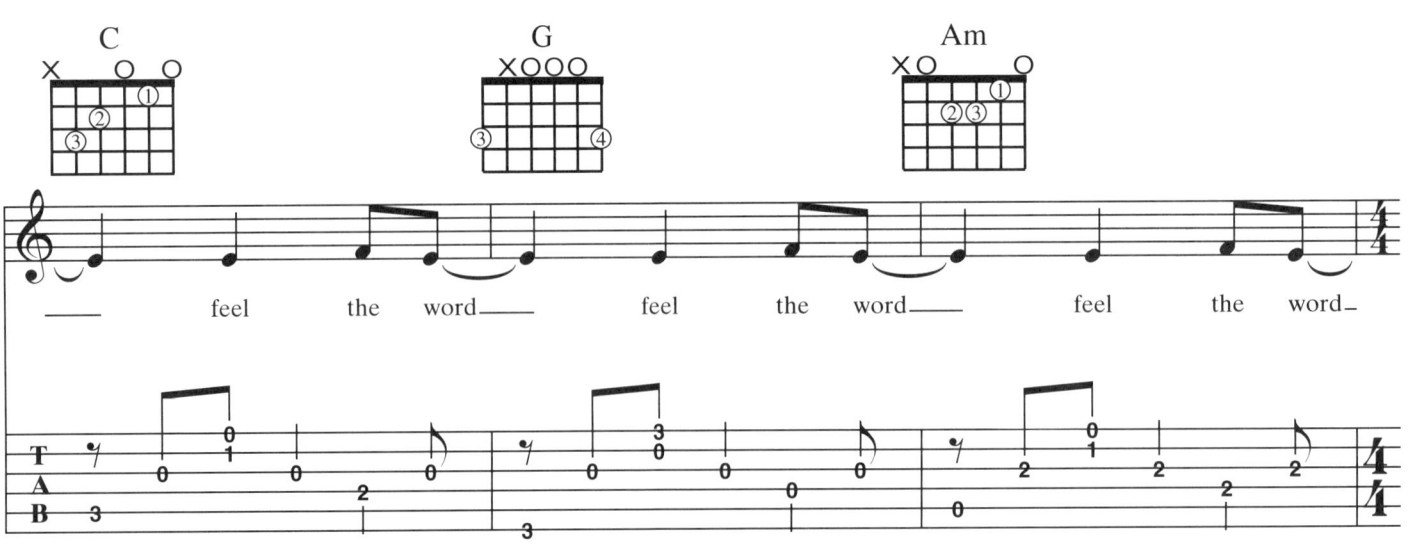

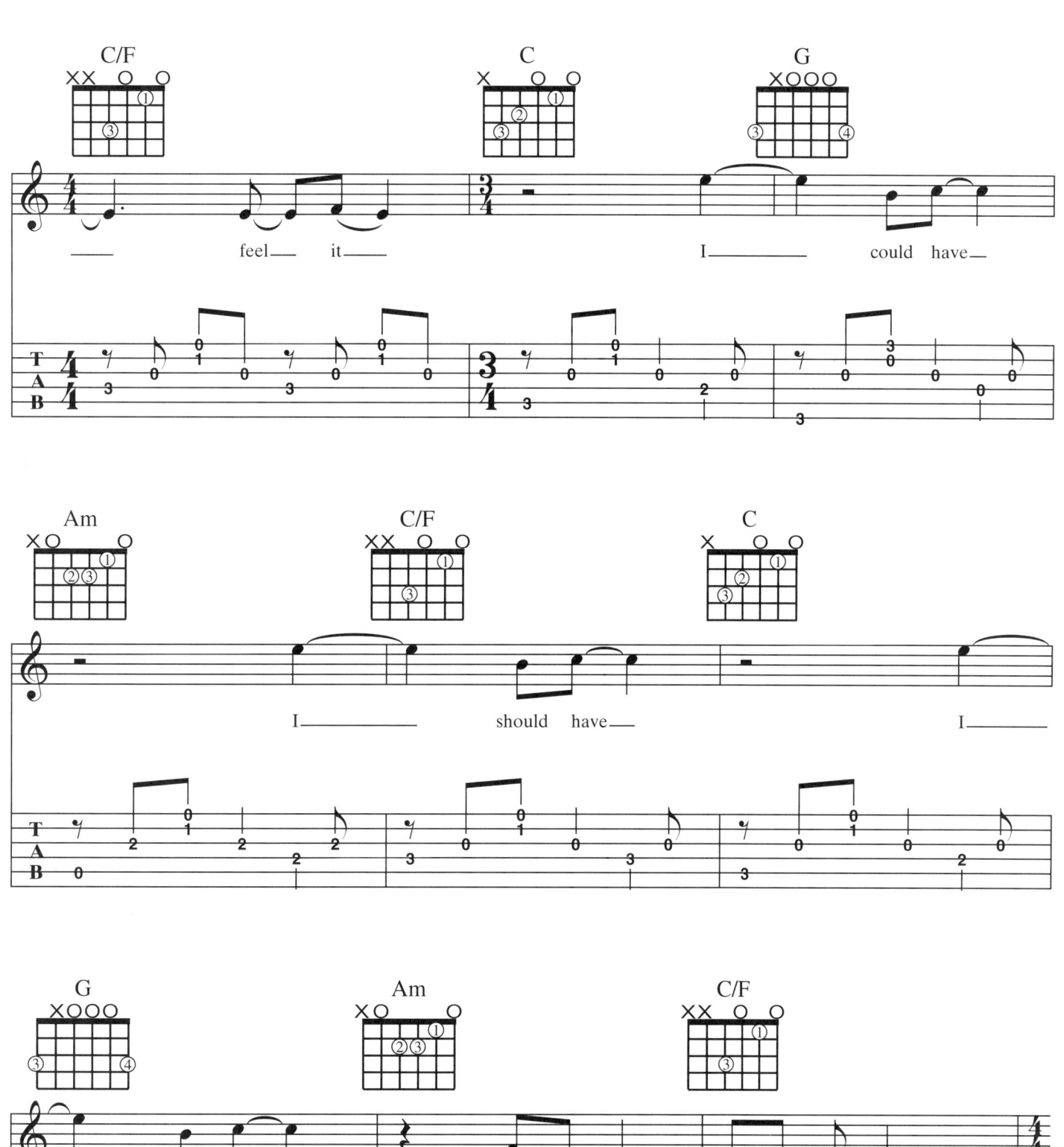

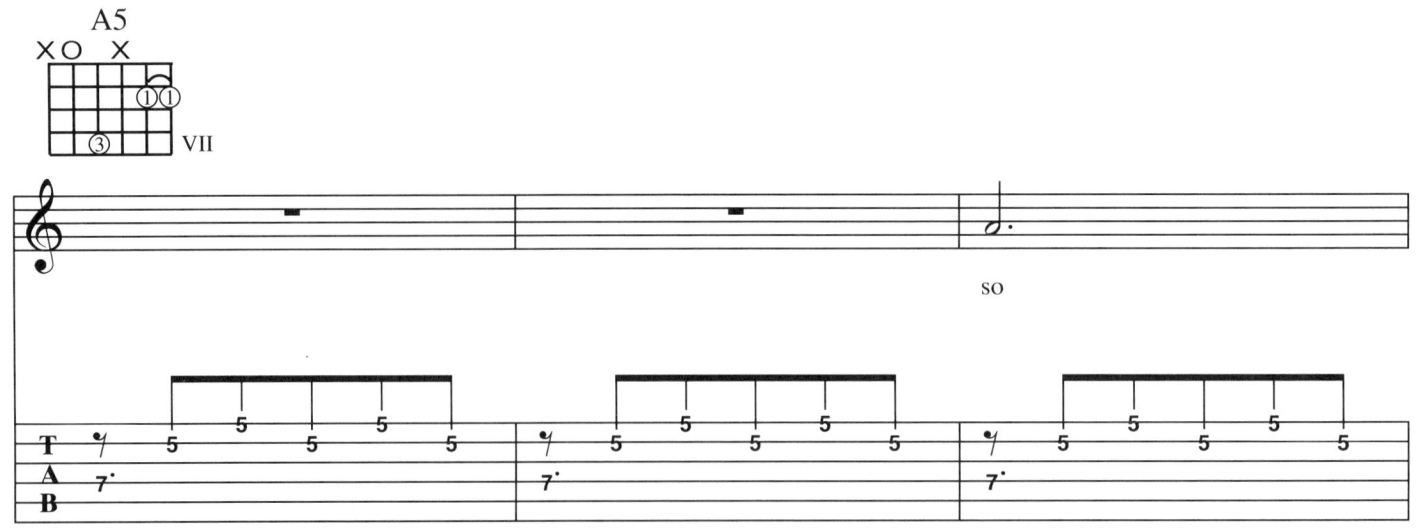

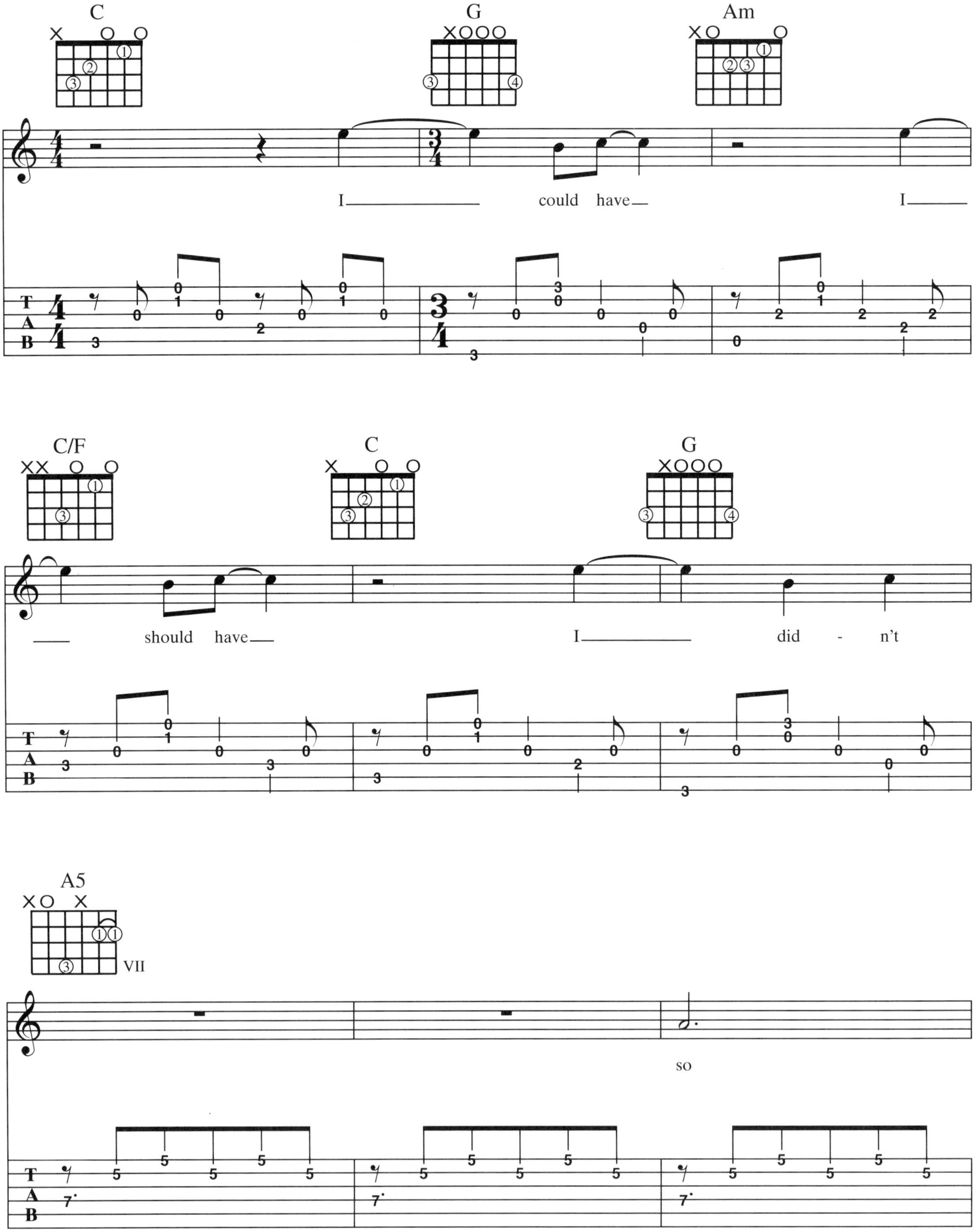
C
G
Am
I could have I
C/F
C
G
should have I did - n't
A5
VII
so

Dsus4add9
VII
D.S. al Coda
G♯+
IV
A5
VII
Coda
lay
down
I'm gon - na
Fmaj7
VIII
A5
lay
down

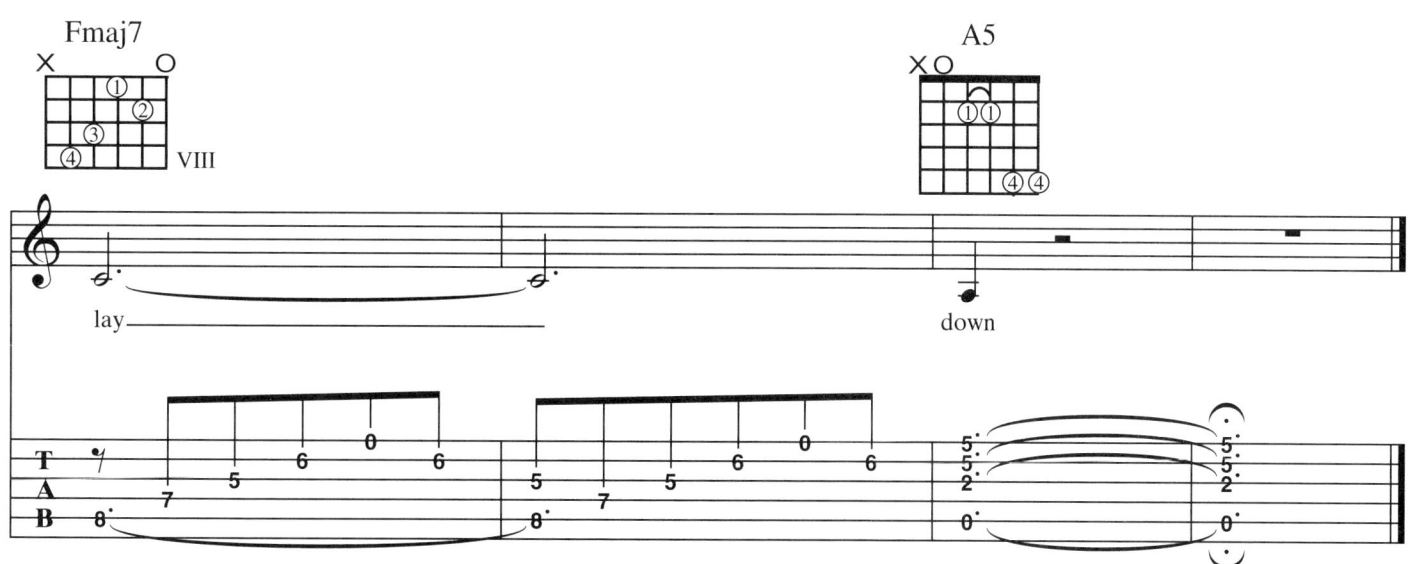

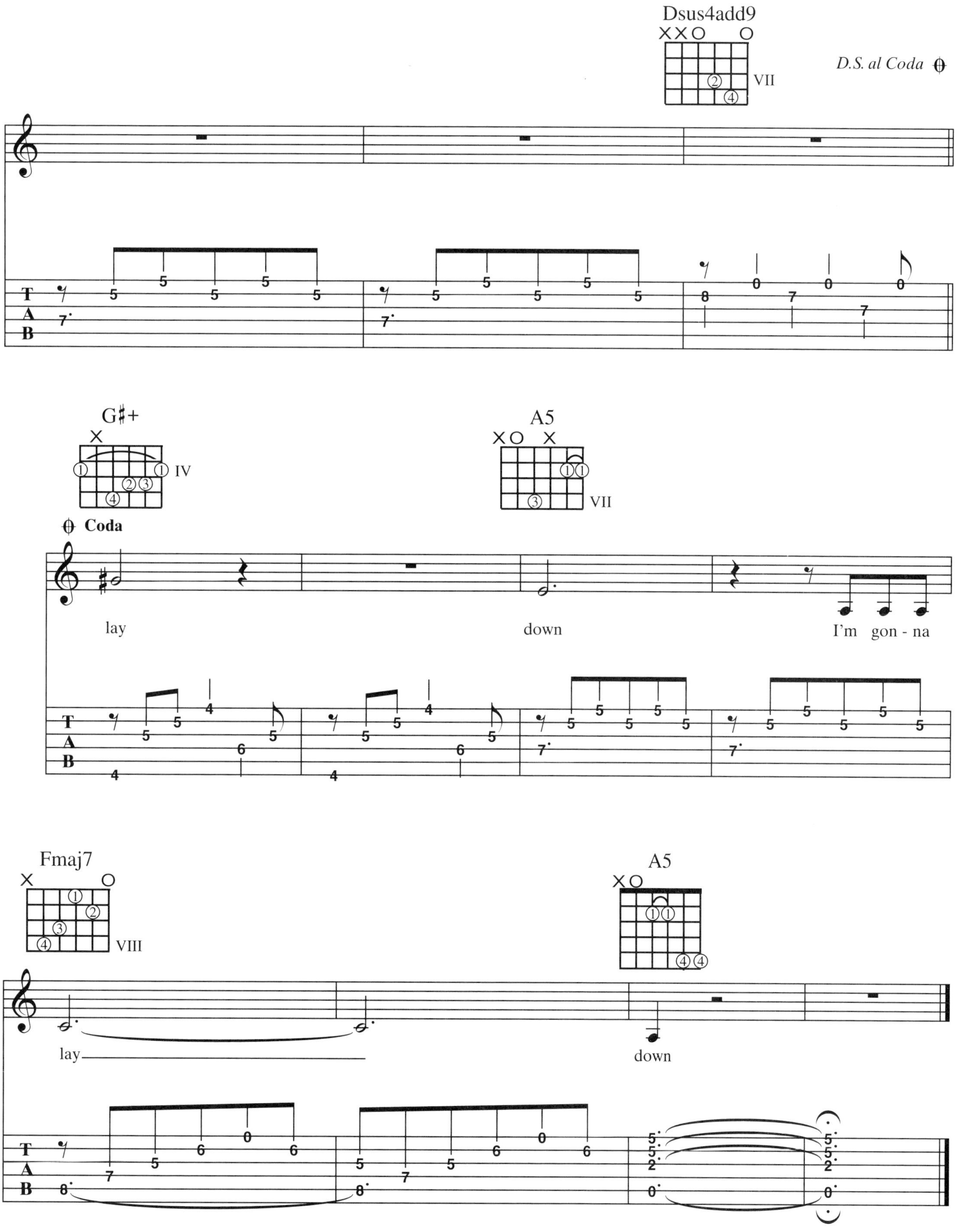

18

Silent All These Years
Words and Music by Tori Amos

melody note for voice
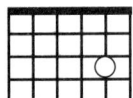

Moderately flowing

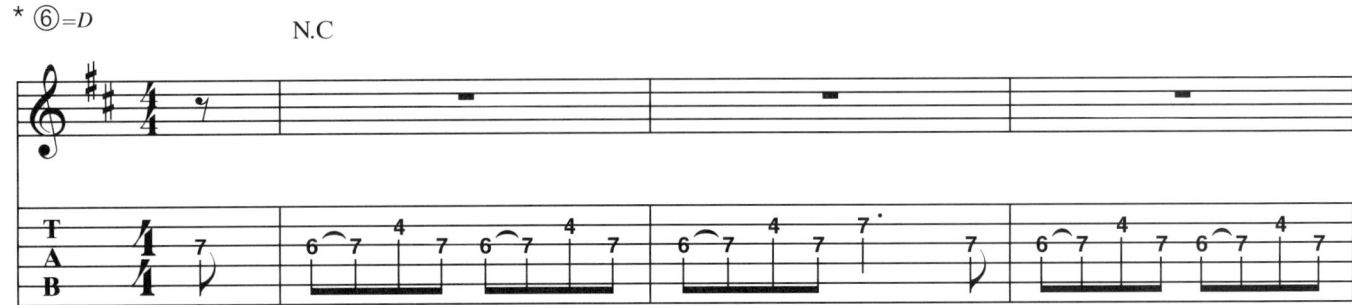

*Capo at second fret. Actual key: E
Drop D: ⑥D ⑤A ④D ③G ②B ①E

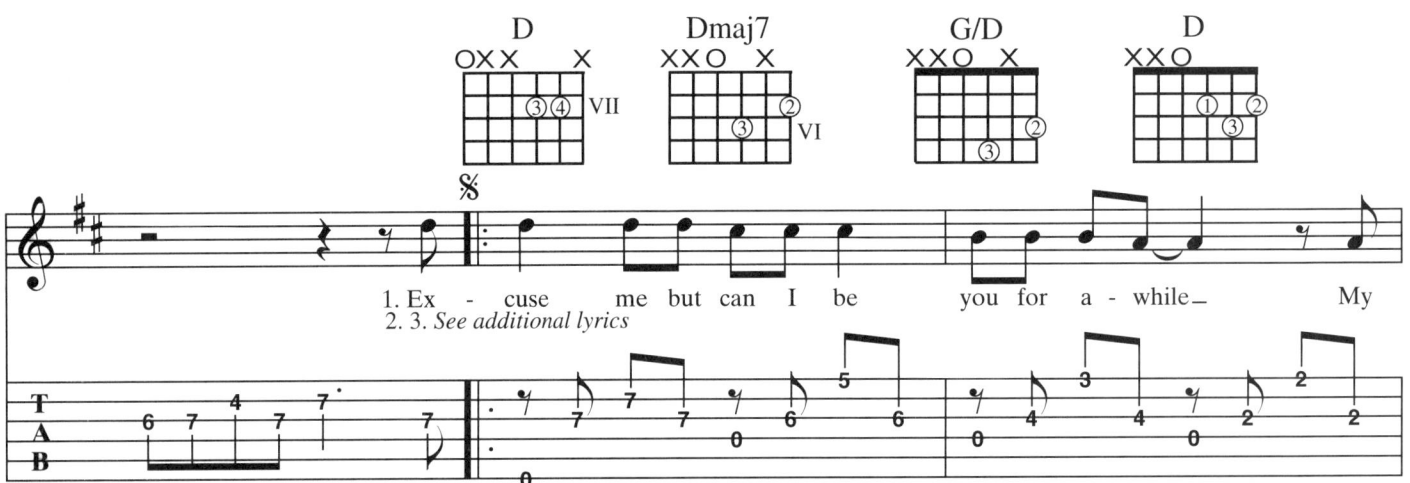

1. Ex - cuse me but can I be you for a - while My
2. 3. *See additional lyrics*

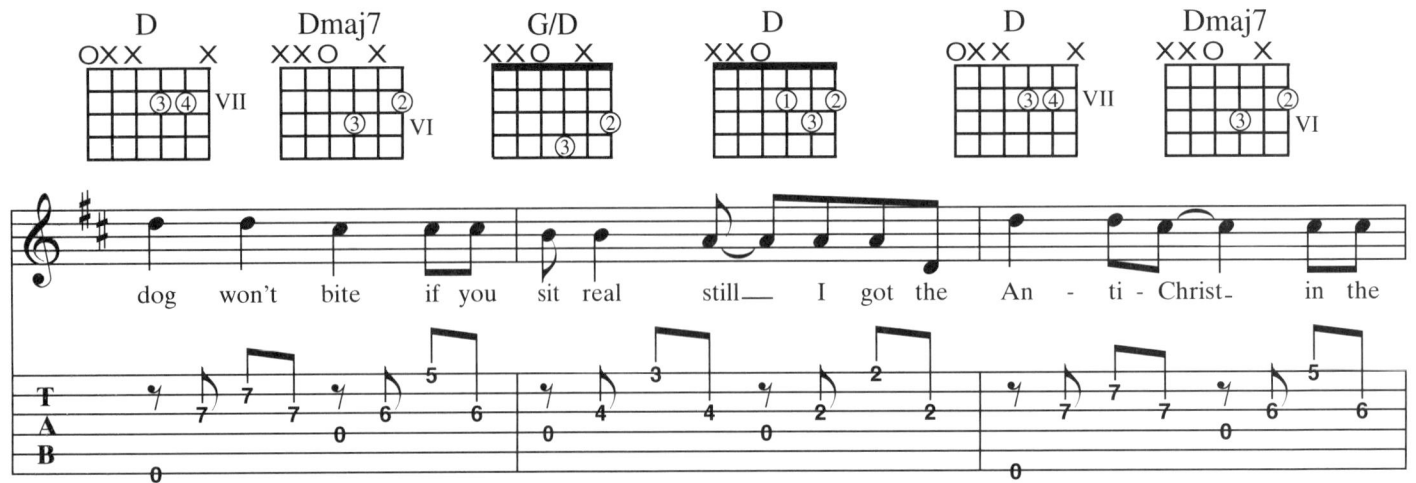

dog won't bite if you sit real still I got the An - ti - Christ in the

Copyright © 1990 Sword and Stone Publishing Inc. (ASCAP)
International Copyright Secured. All Rights Reserved.

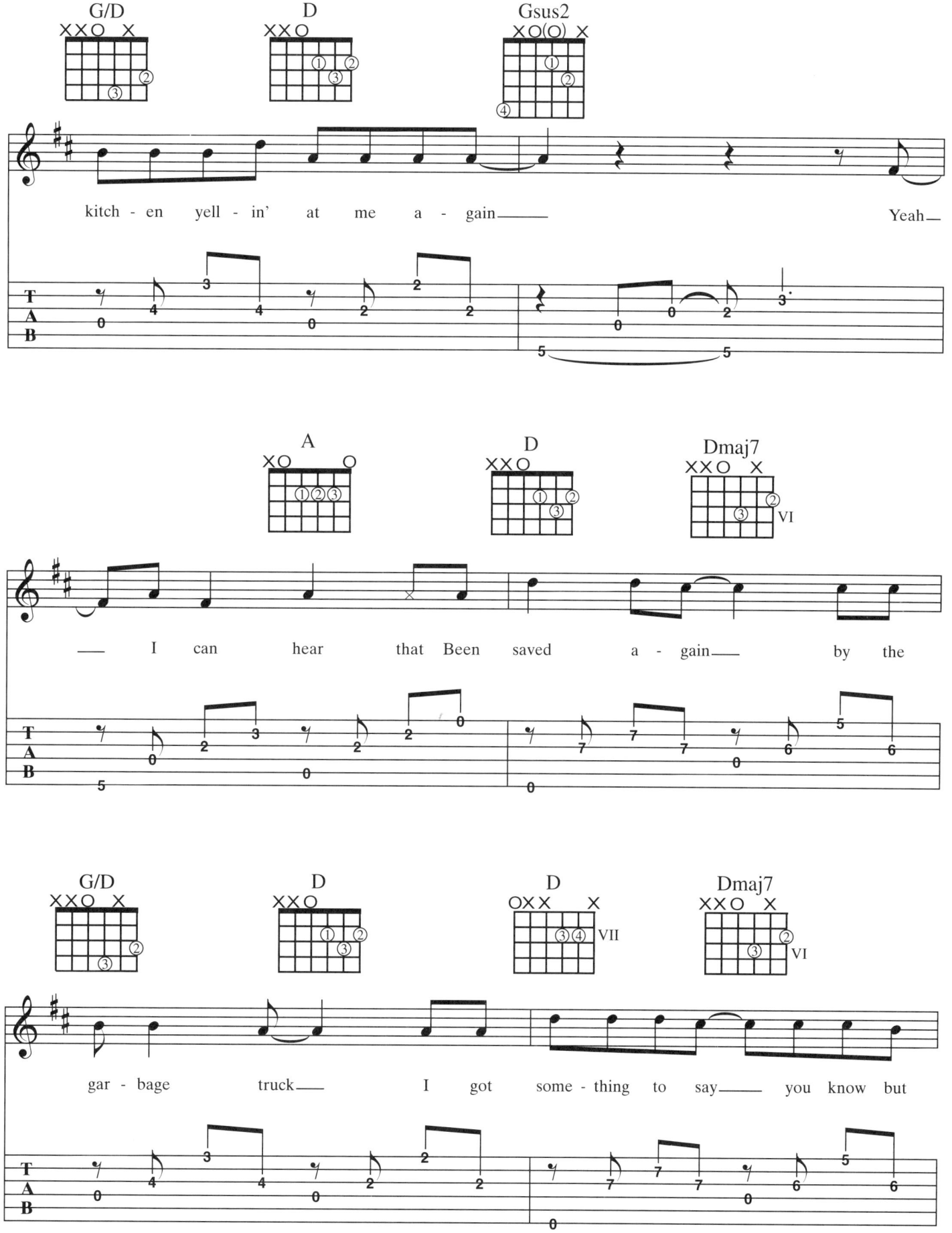

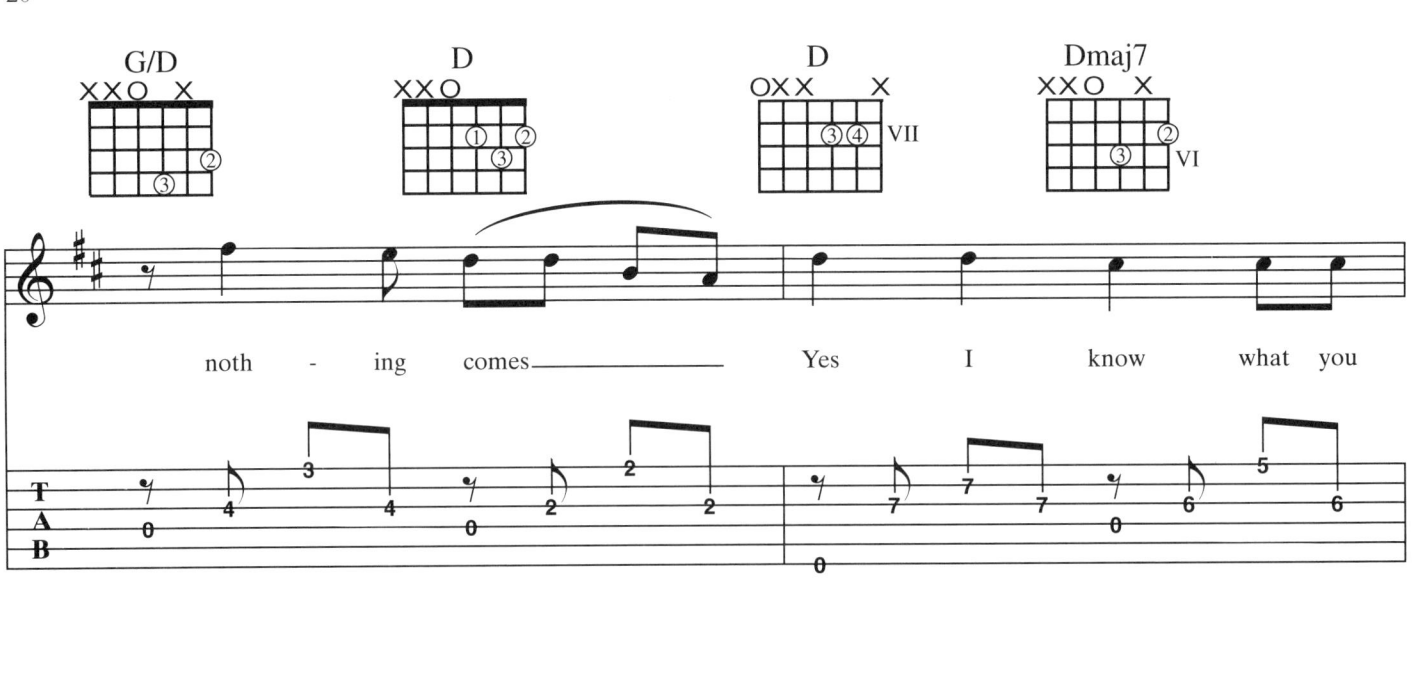
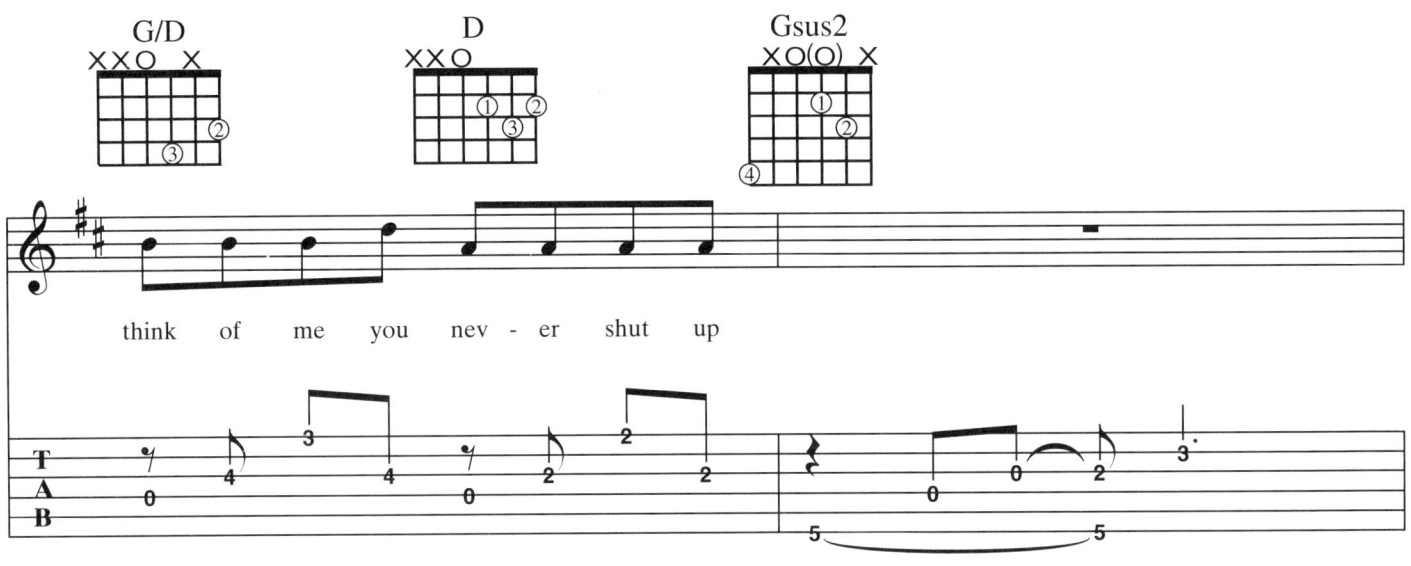
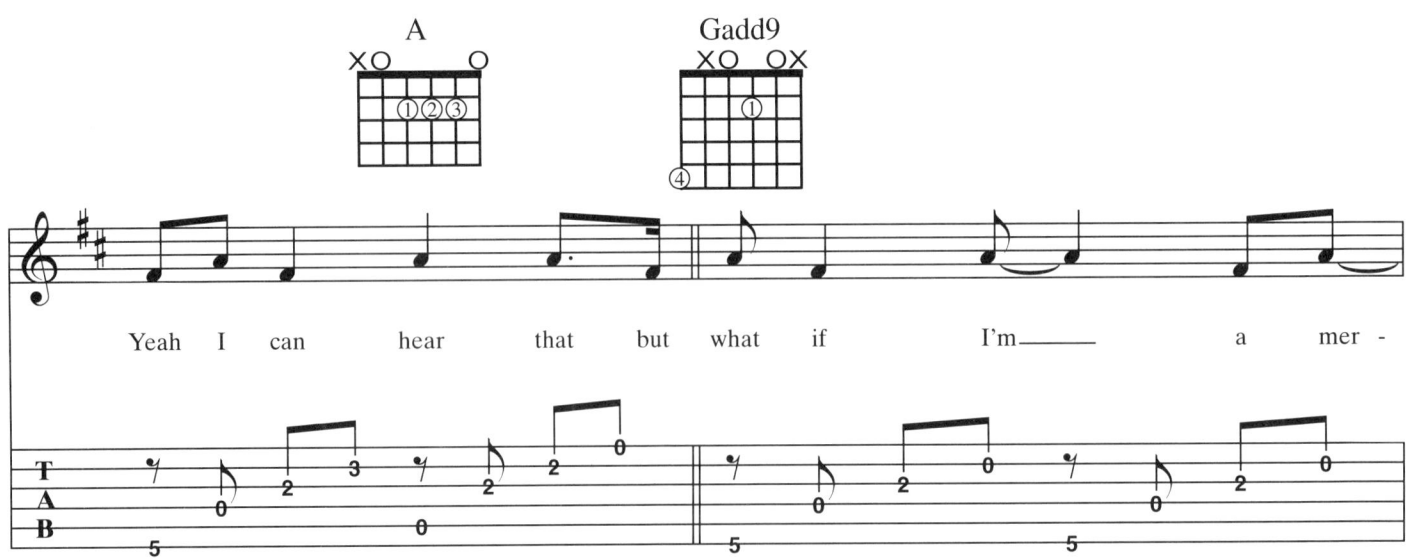

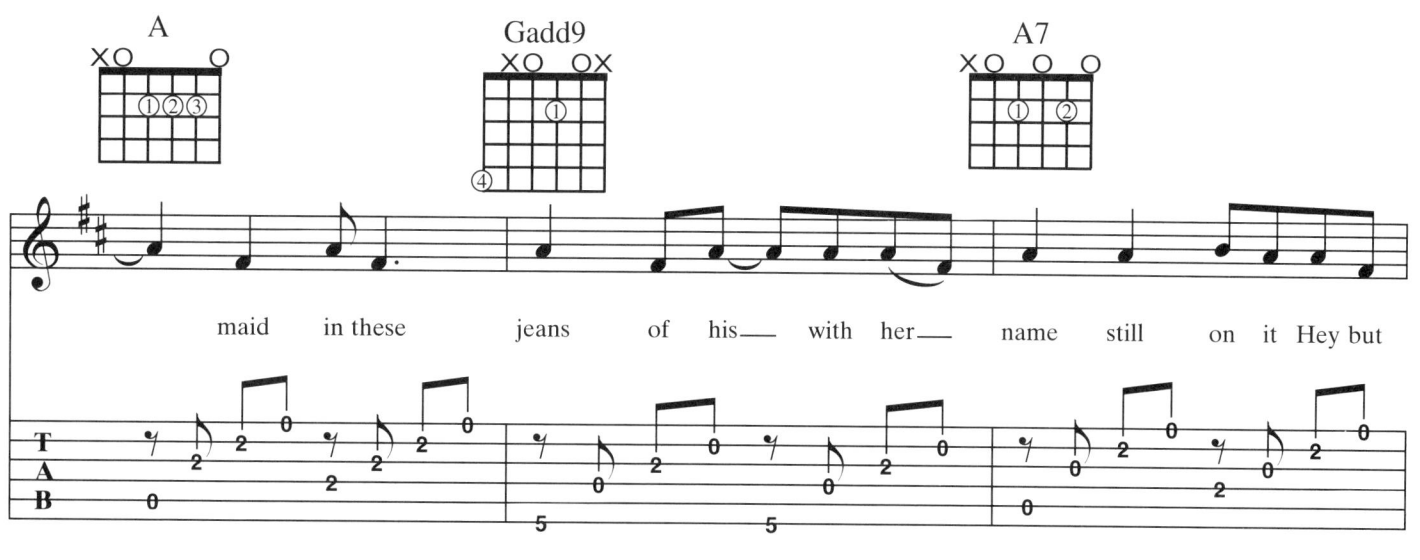
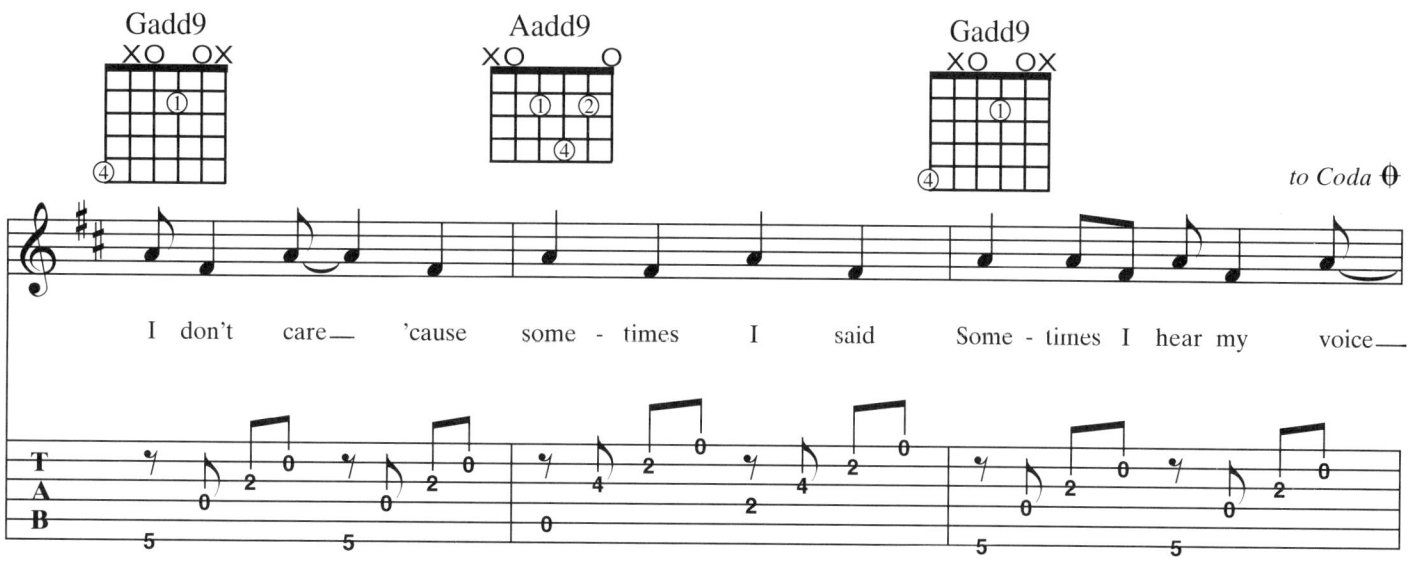
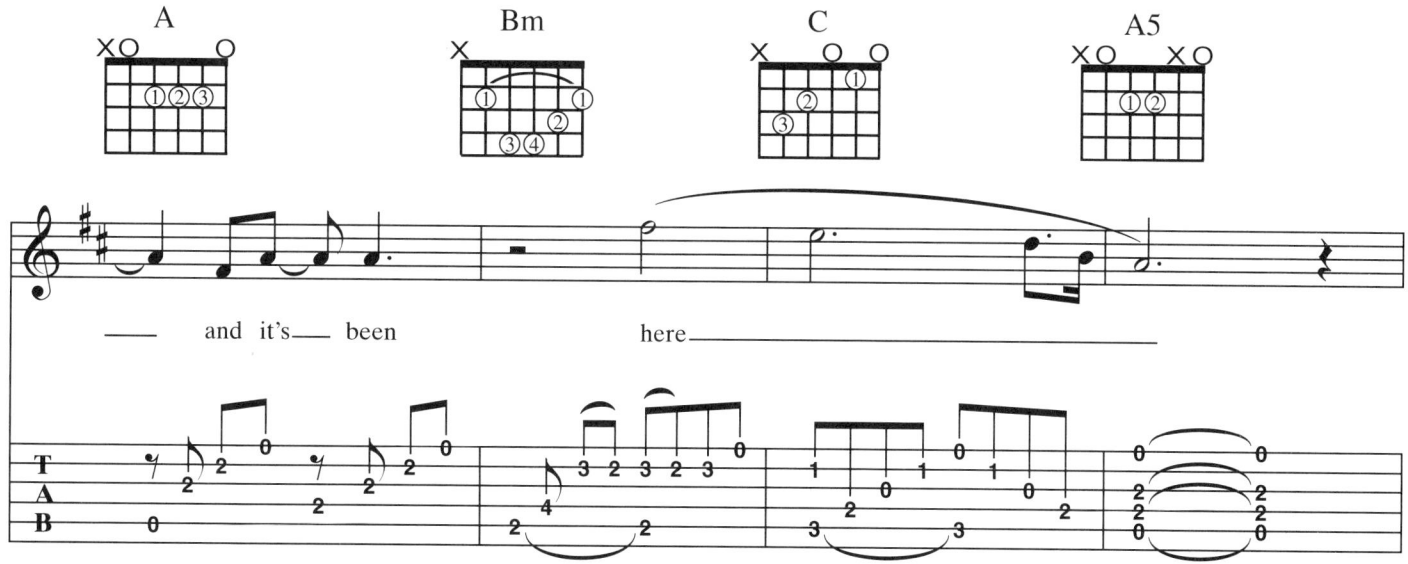

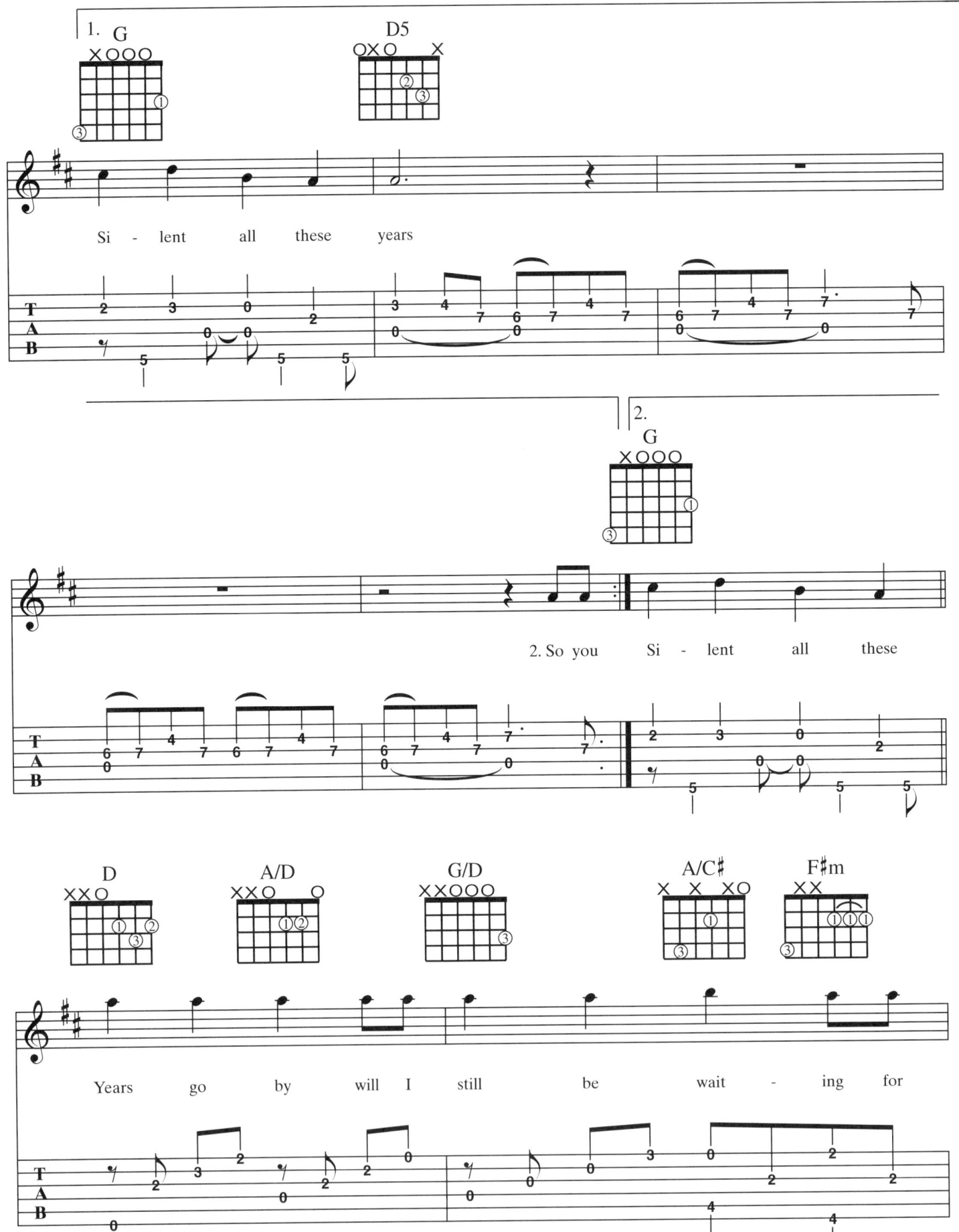

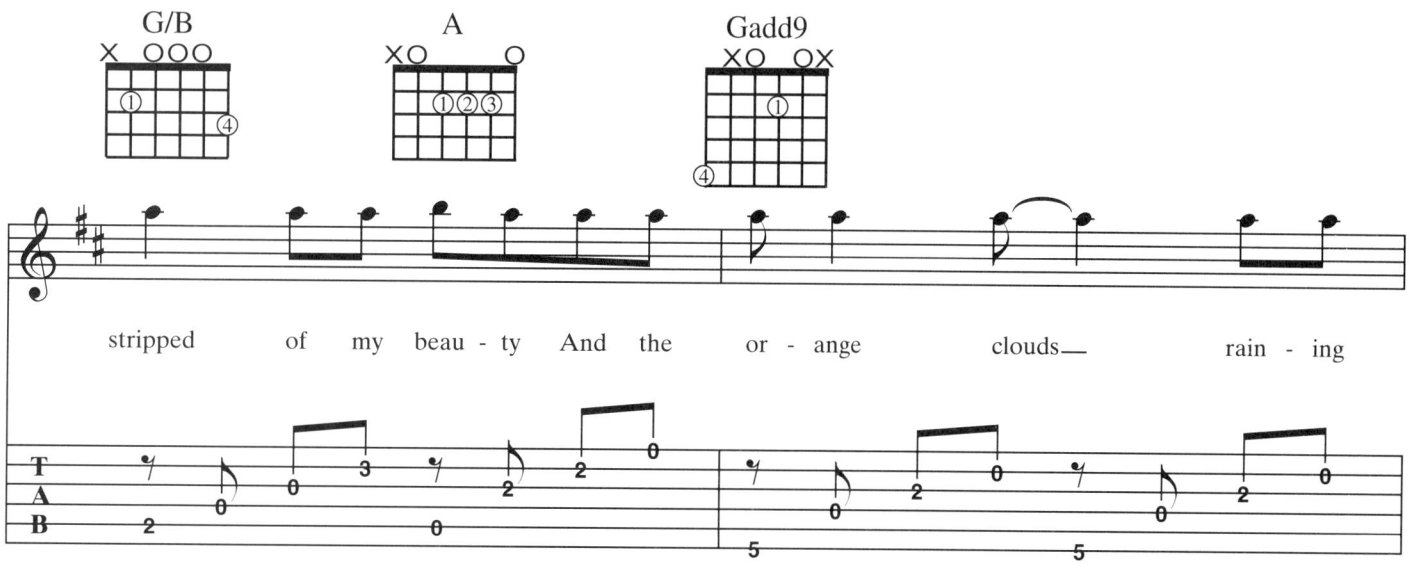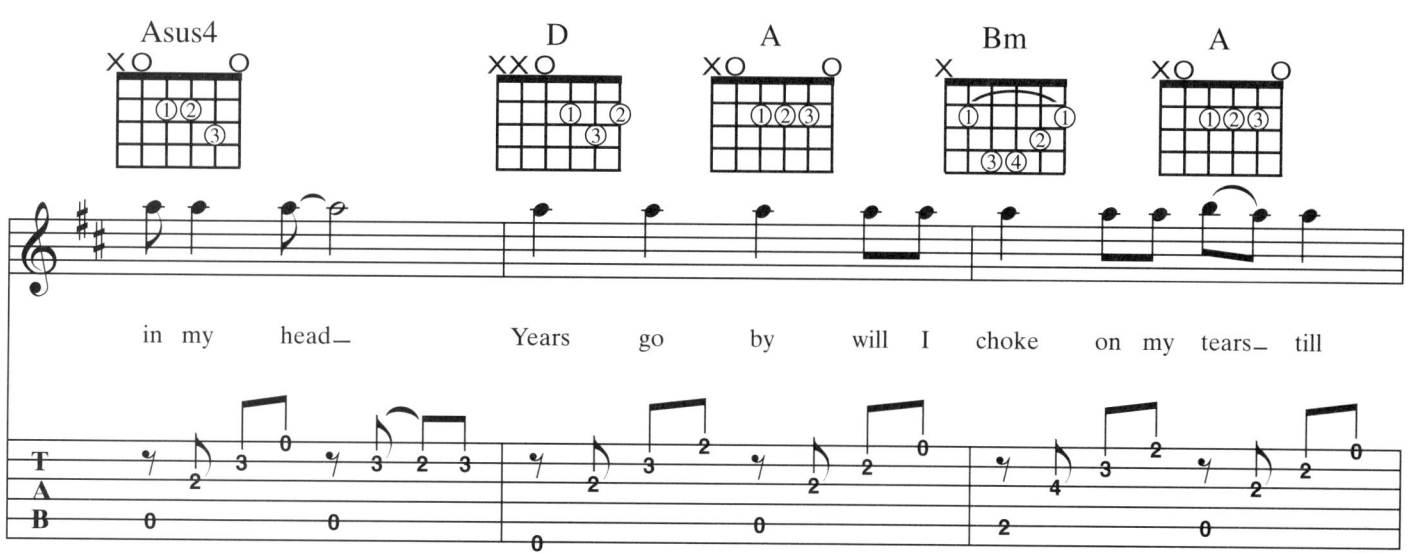

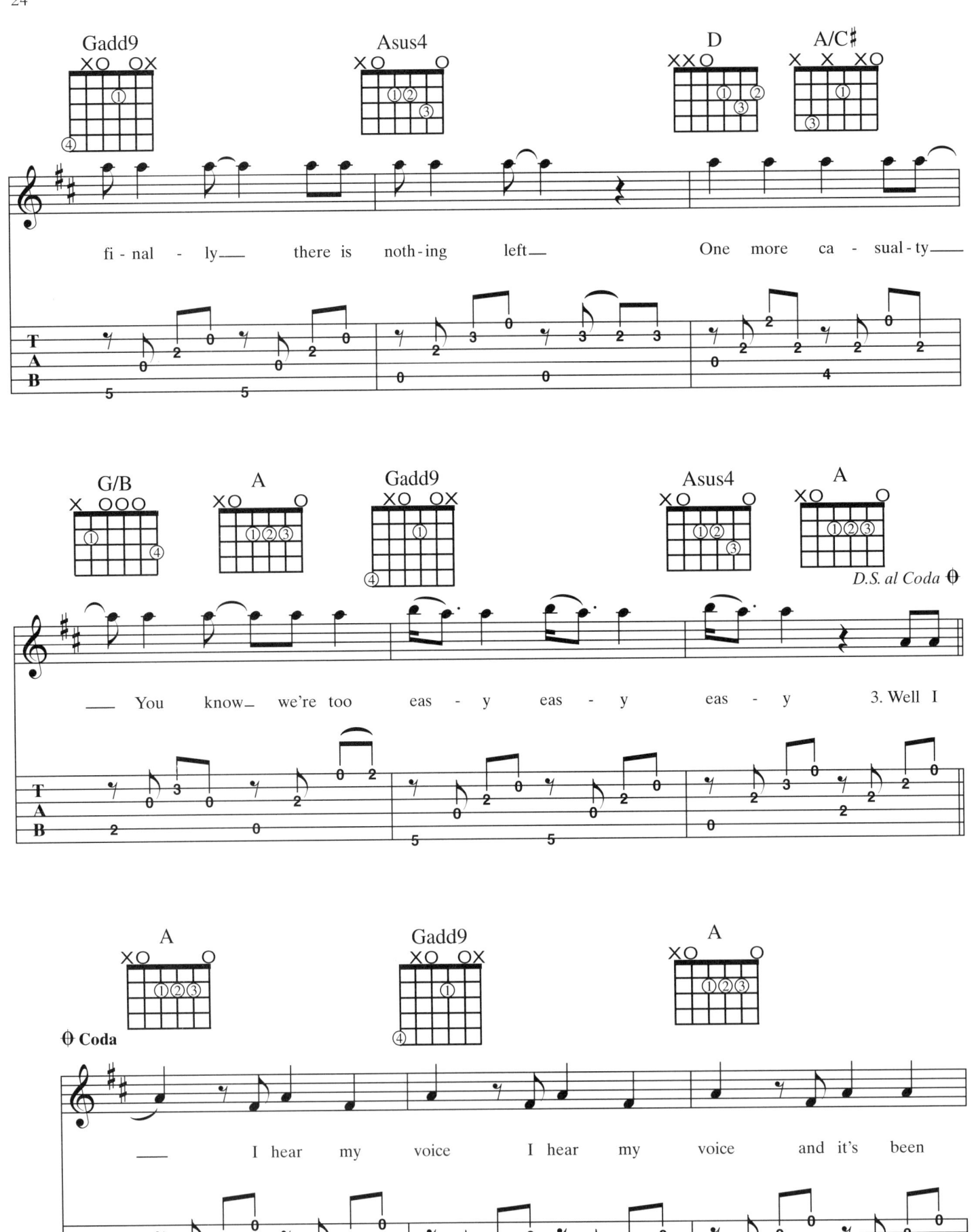

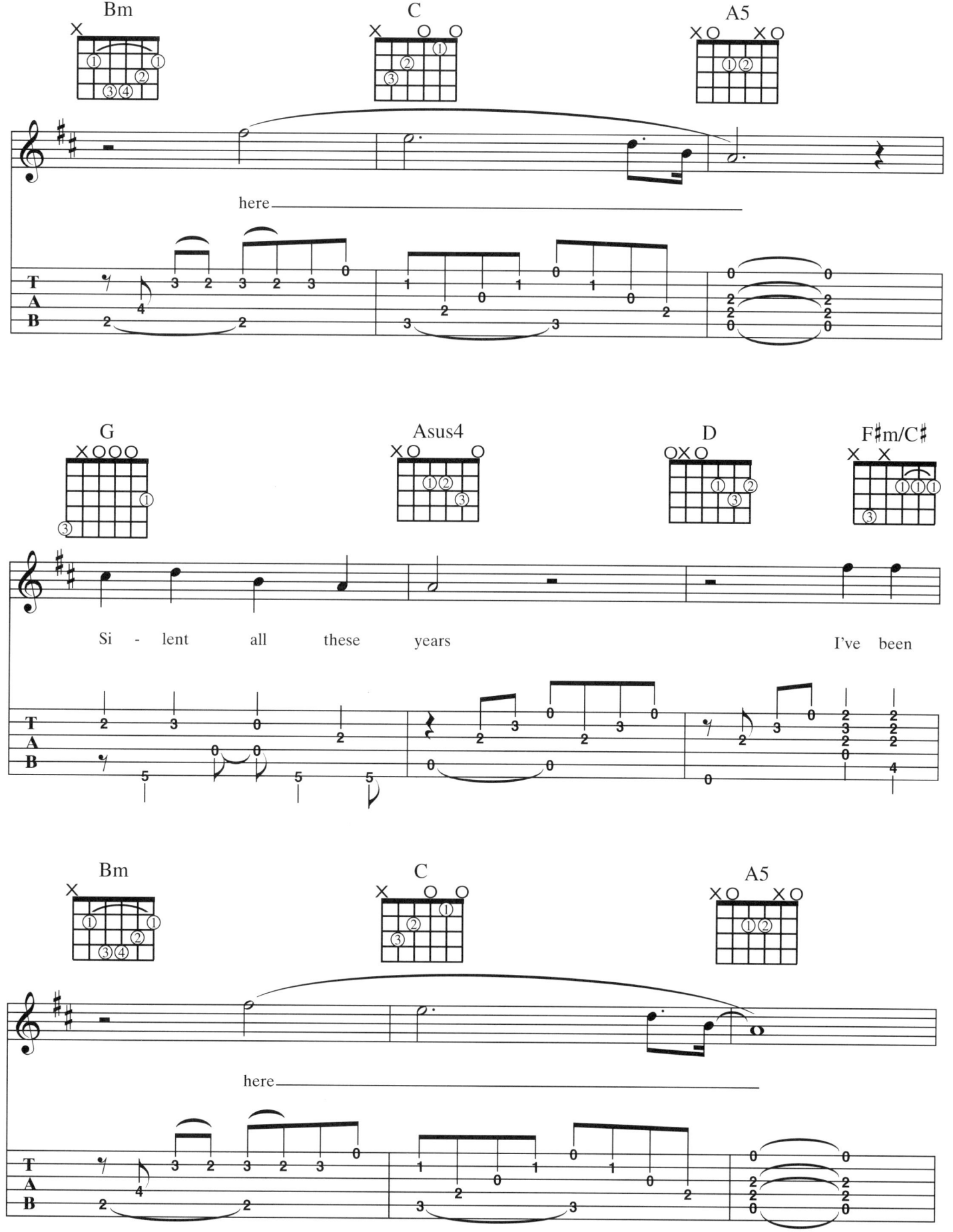

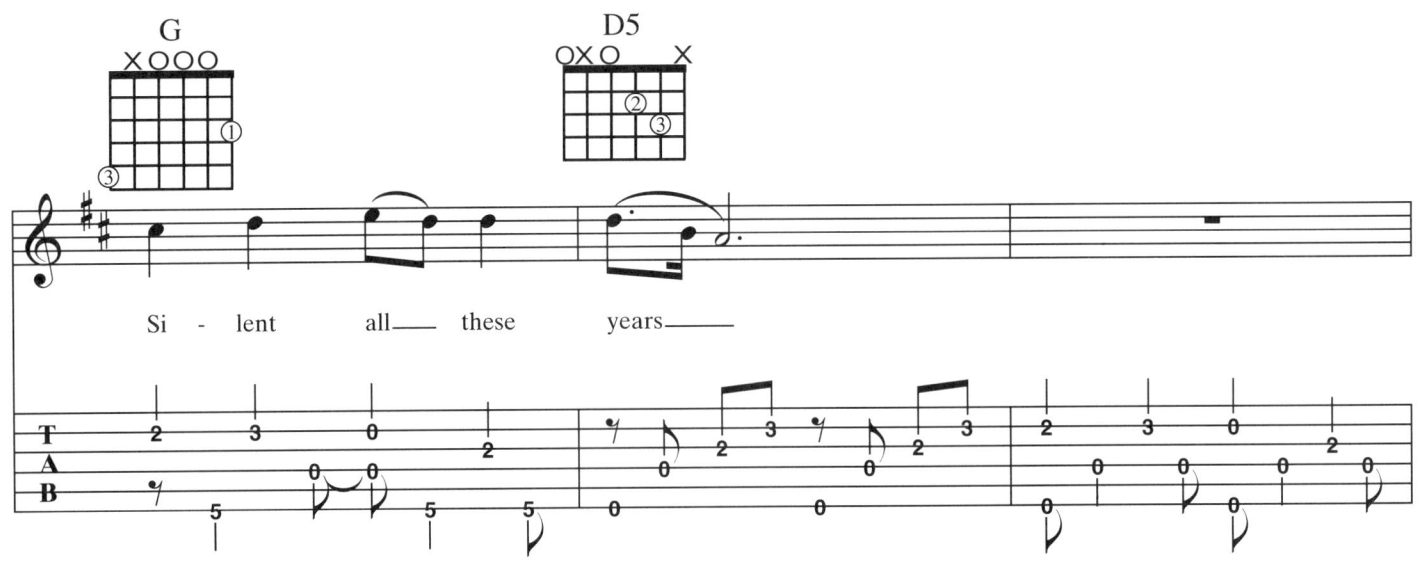
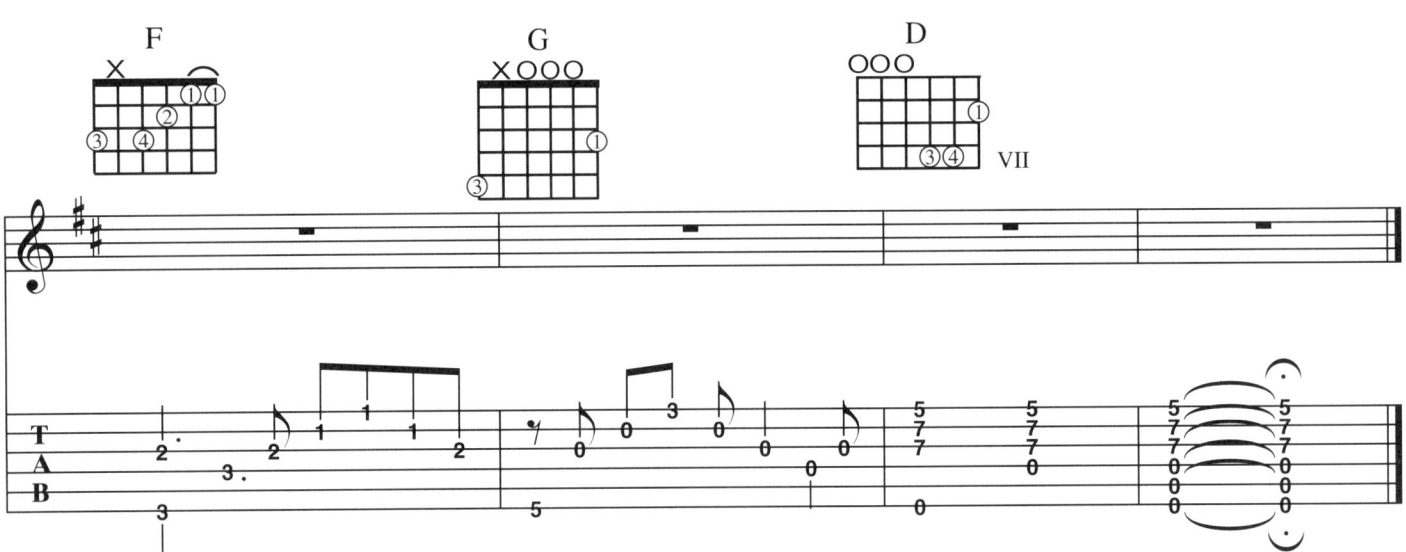

Additional lyrics

2. So you found a girl who thinks really deep thoughts
   What's so amazing about really deep thoughts
   Boy you best pray that I bleed real soon
   How's that thought for you

   My scream got lost in a paper cup
   You think there's a heaven where some screams have gone
   I got twenty-five bucks and a cracker
   Do you think it's enough... to get us there
   Cause

3. Well, I love the way we communicate
   Your eyes focus on my funny lip shape
   Let's hear what you think of me now
   But baby don't look up the sky is falling

   Your mother shows up in a nasty dress
   It's your turn now to stand where I stand
   And everybody lookin' at you
   Here take hold of my hand... yeah, I can hear them
   But

Pretty Good Year
Words and Music by Tori Amos

melody note for voice

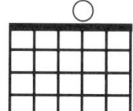

Moderately flowing

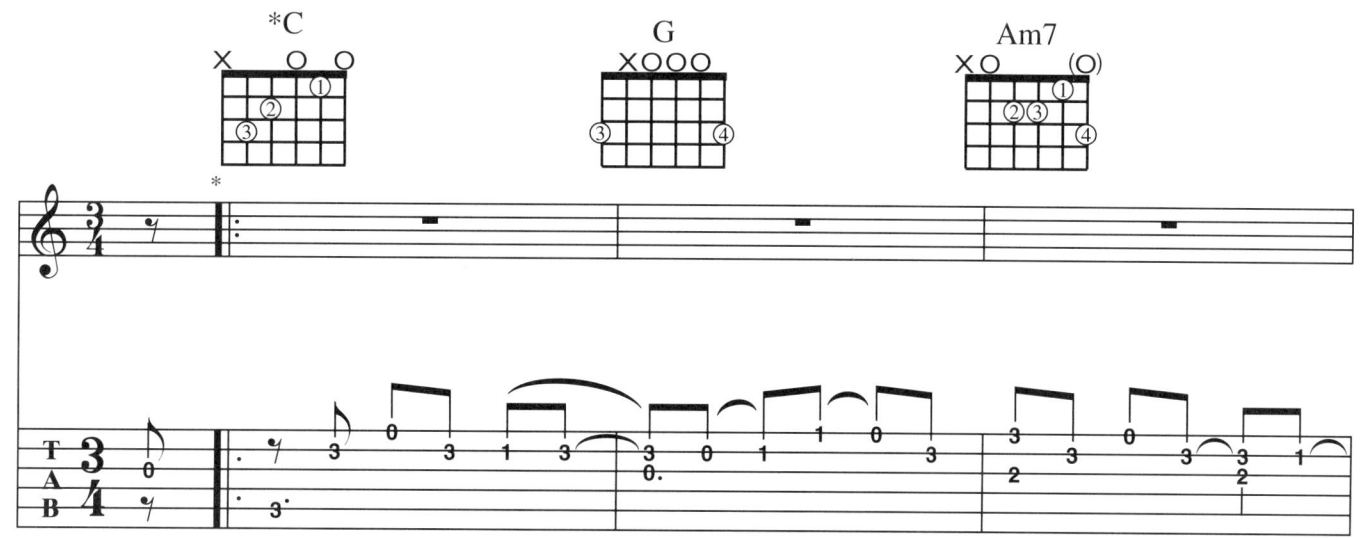

*Capo at sixth fret. Actual key: G♭

Tears on the sleeve of a ___ man

Copyright © 1993 Sword and Stone Publishing Inc. (ASCAP)
International Copyright Secured. All Rights Reserved.

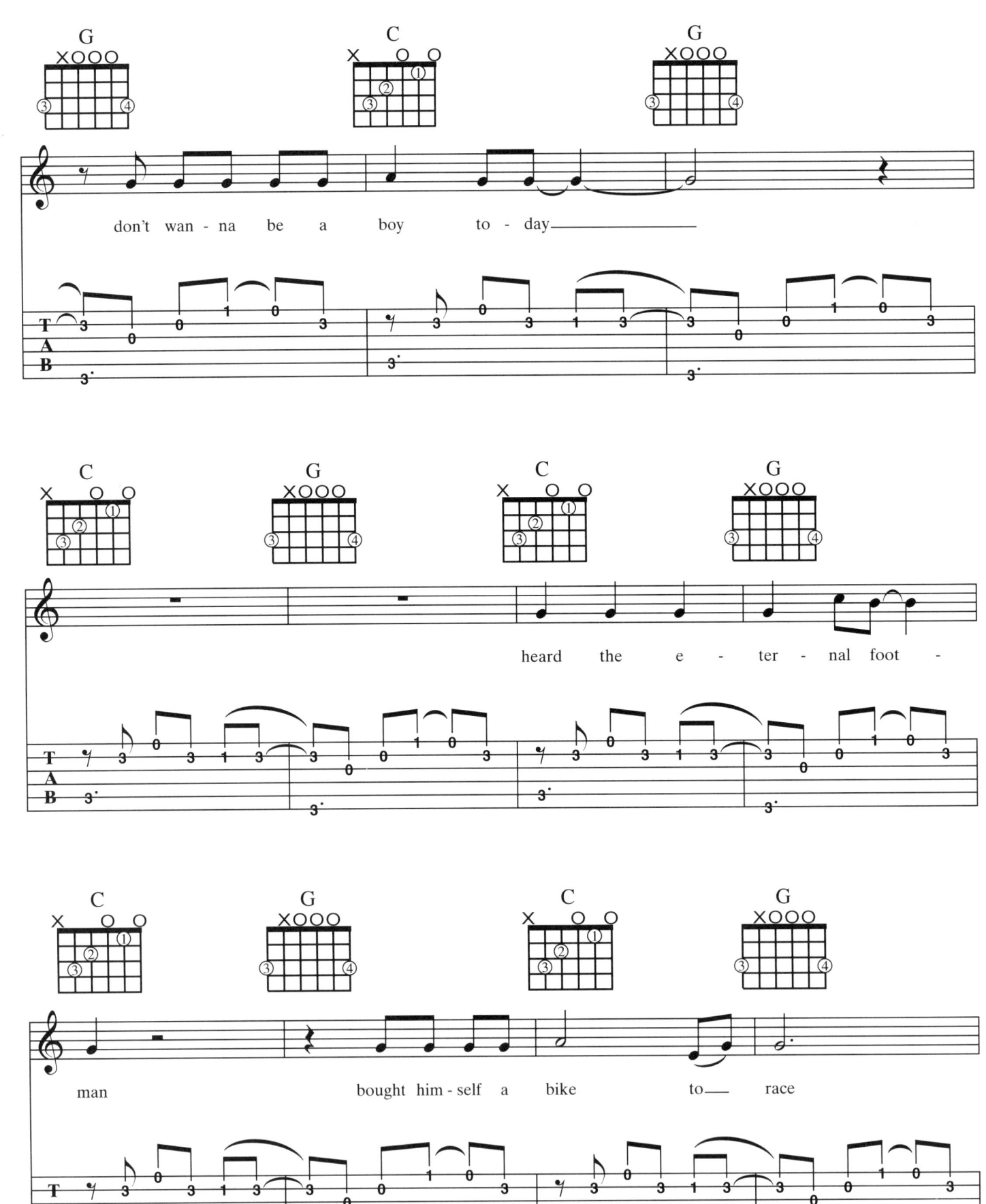

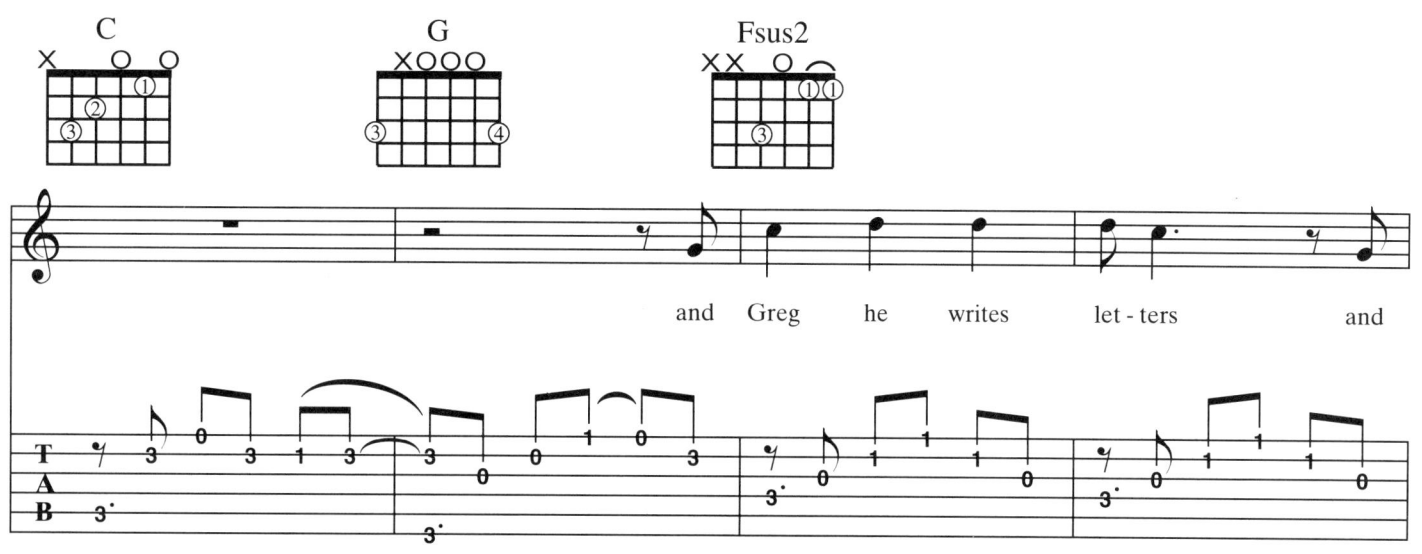
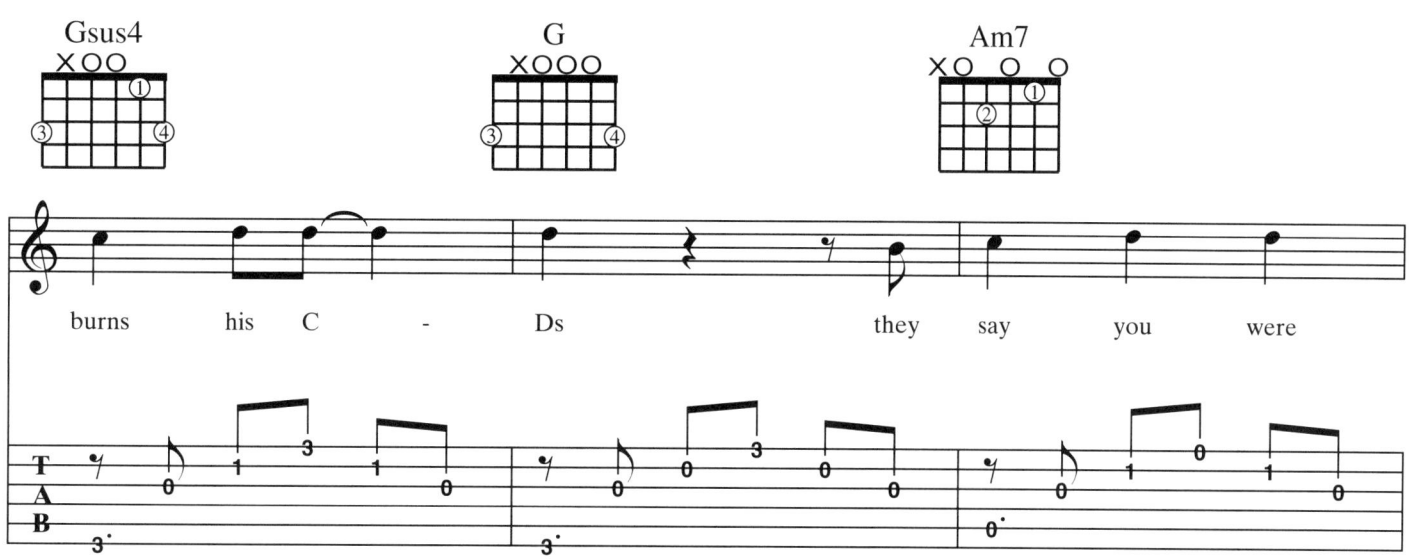

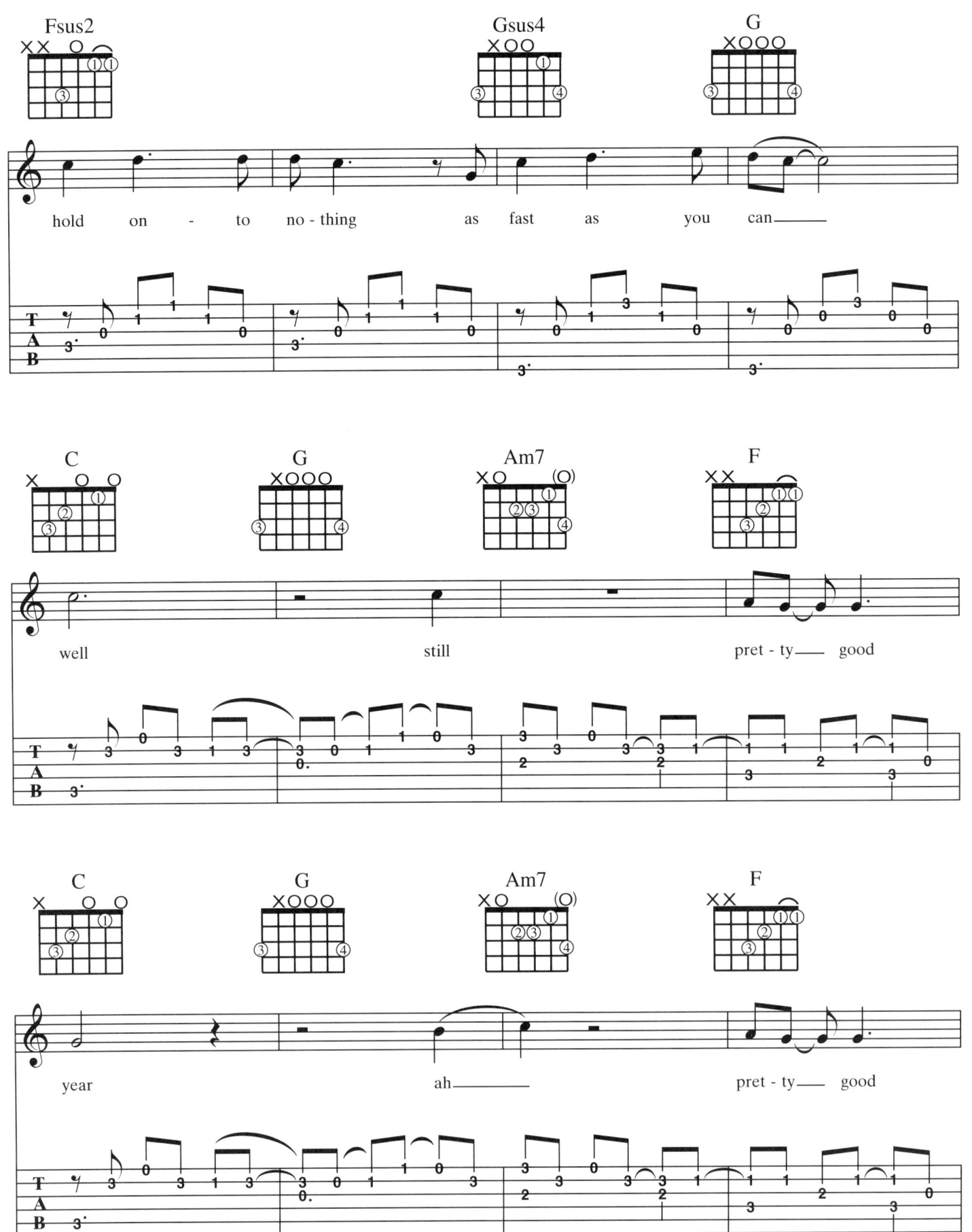

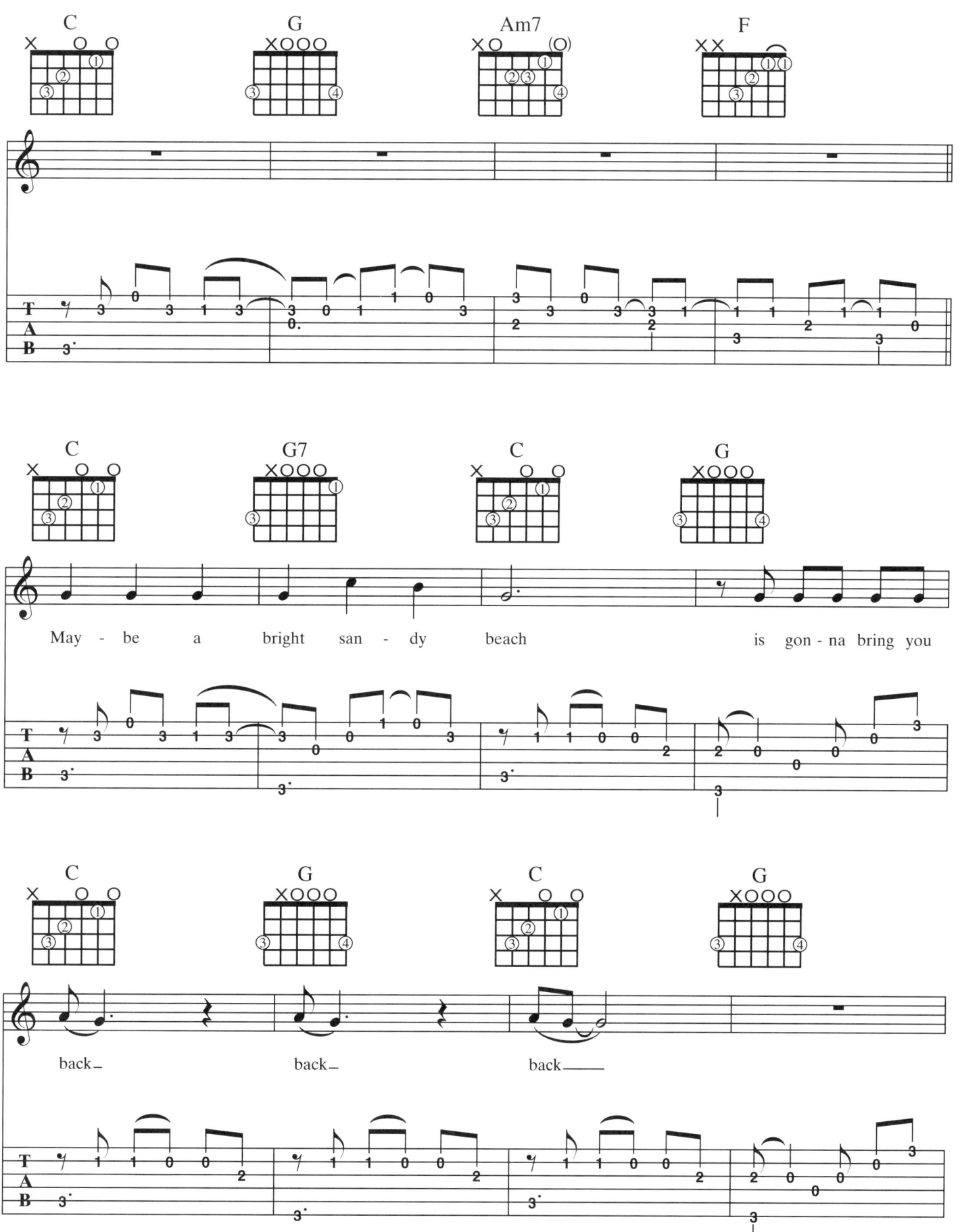

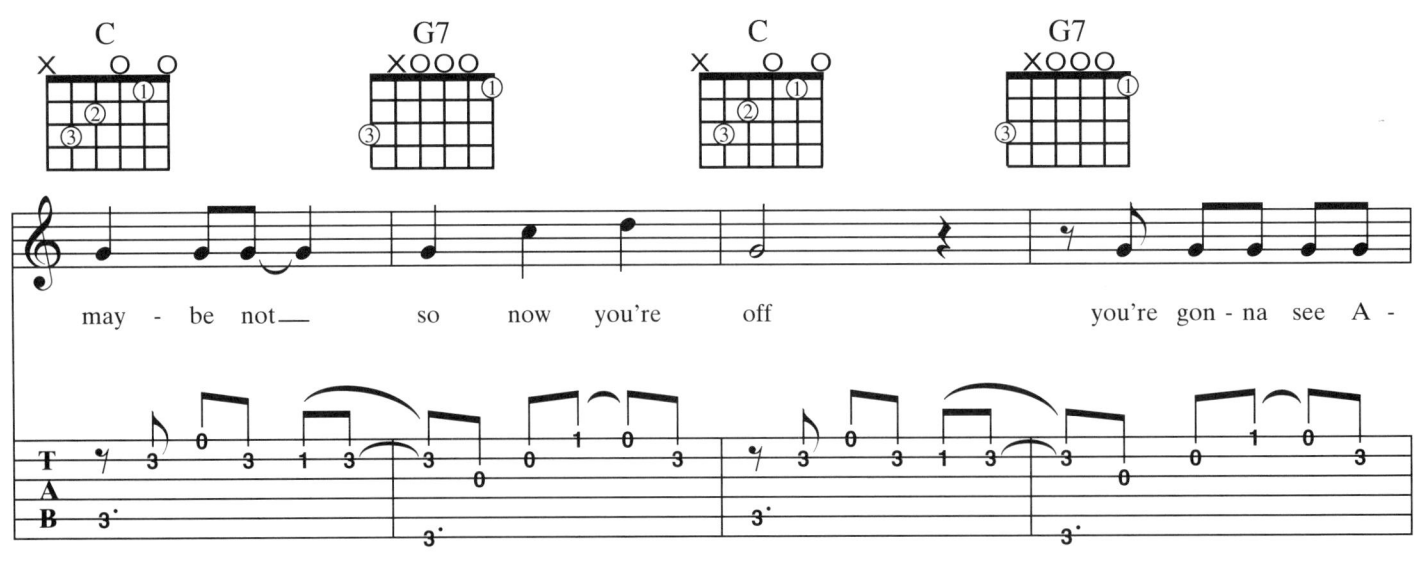
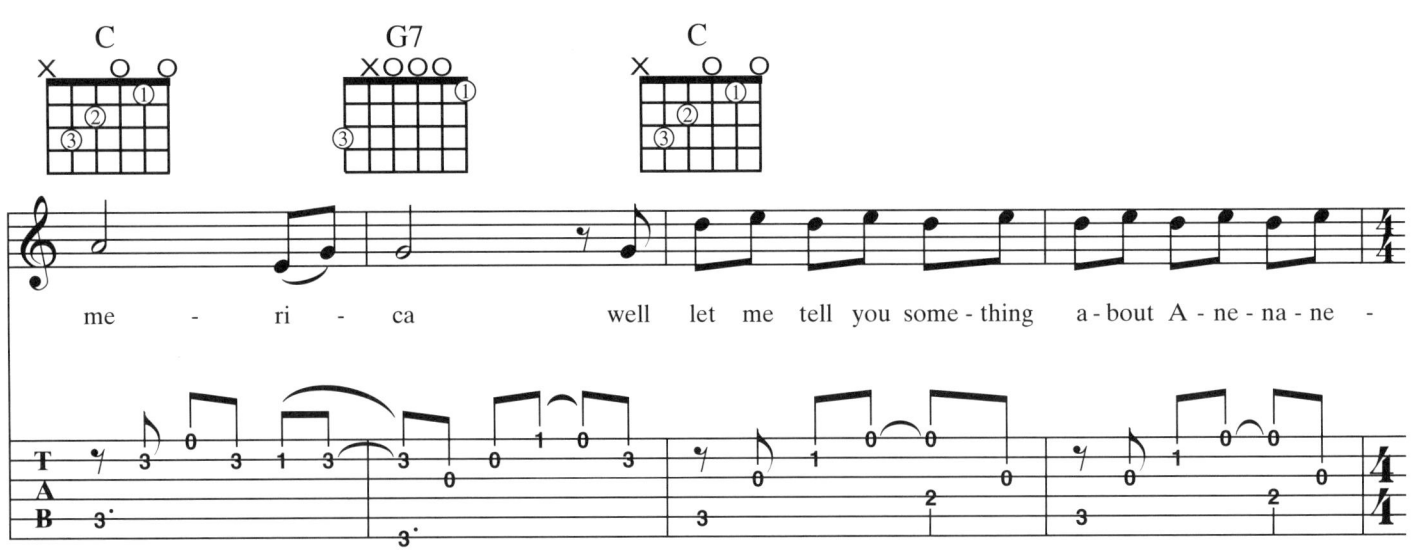

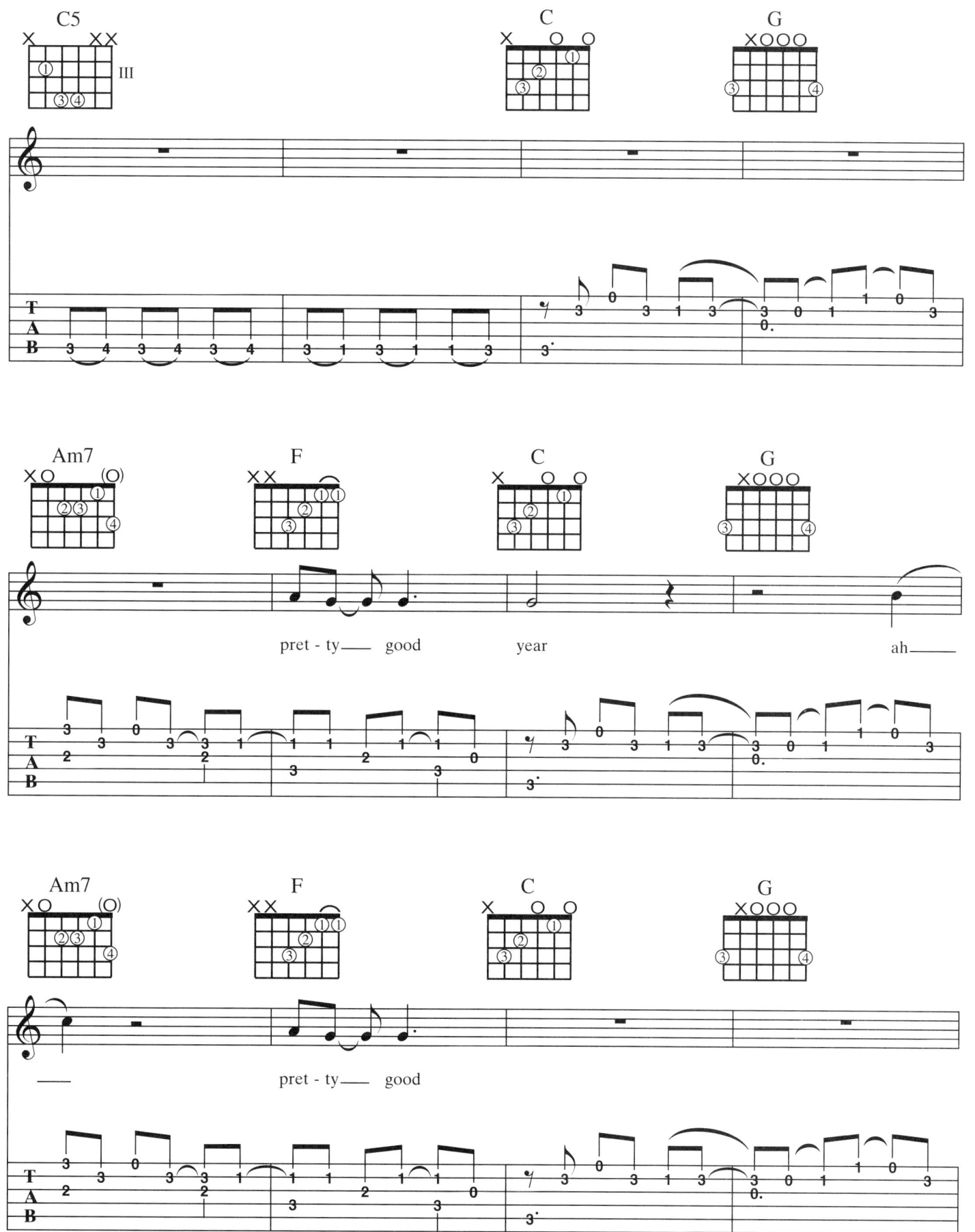

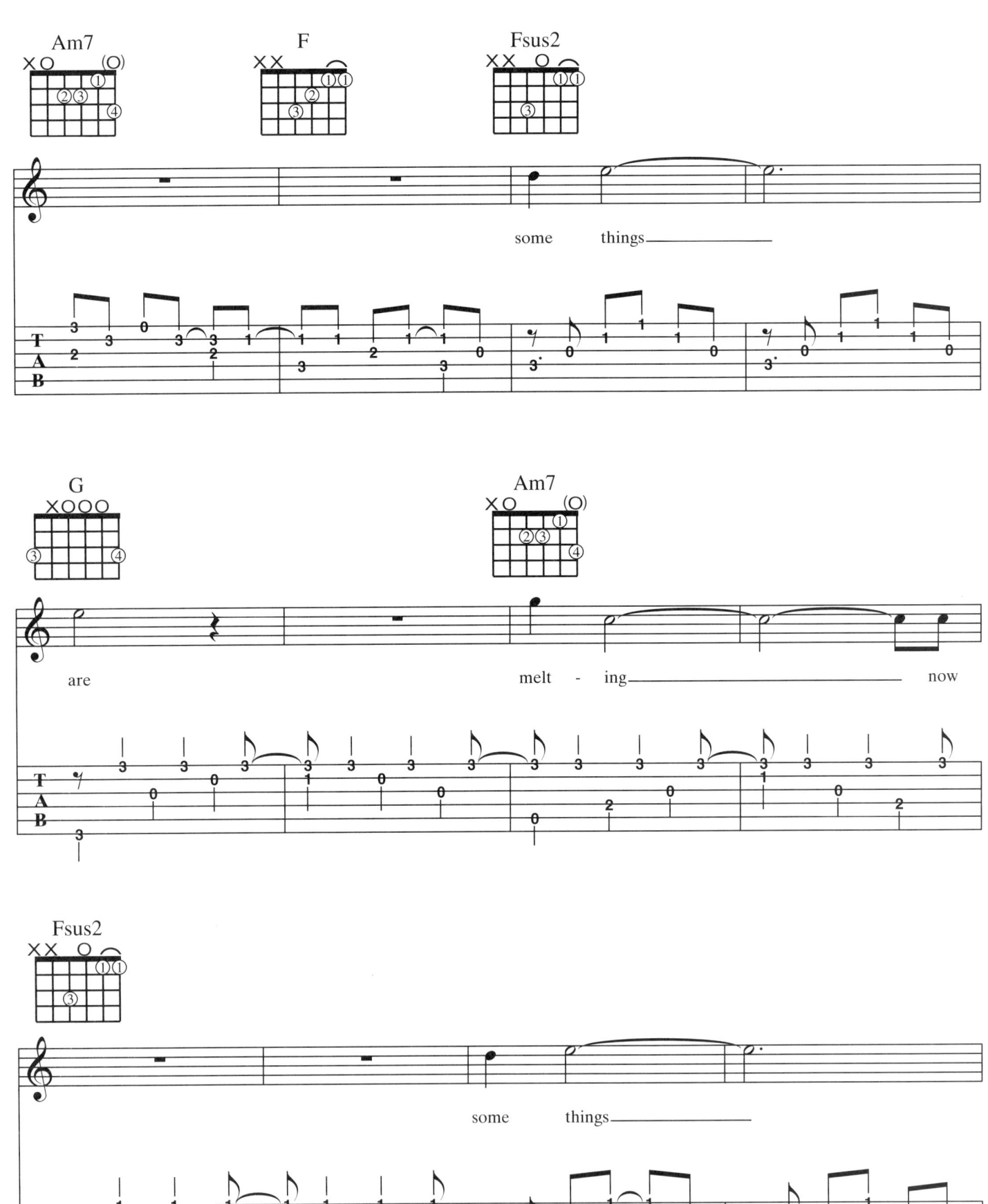

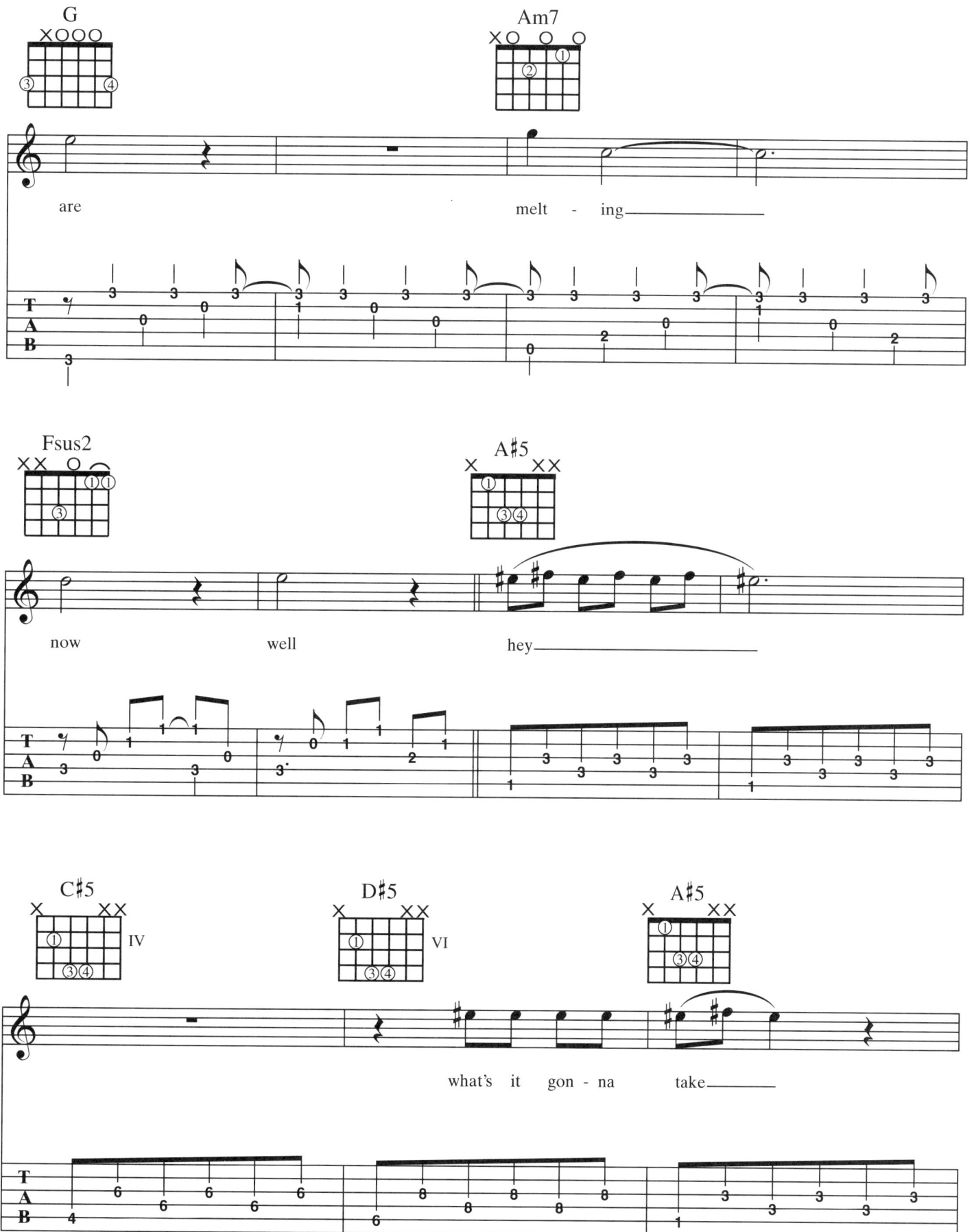

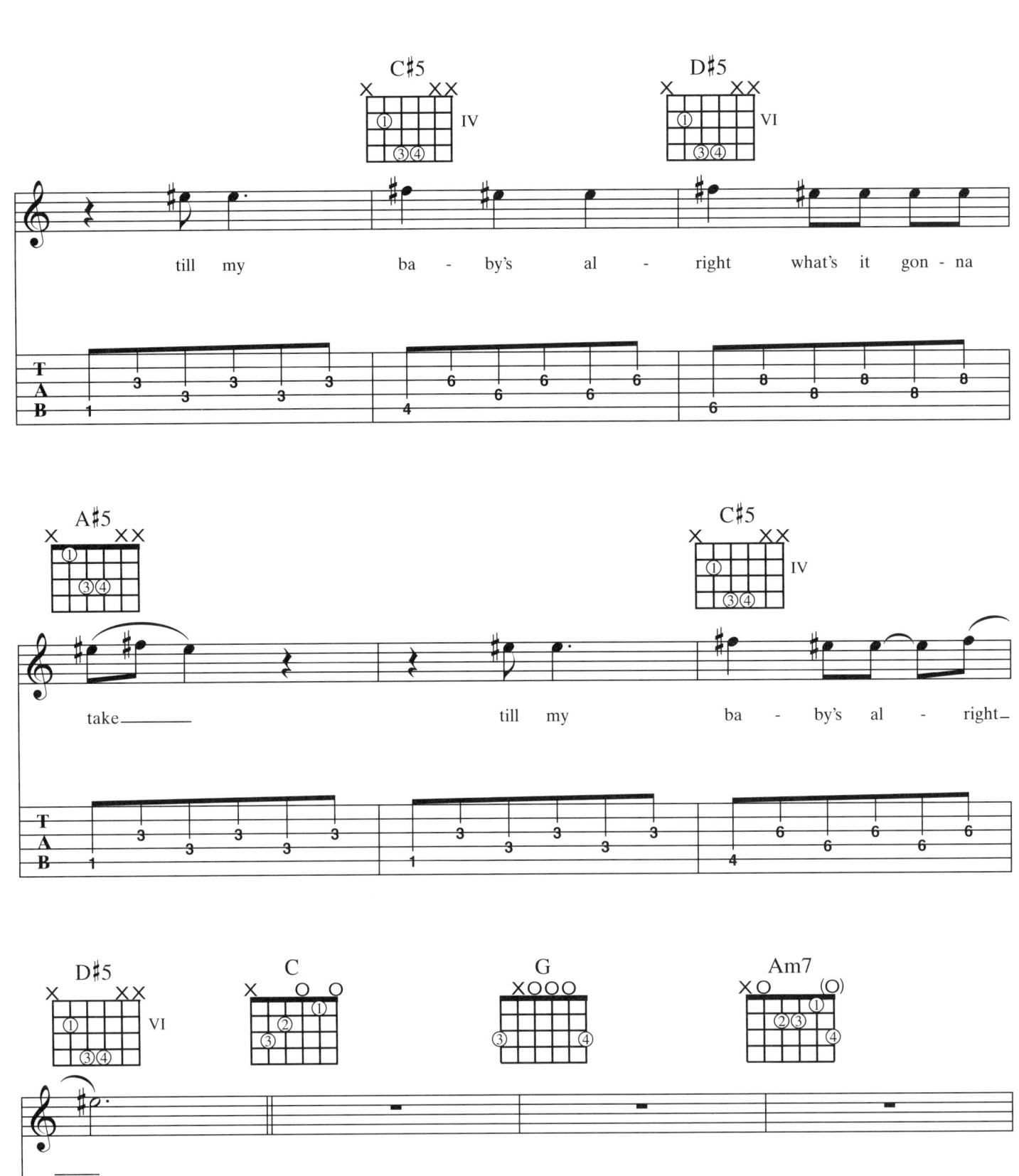

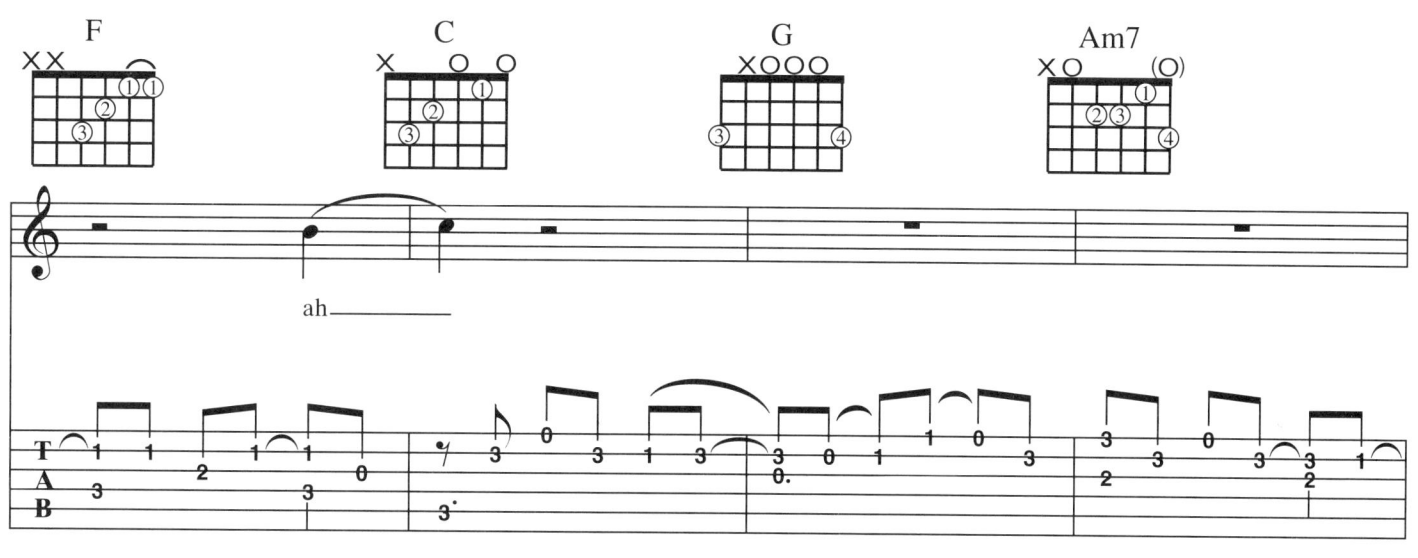

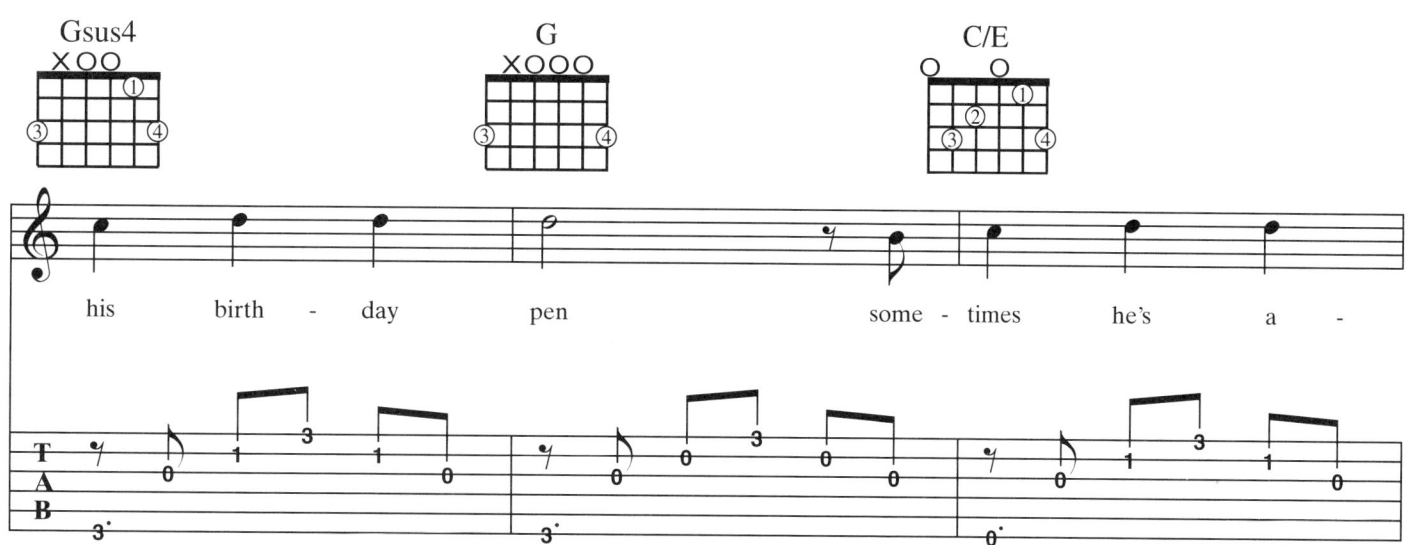

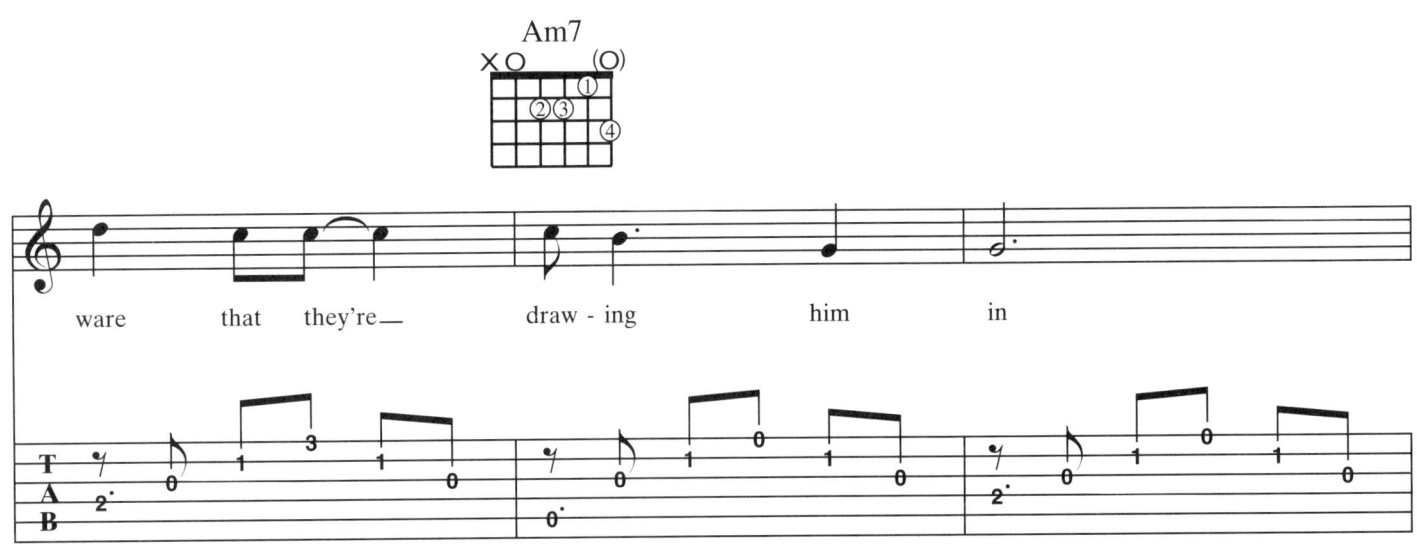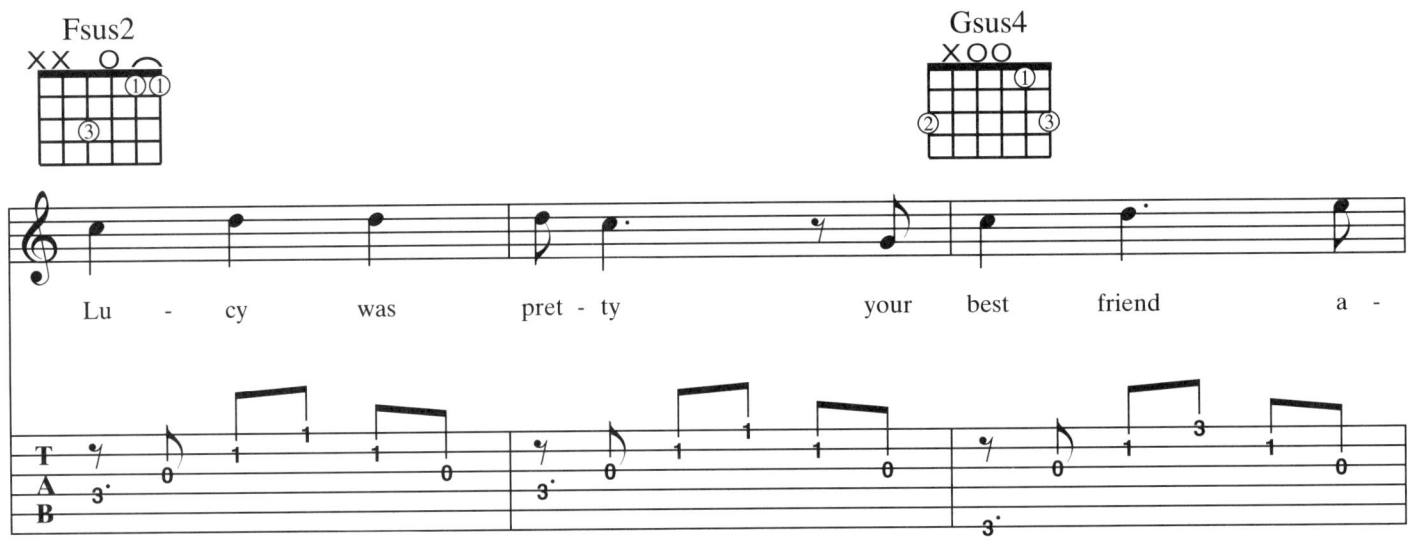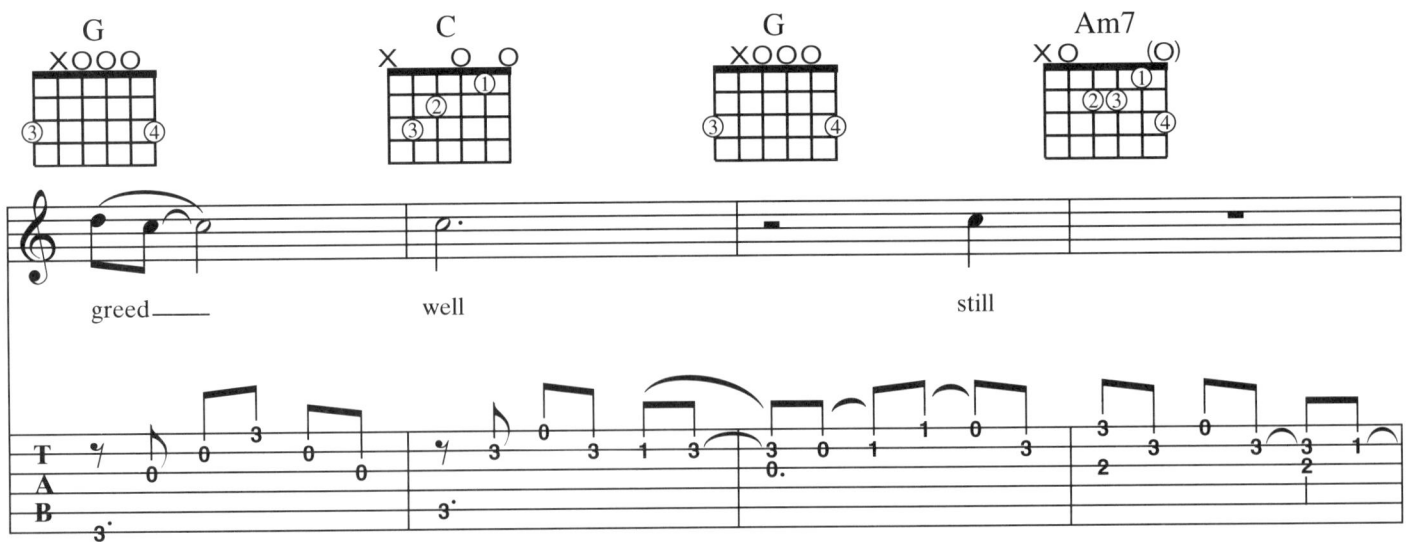

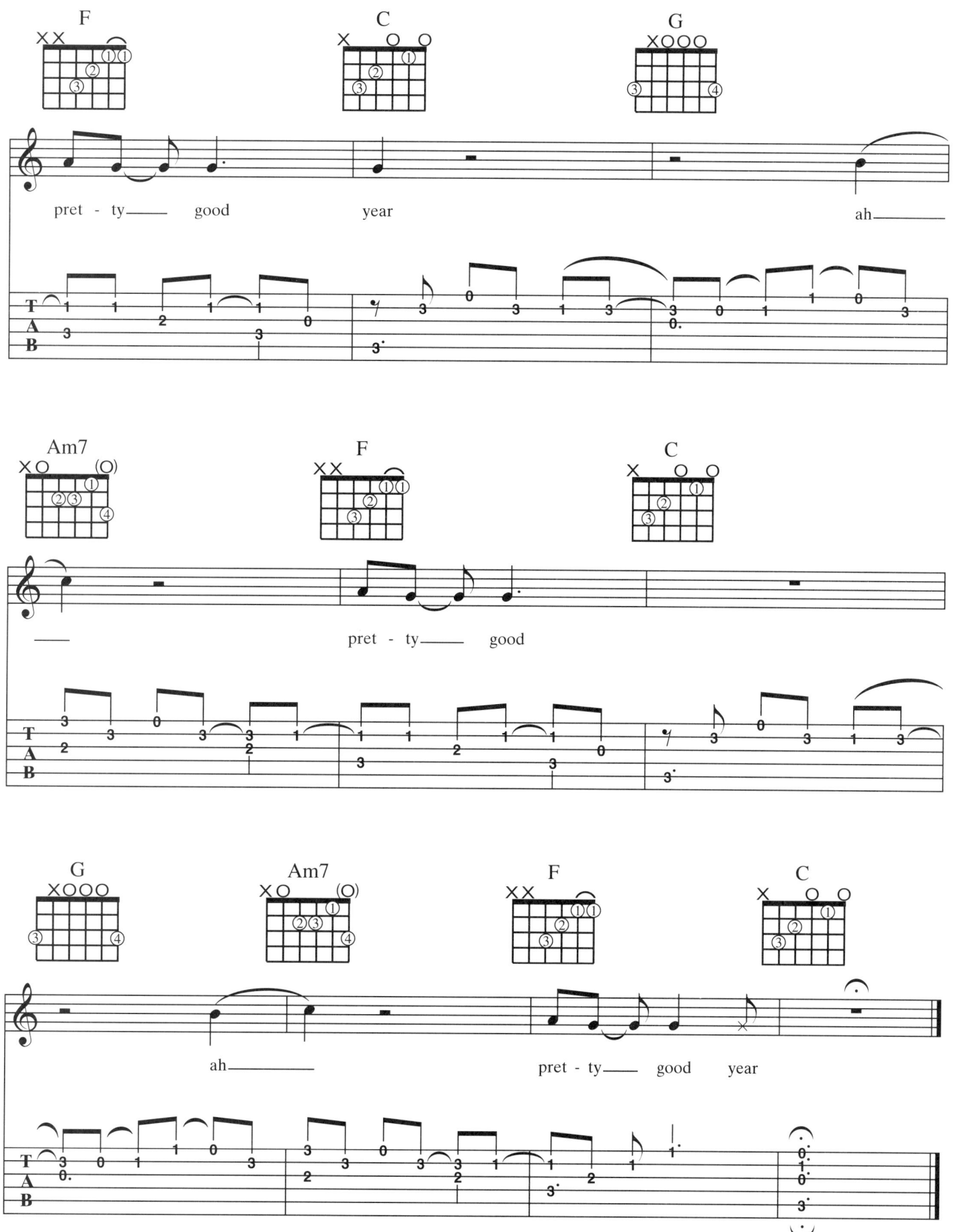

Caught a Lite Sneeze
Words and Music by Tori Amos

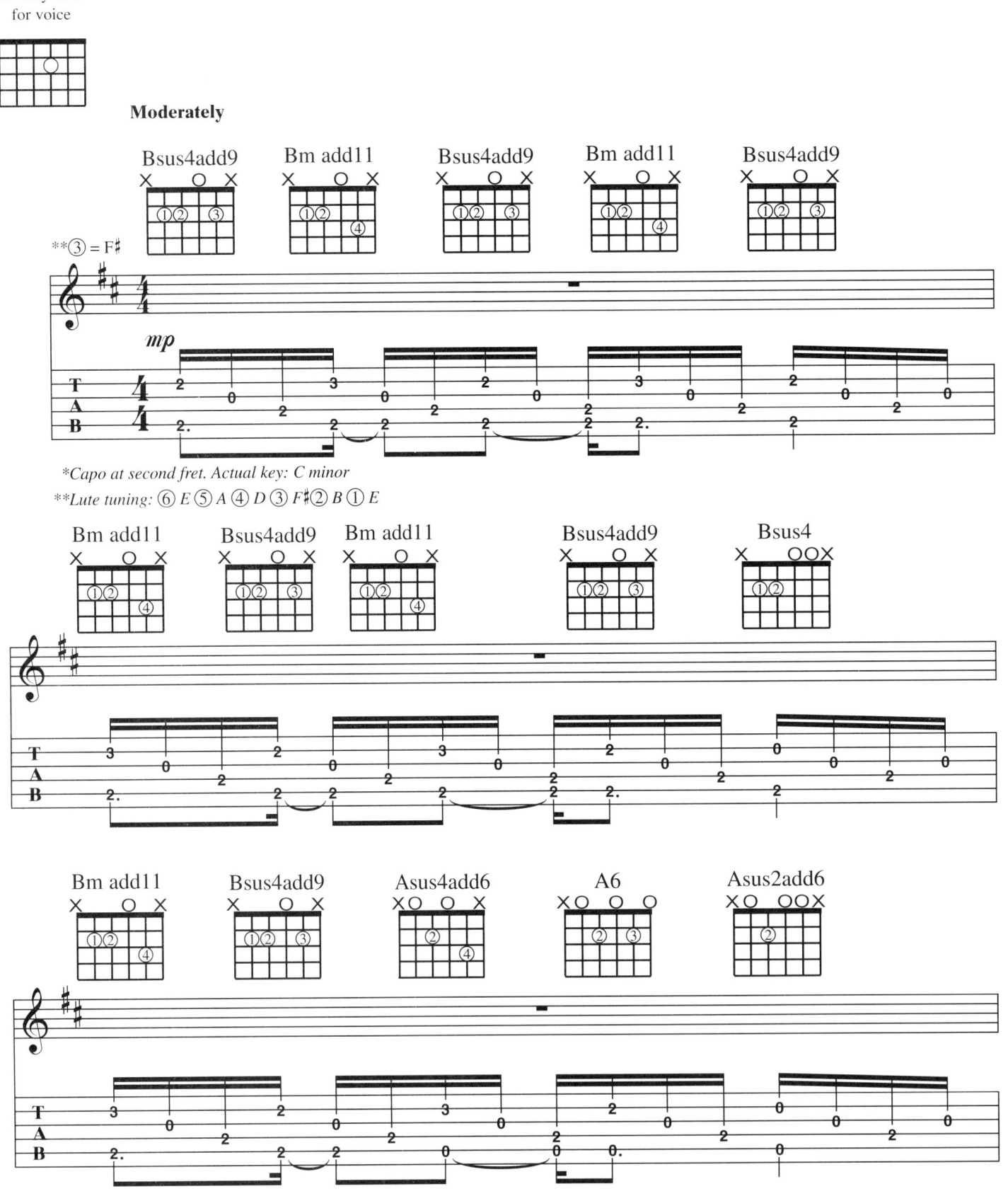

*Capo at second fret. Actual key: C minor
**Lute tuning: ⑥ E ⑤ A ④ D ③ F♯ ② B ① E

Copyright © 1995 SWORD AND STONE PUBLISHING INC. (ASCAP)
INTERNATIONAL COPYRIGHT SECURED. ALL RIGHTS RESERVED.

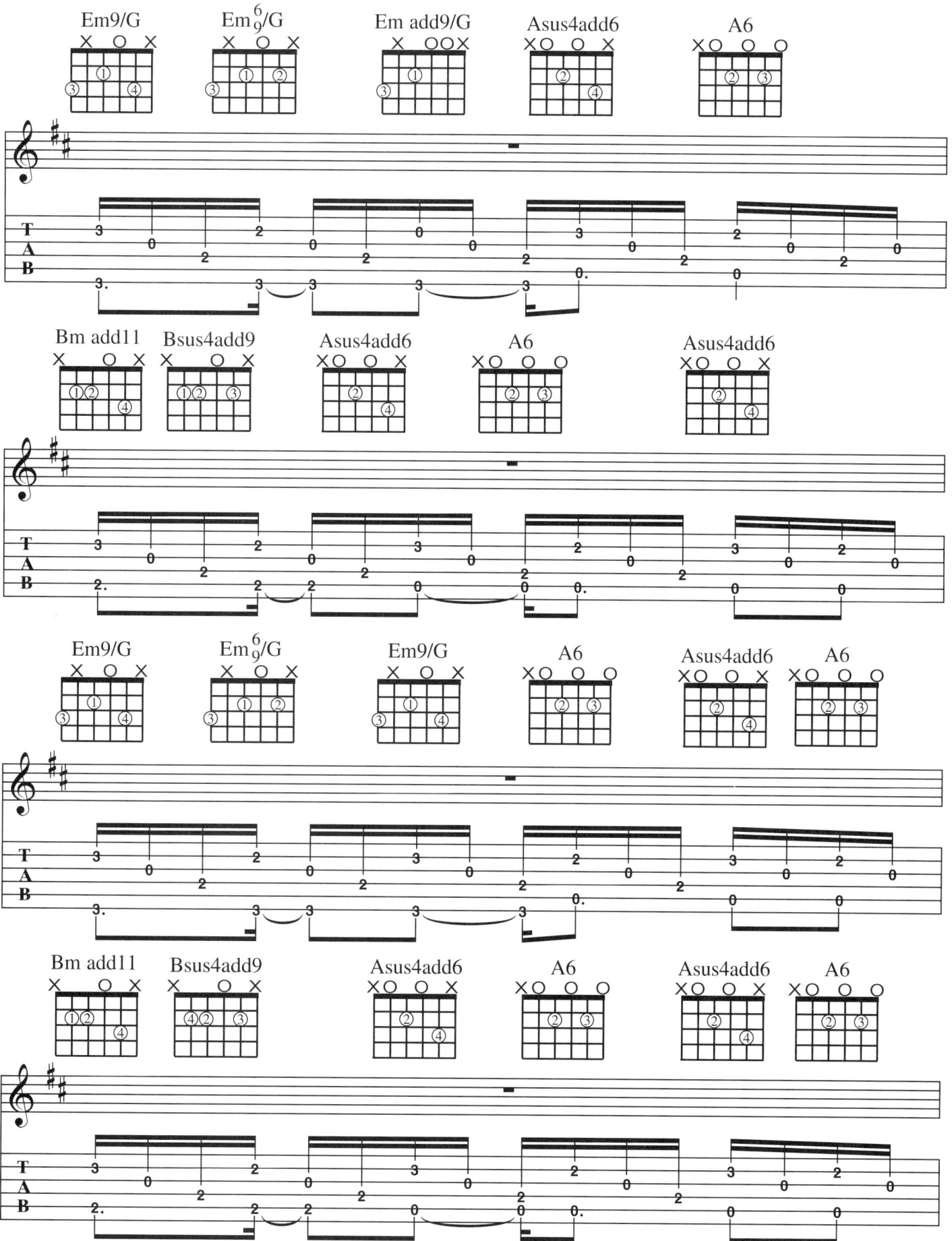

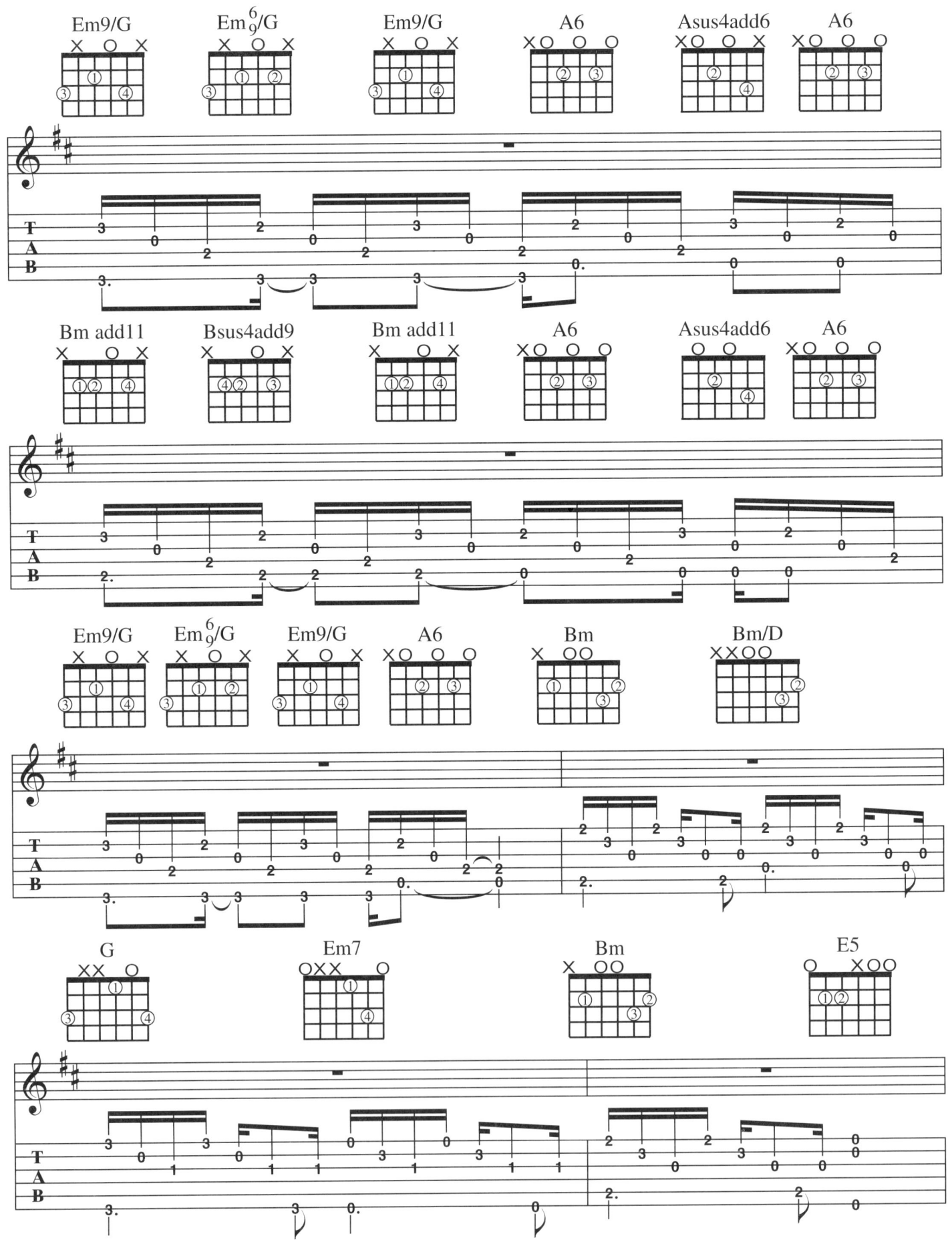

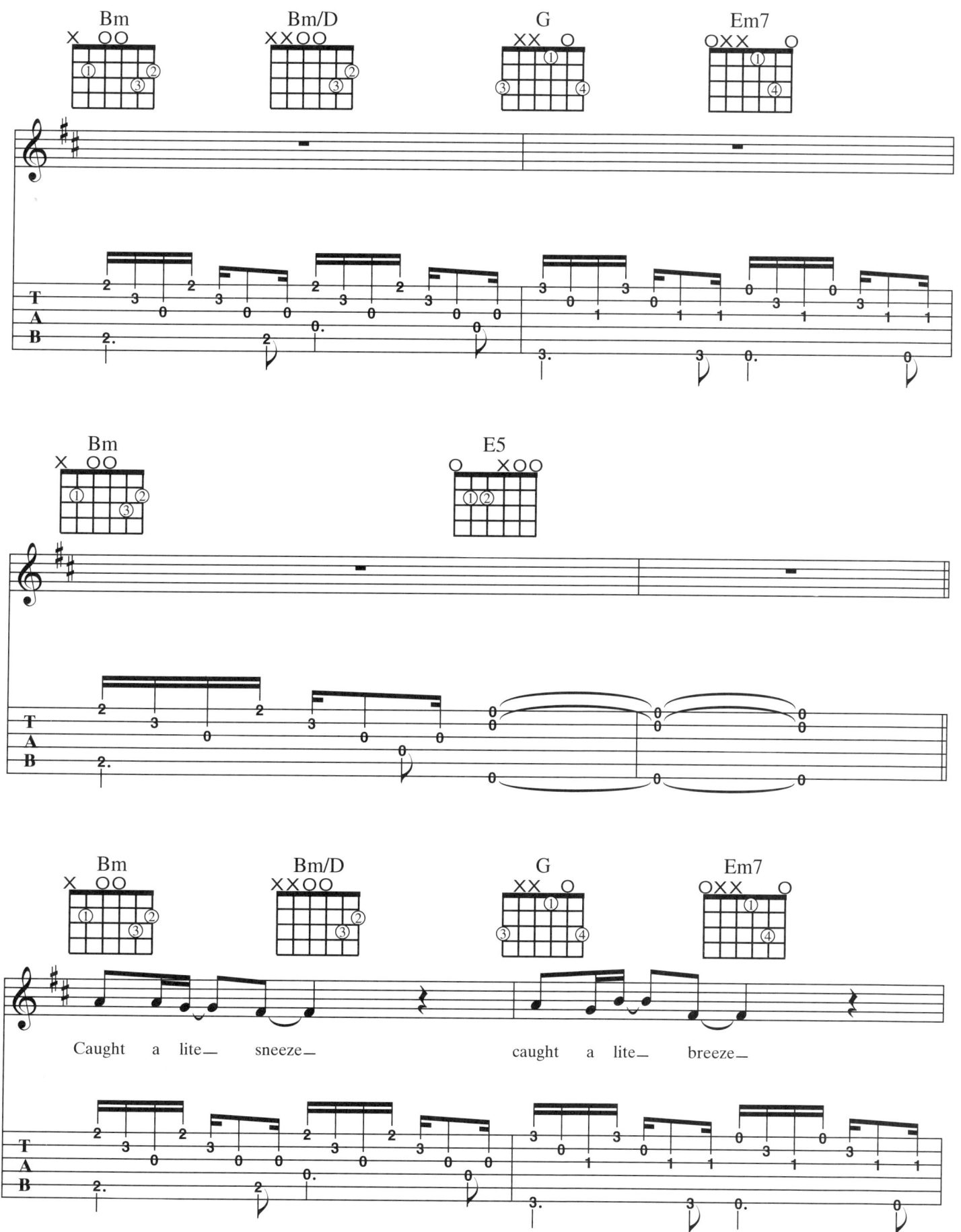

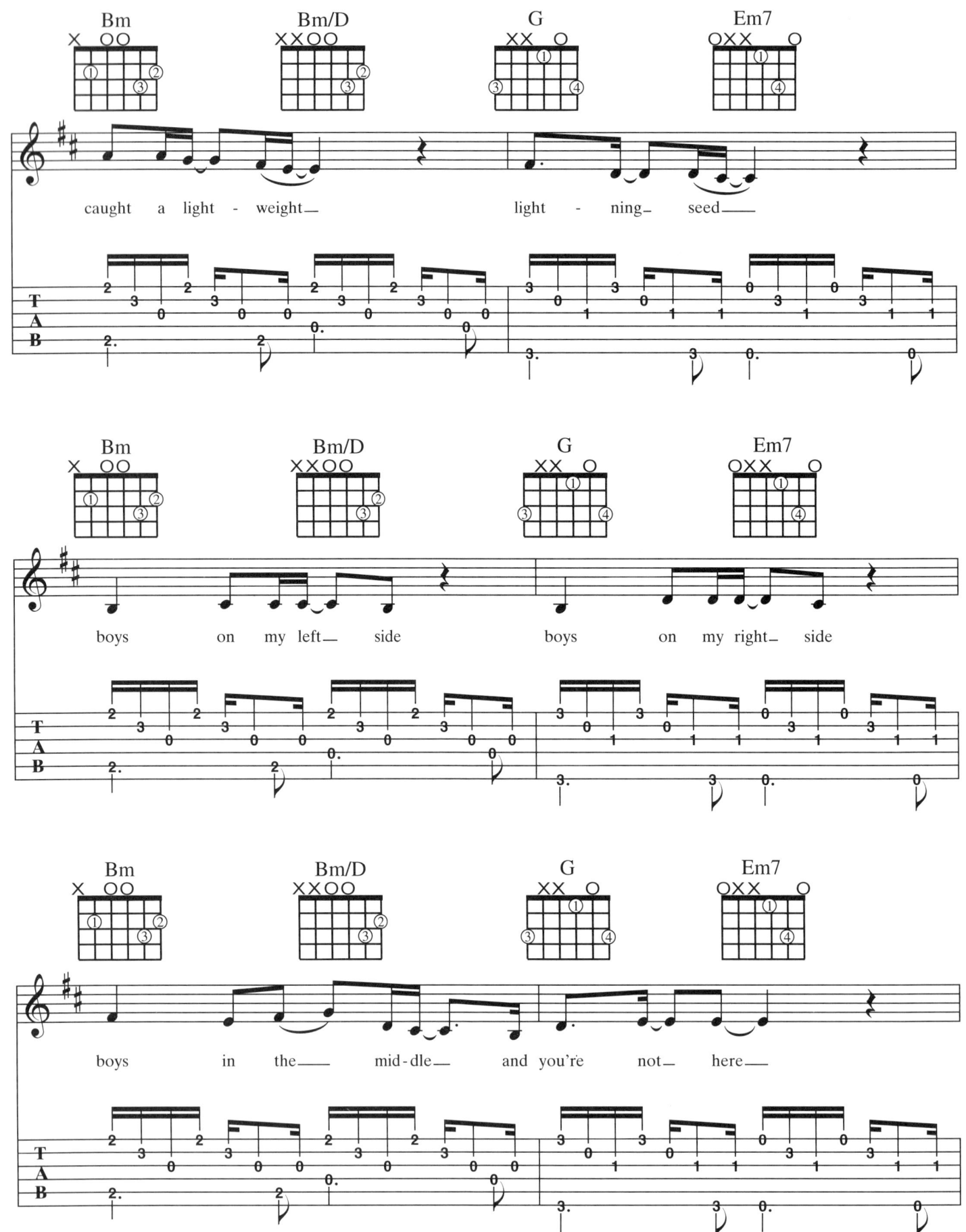

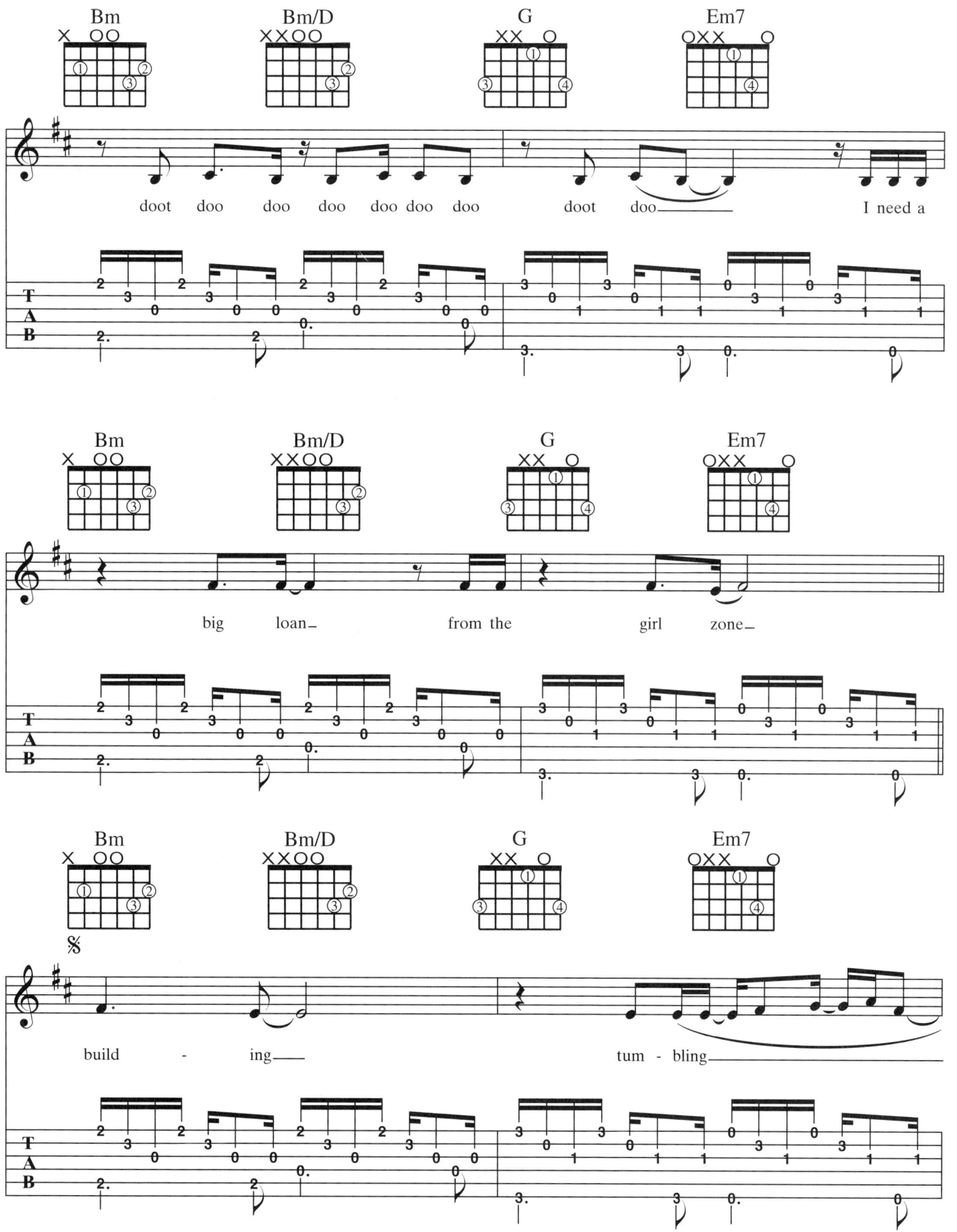

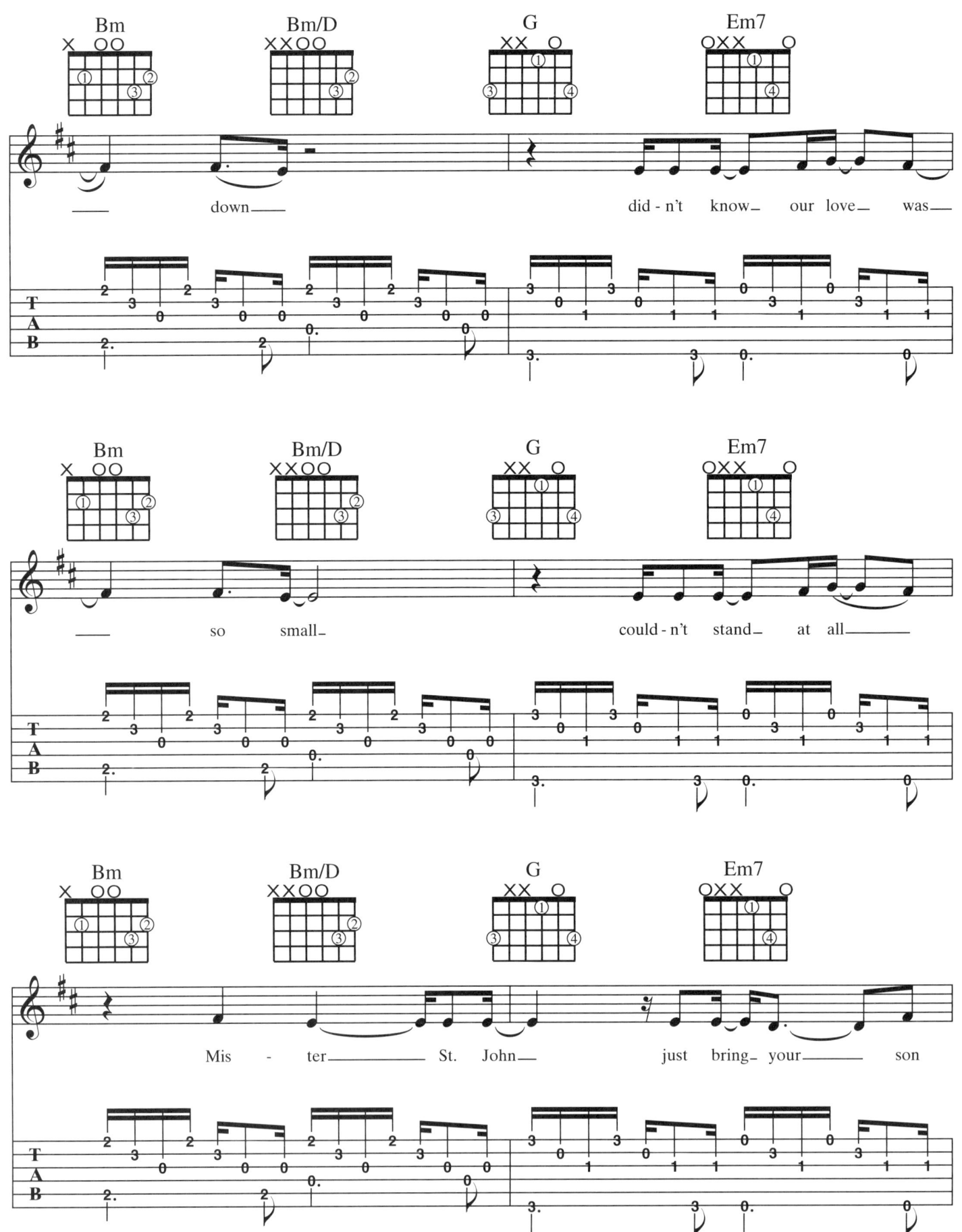

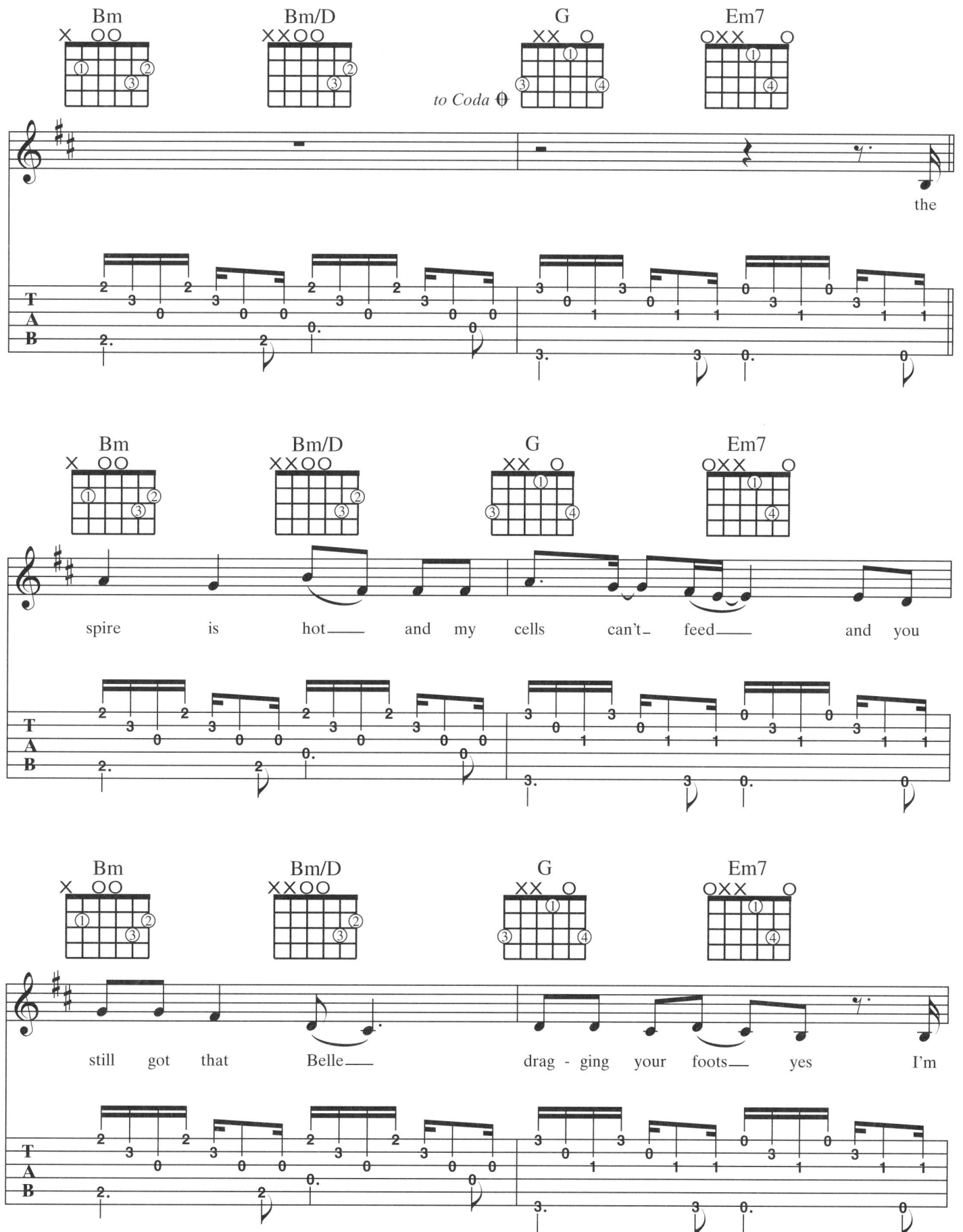

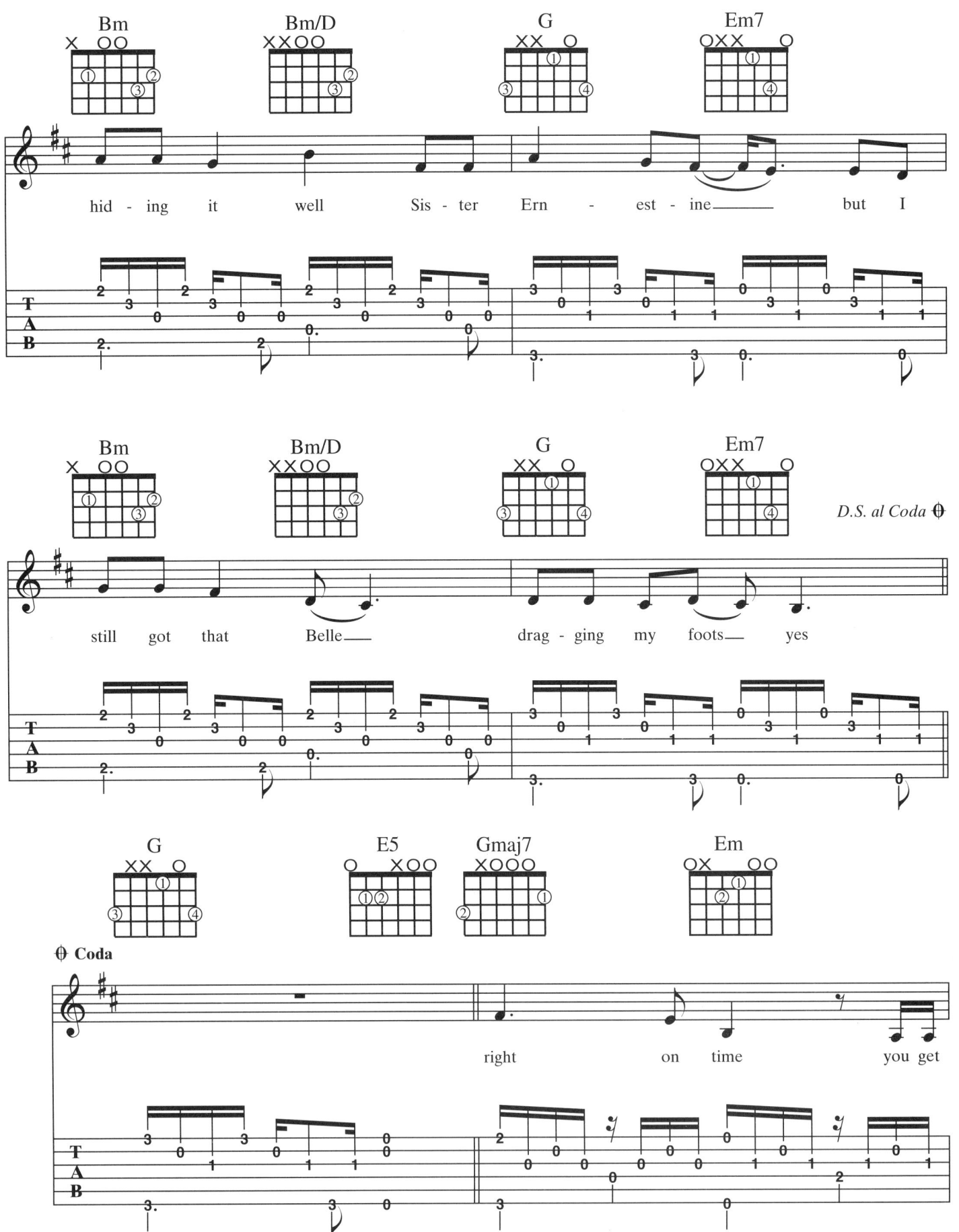

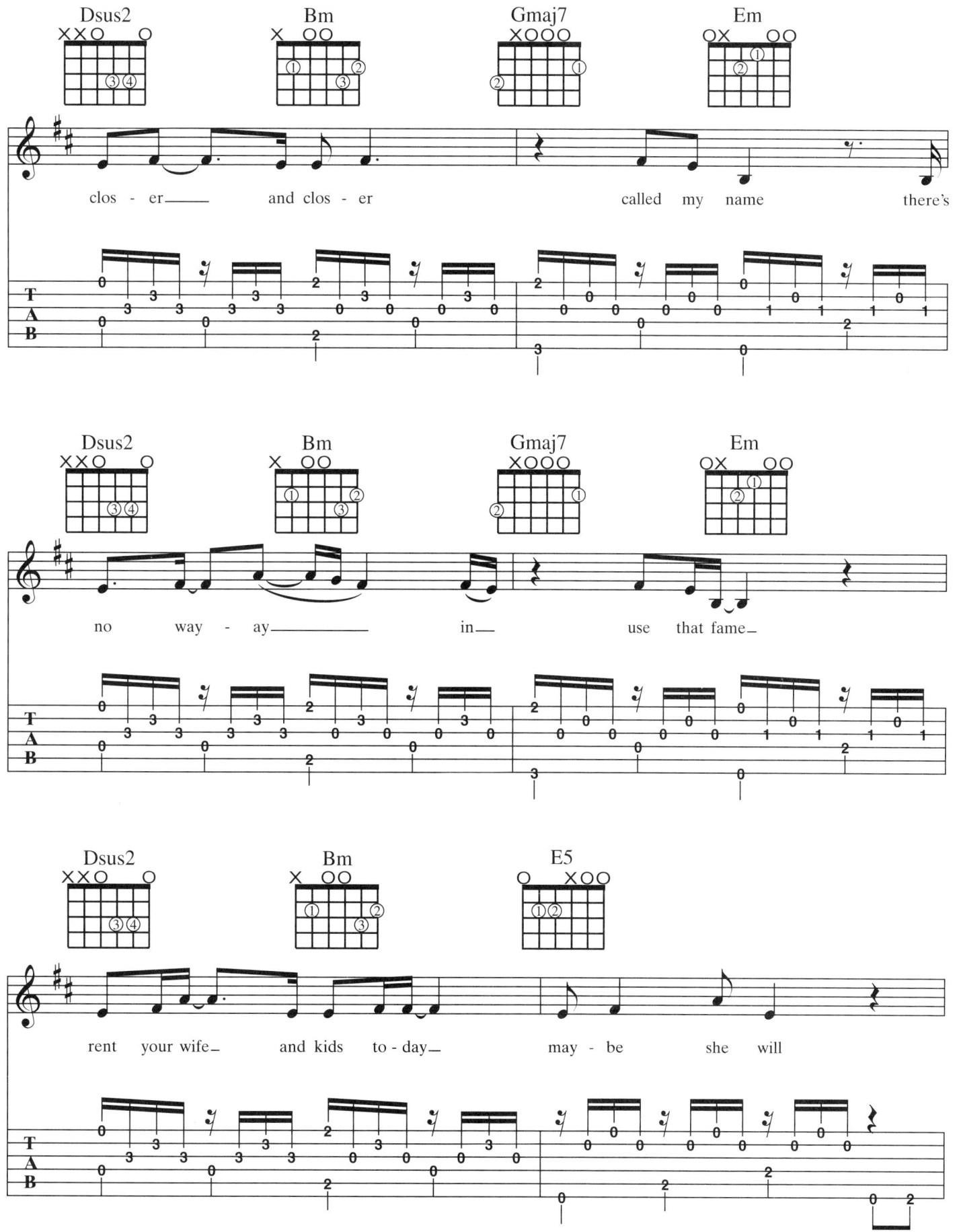

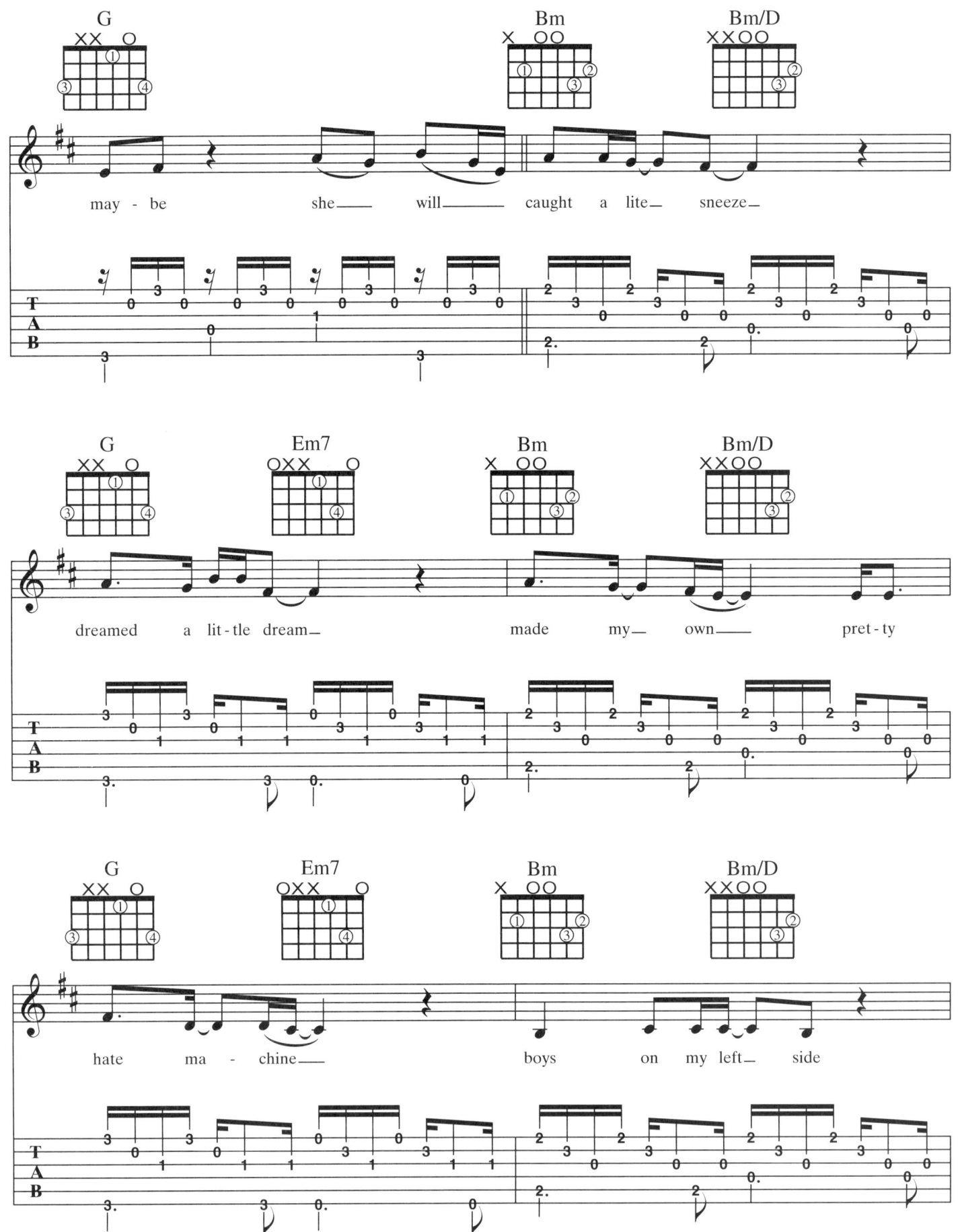

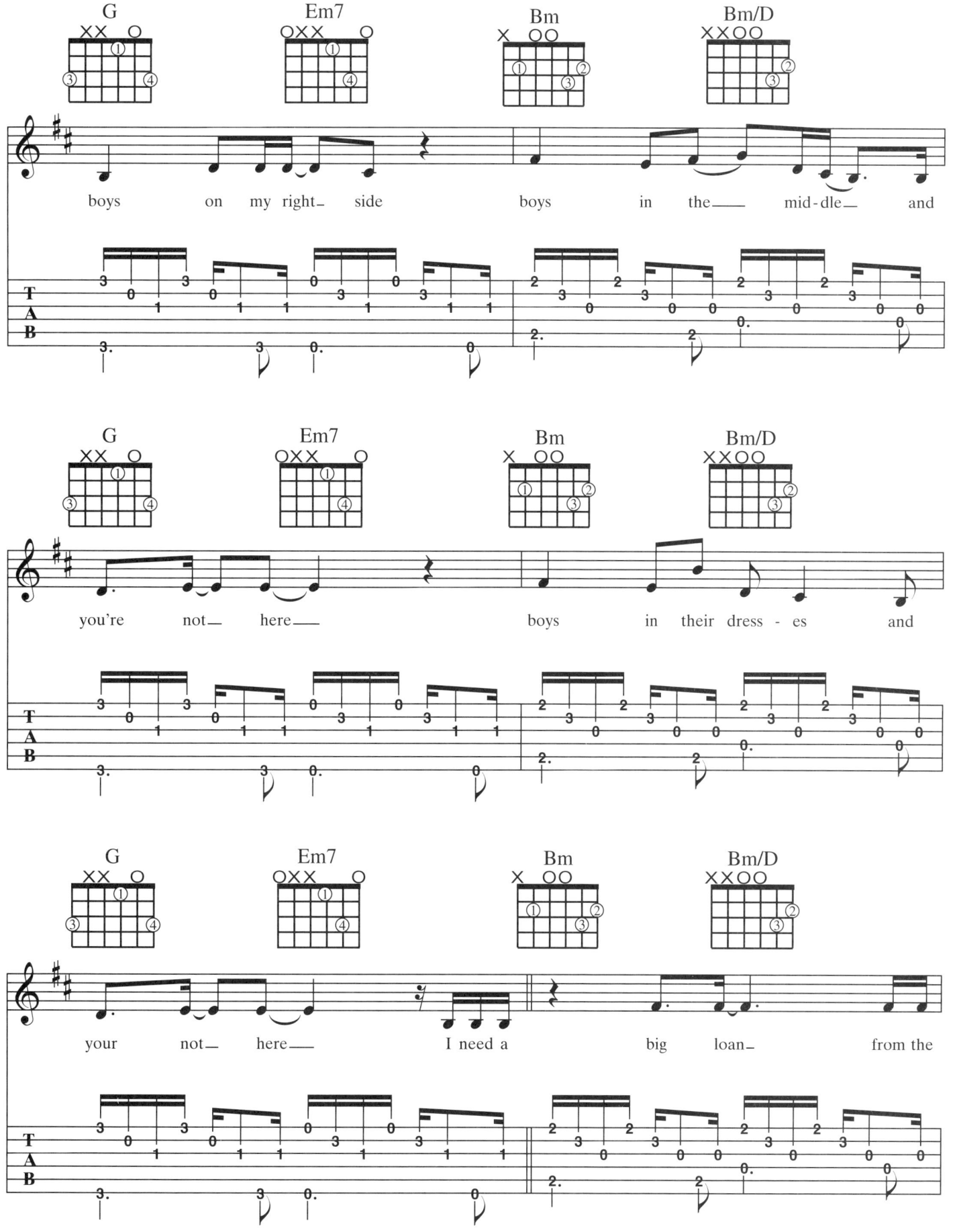

52

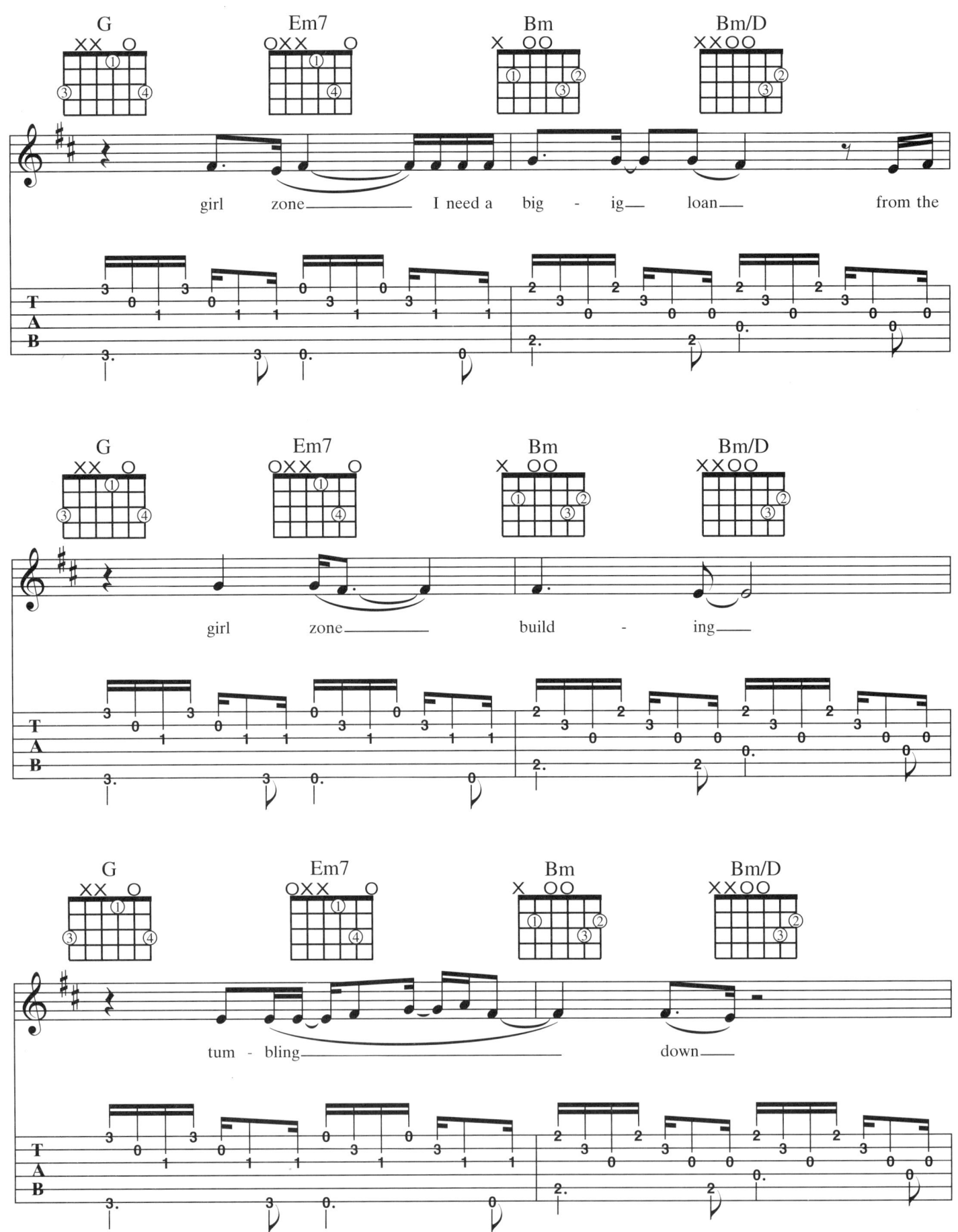

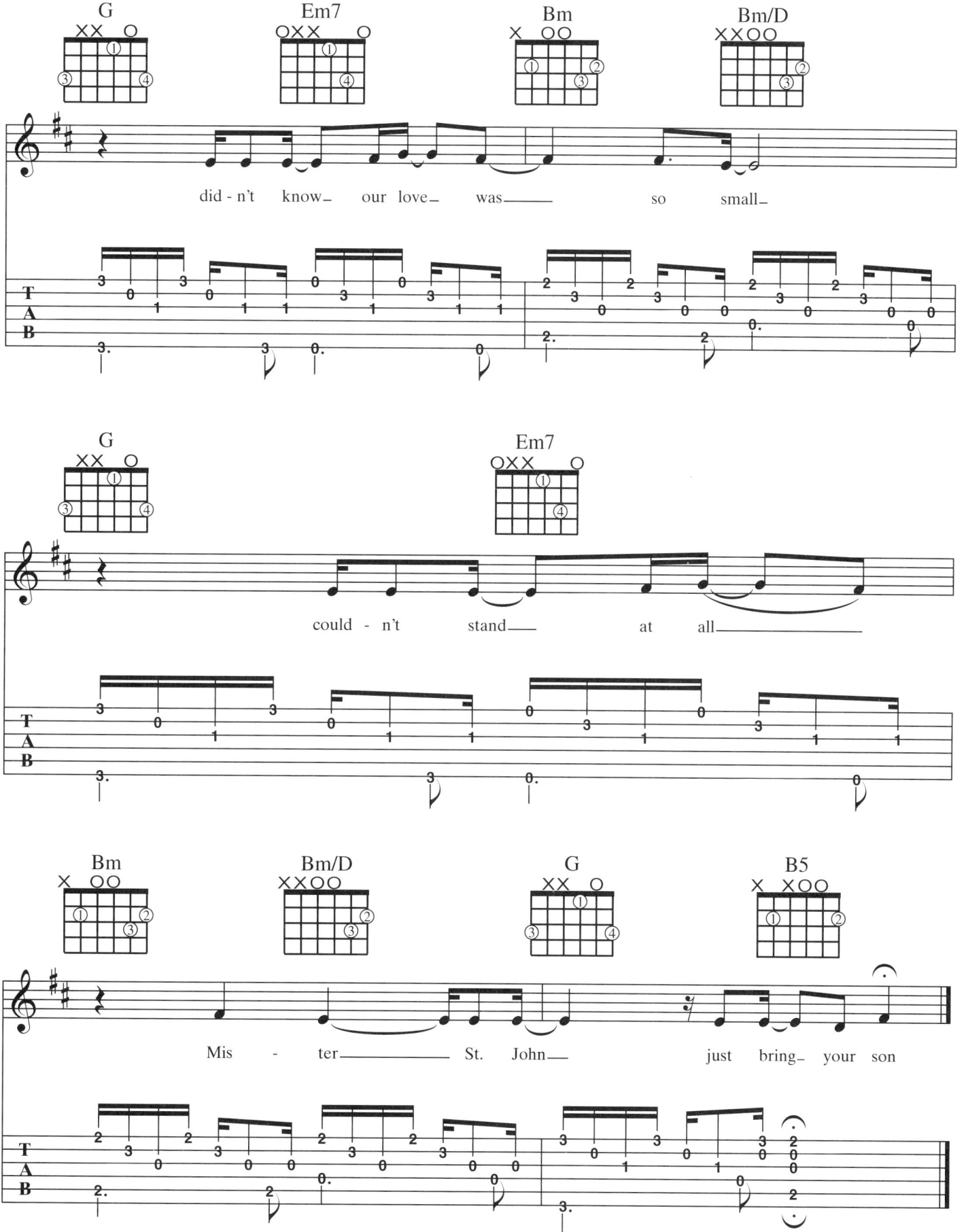

CHINA
Words and Music by Tori Amos

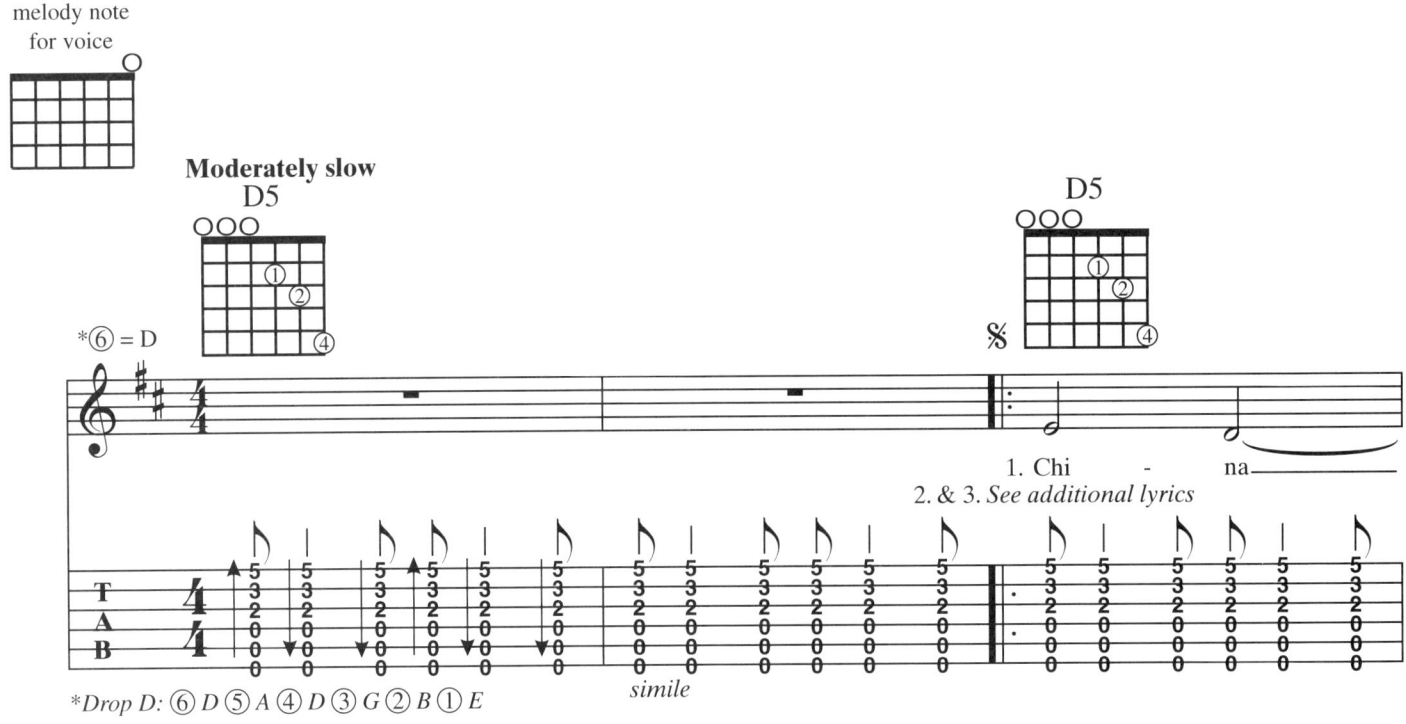

Copyright © 1991 Sword and Stone Publishing Inc. (ASCAP)
International Copyright Secured. All Rights Reserved.

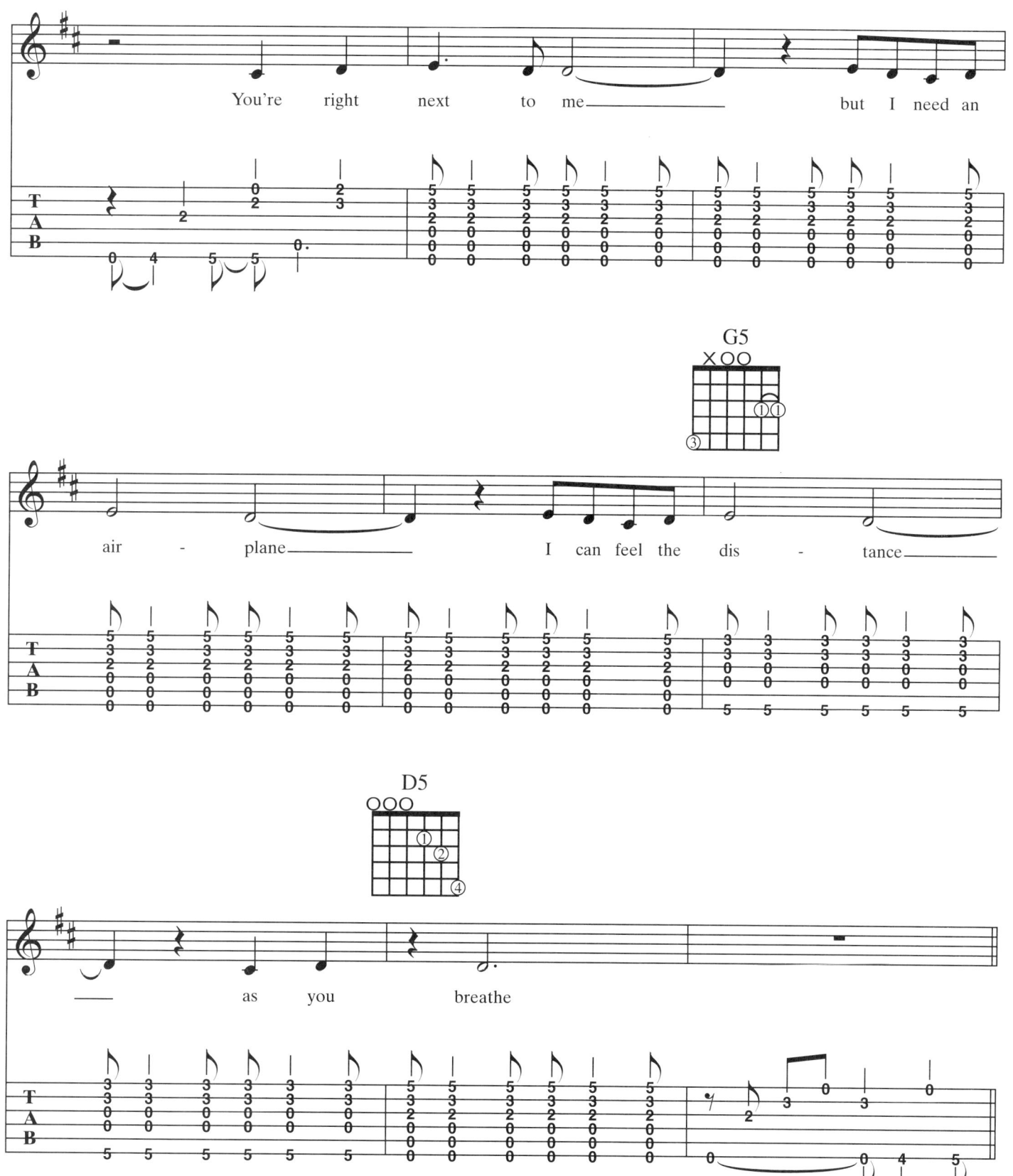

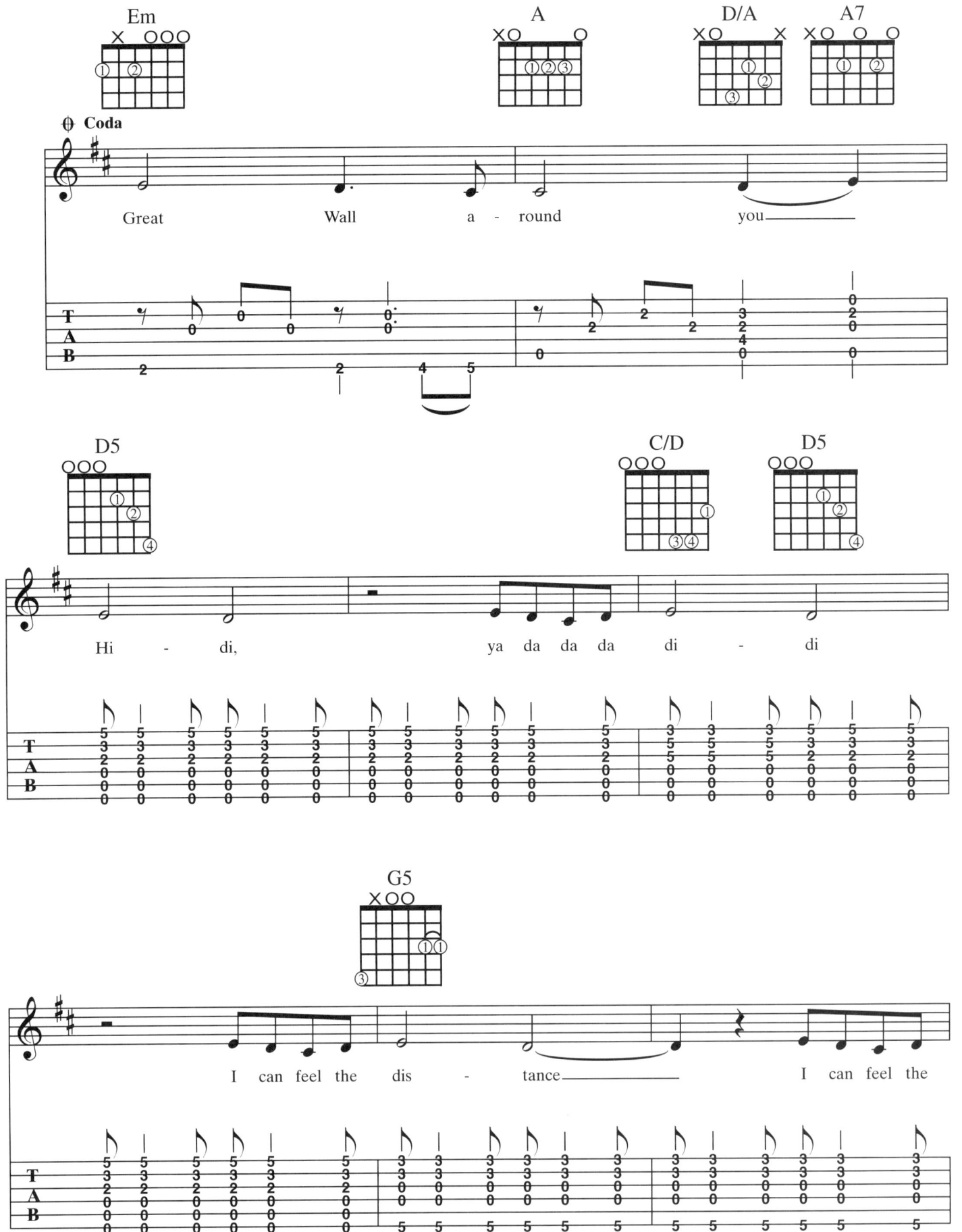

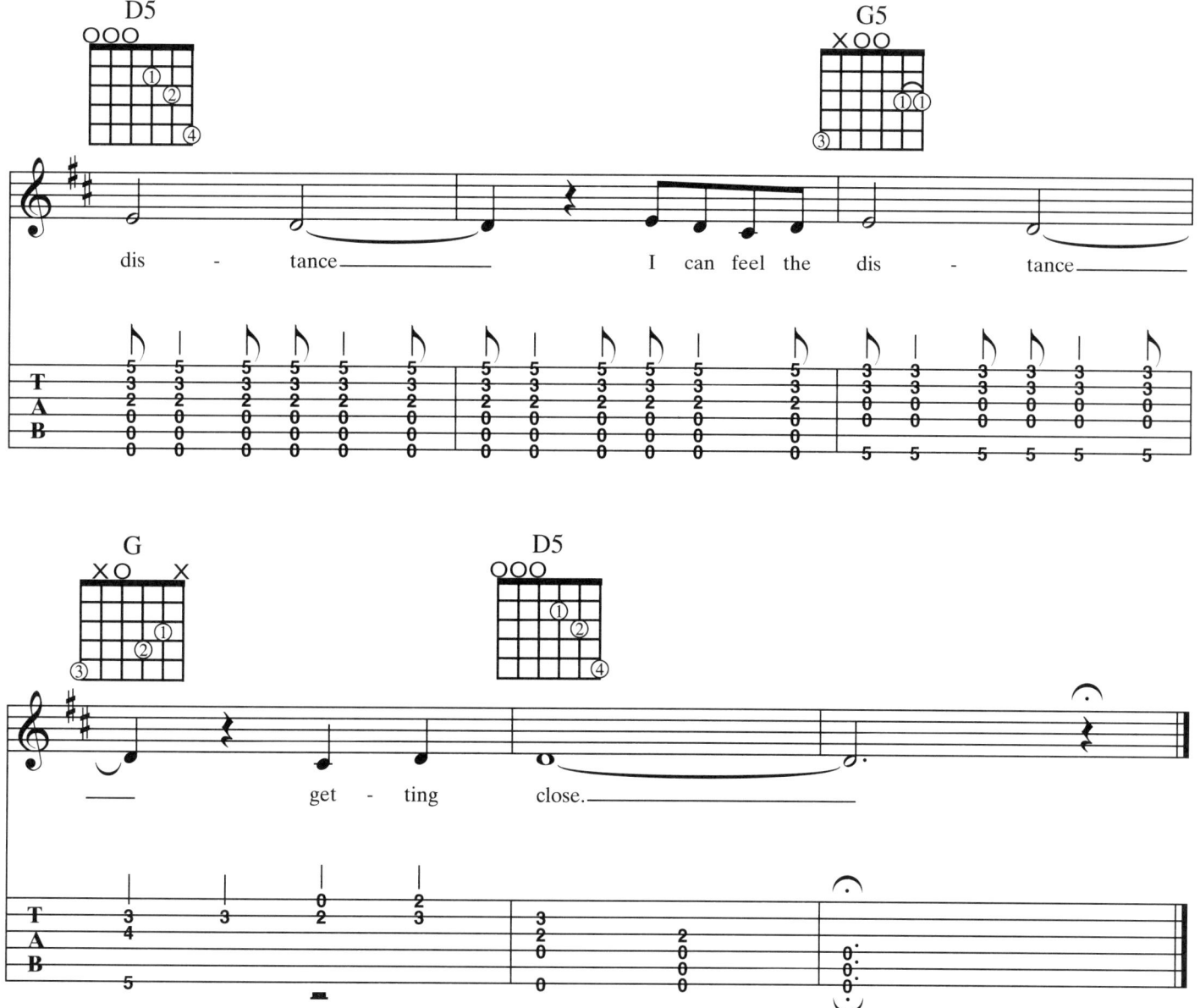

Additional lyrics

2. China decorates our table
   Funny how the cracks don't seem to show
   Pour the wine dear you say we'll take a holiday
   But we never can agree on where to go
   Sometimes... *etc.*

3. China all the way to New York
   Maybe you got lost in Mexico
   You're right next to me I think that you can hear me
   Funny how the distance learns to grow
   Sometimes... *etc.*

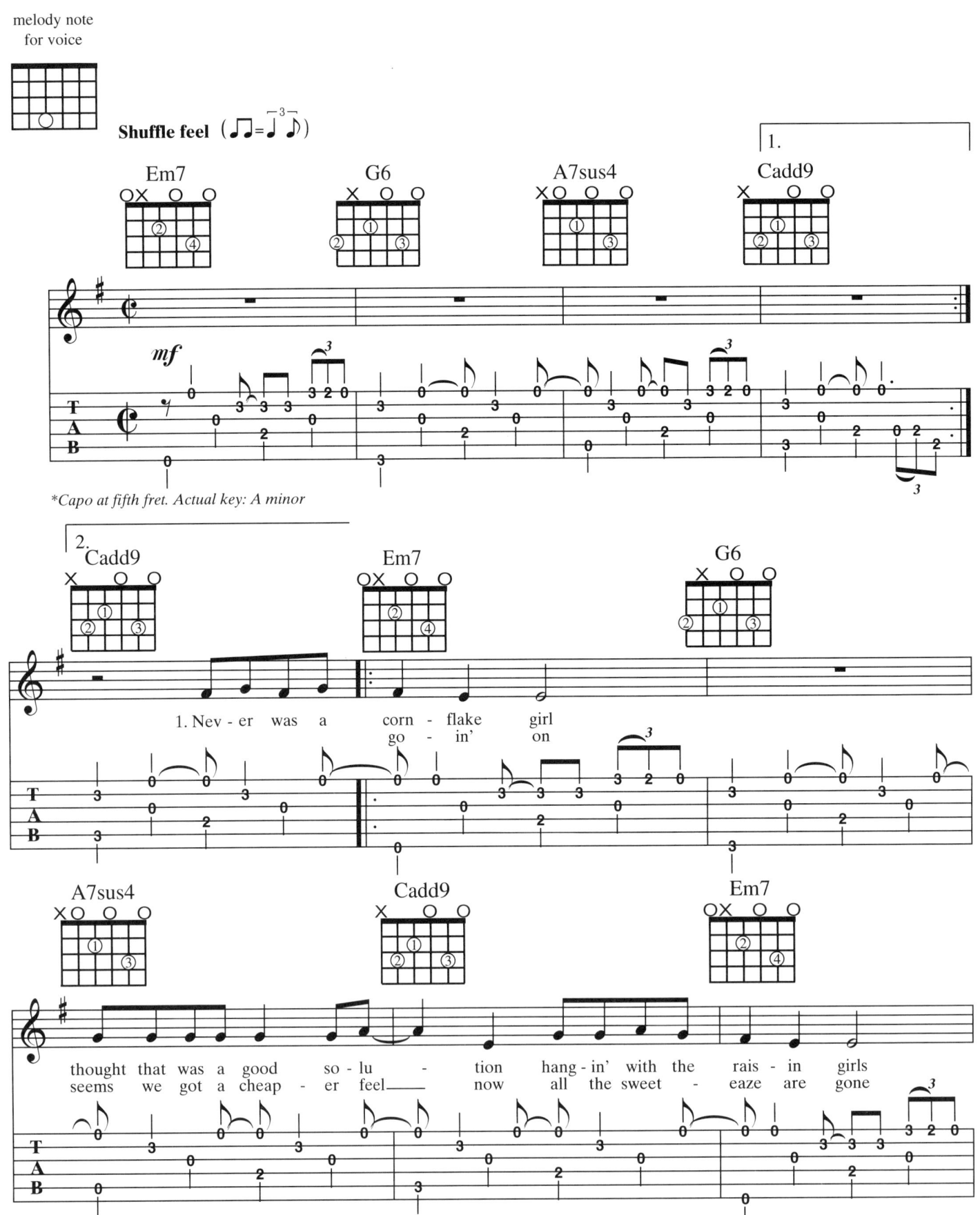

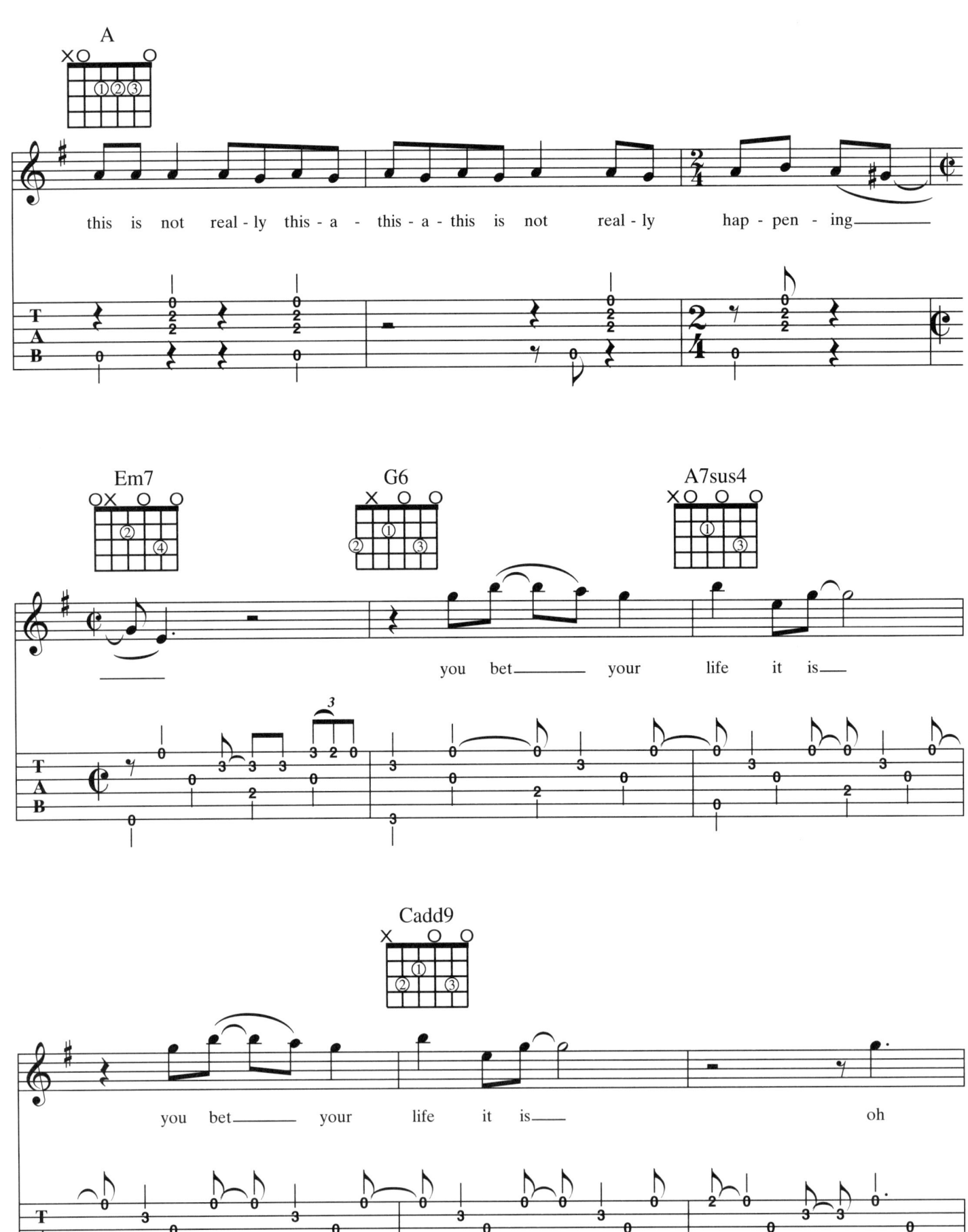

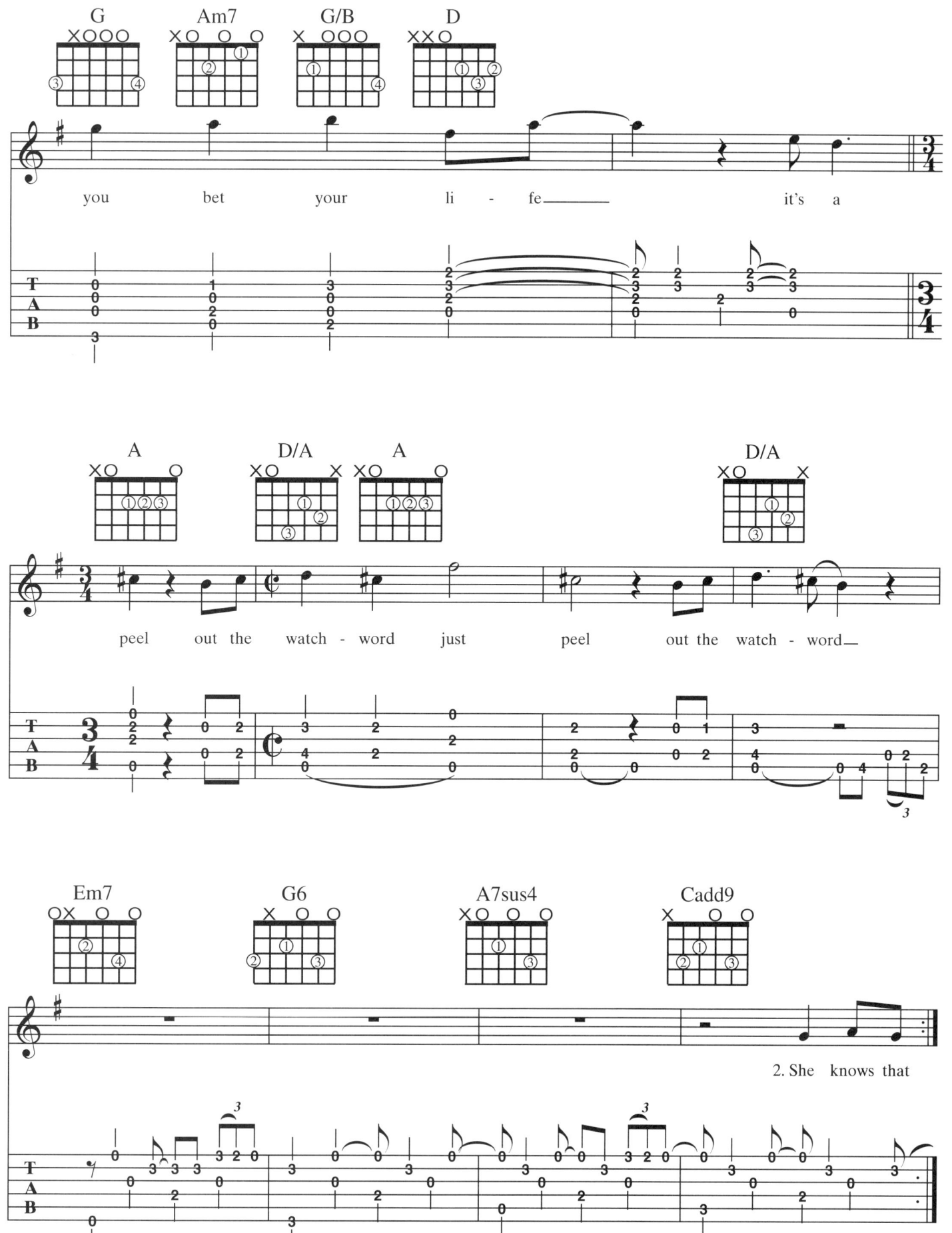

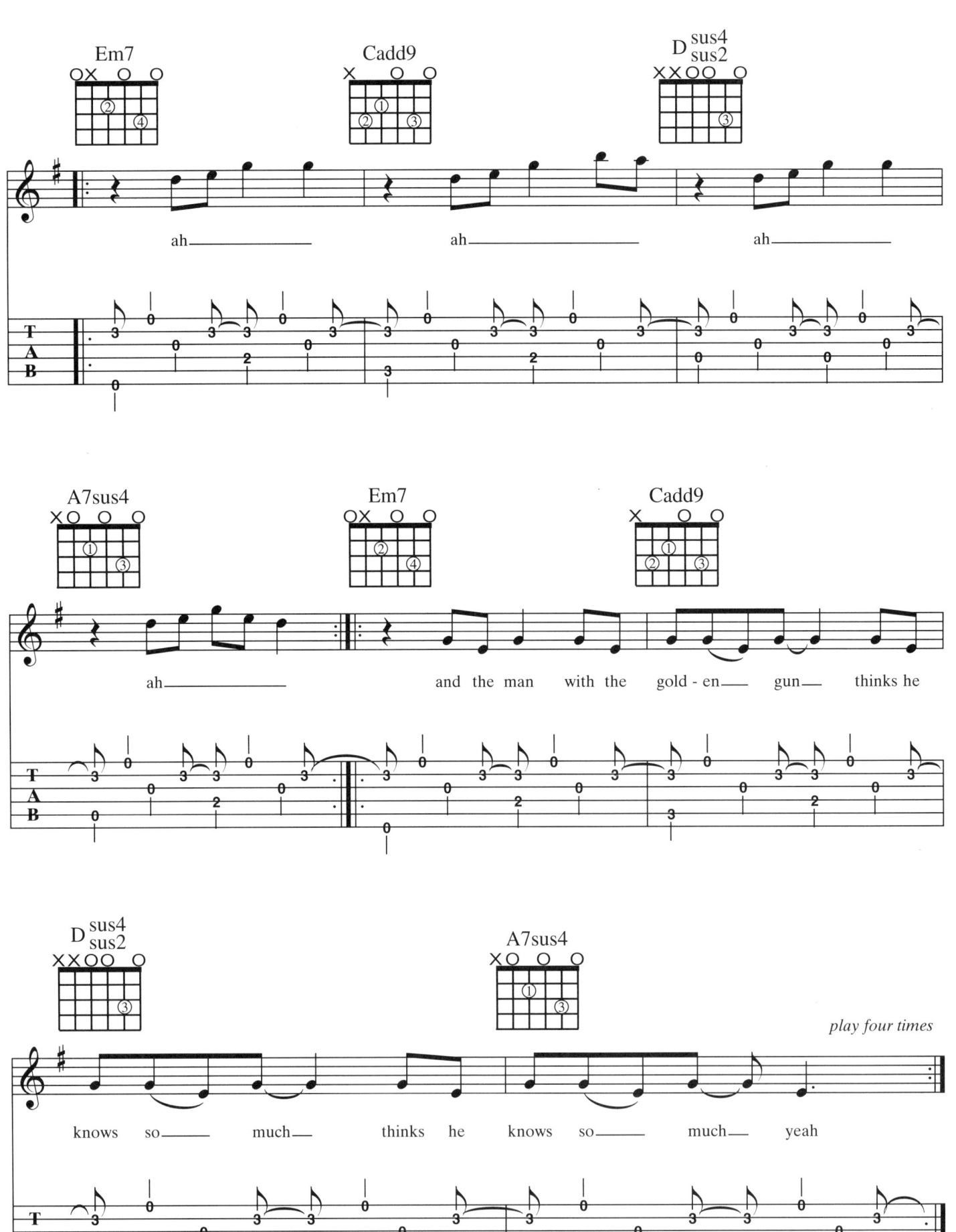

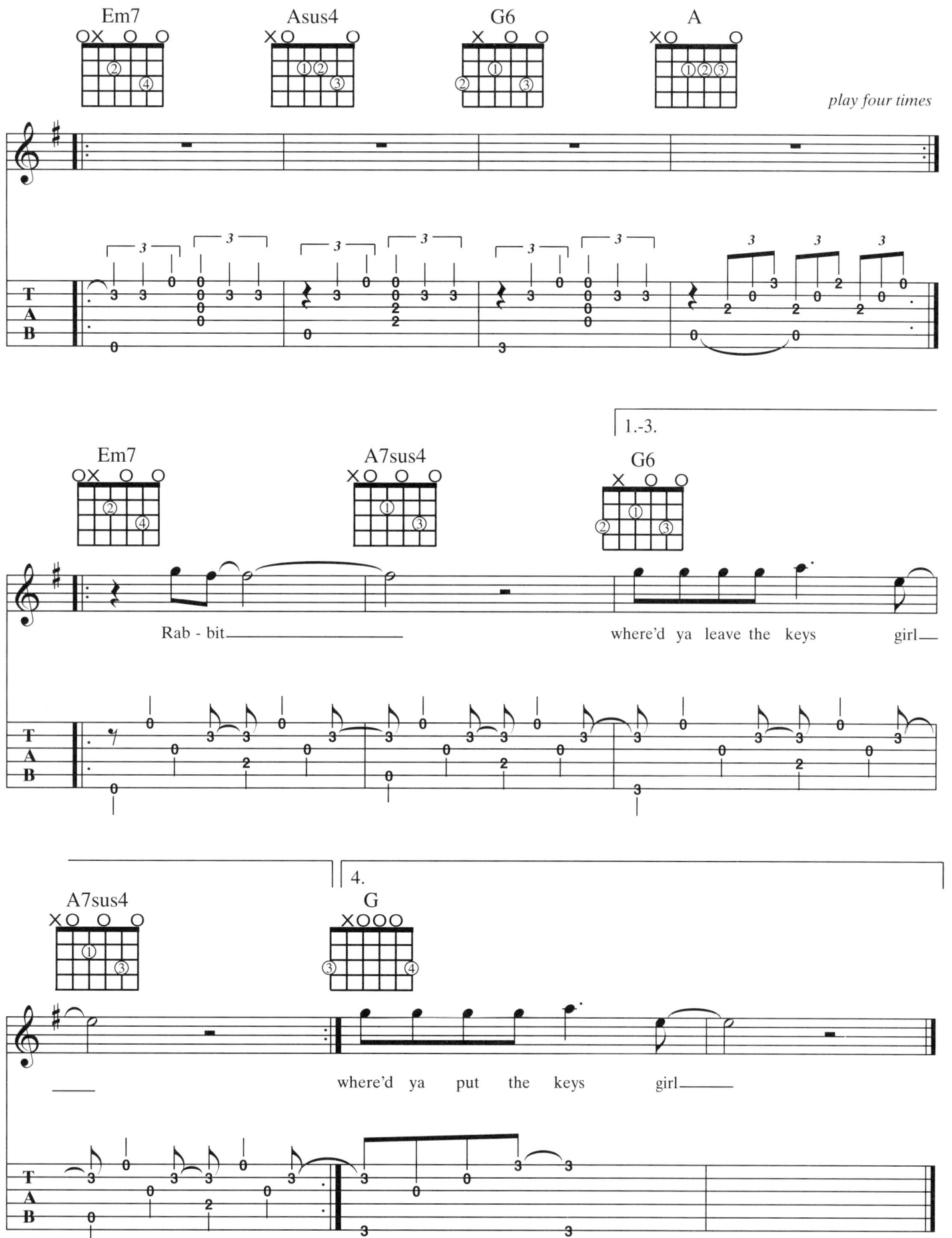

Little Earthquakes
Words and Music by Tori Amos

melody note for voice

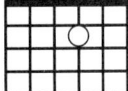

Moderately

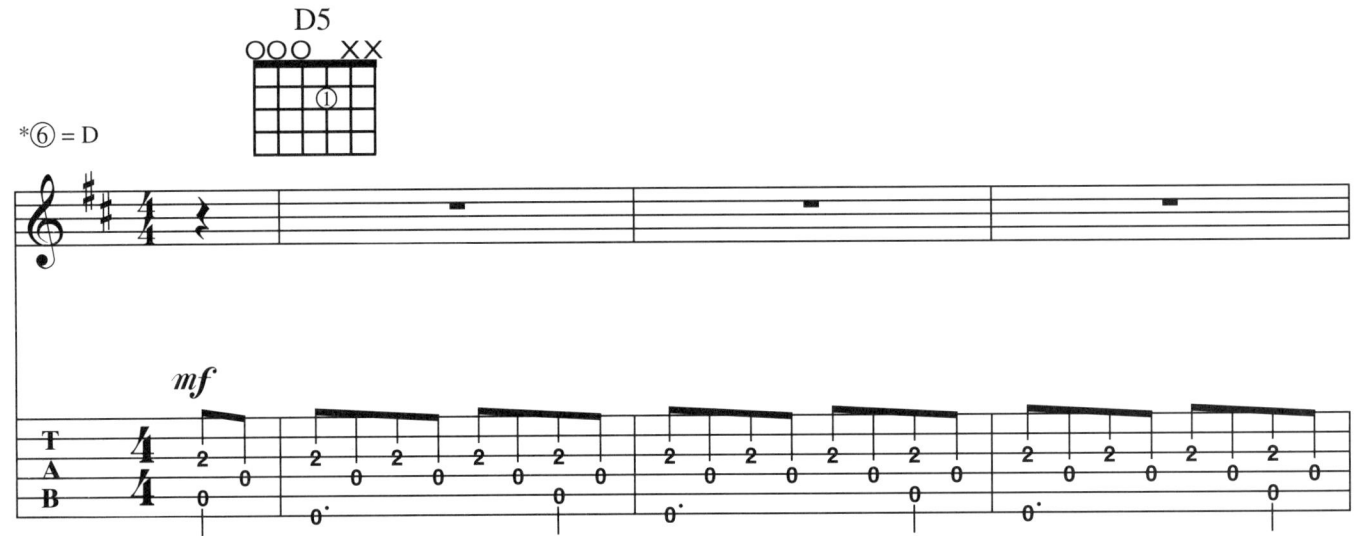

*Capo at second fret. Actual key: E
Drop D: ⑥ D ⑤ A ④ D ③ G ② B ① E

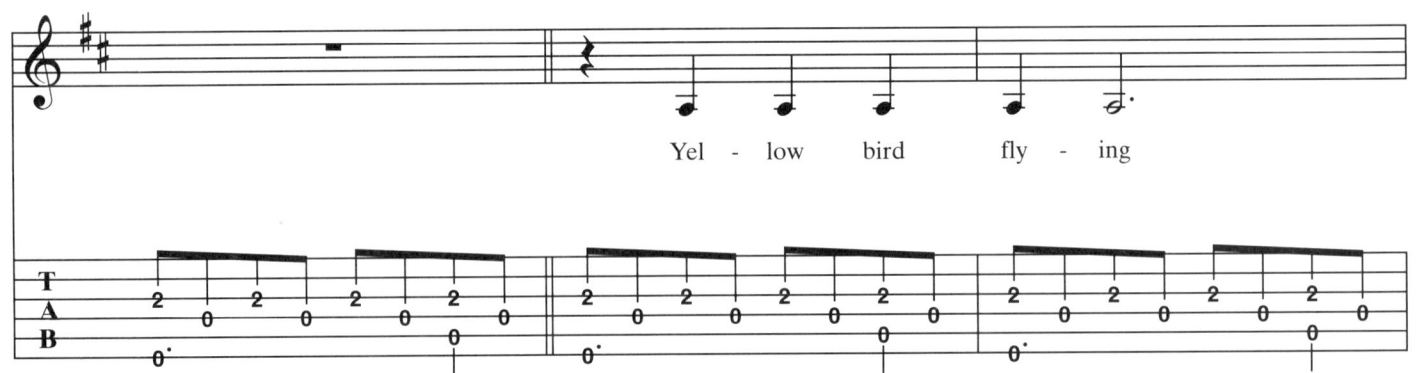

Yel - low bird fly - ing

Copyright © 1990 Sword and Stone Publishing Inc. (ASCAP)
International Copyright Secured. All Rights Reserved.

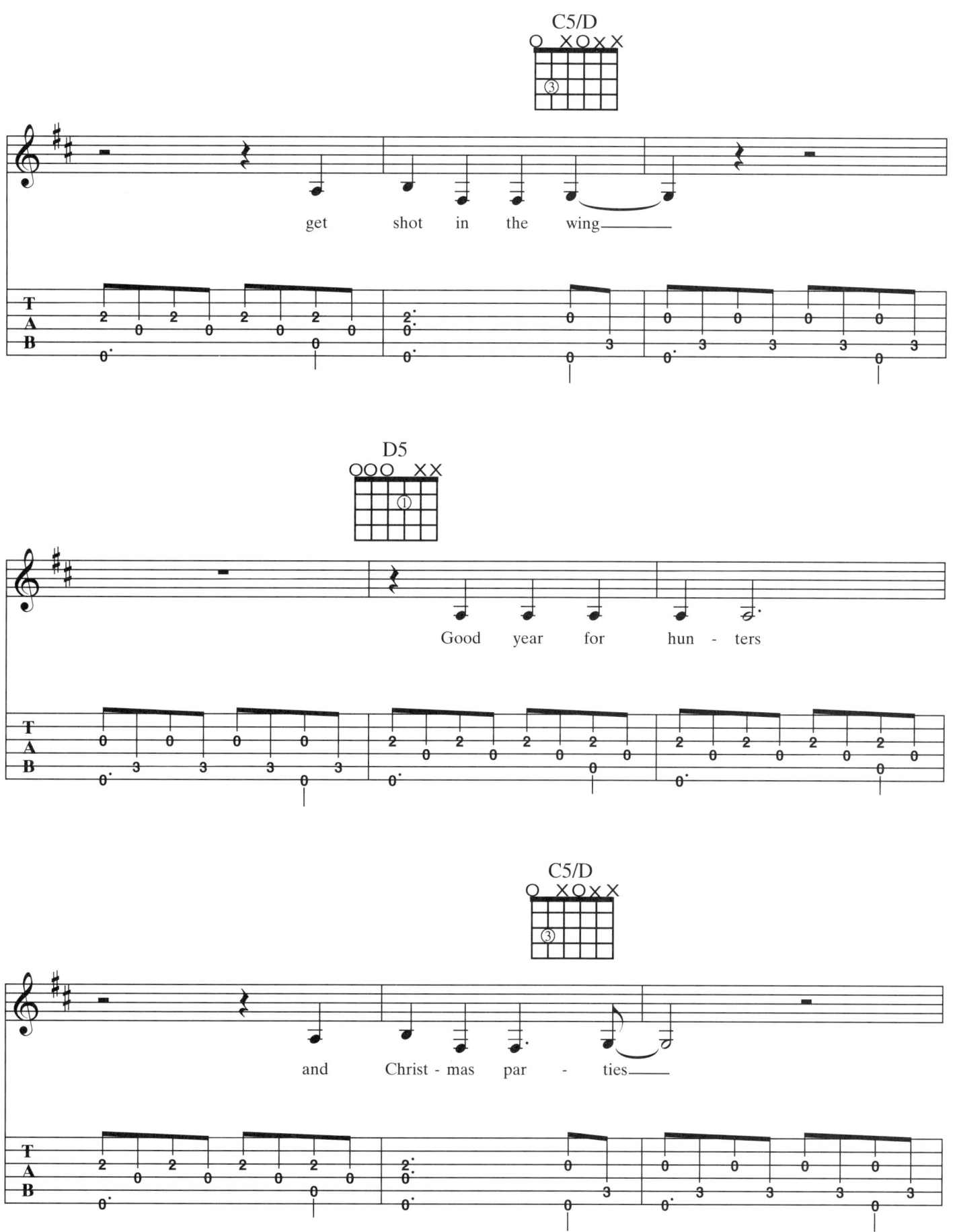

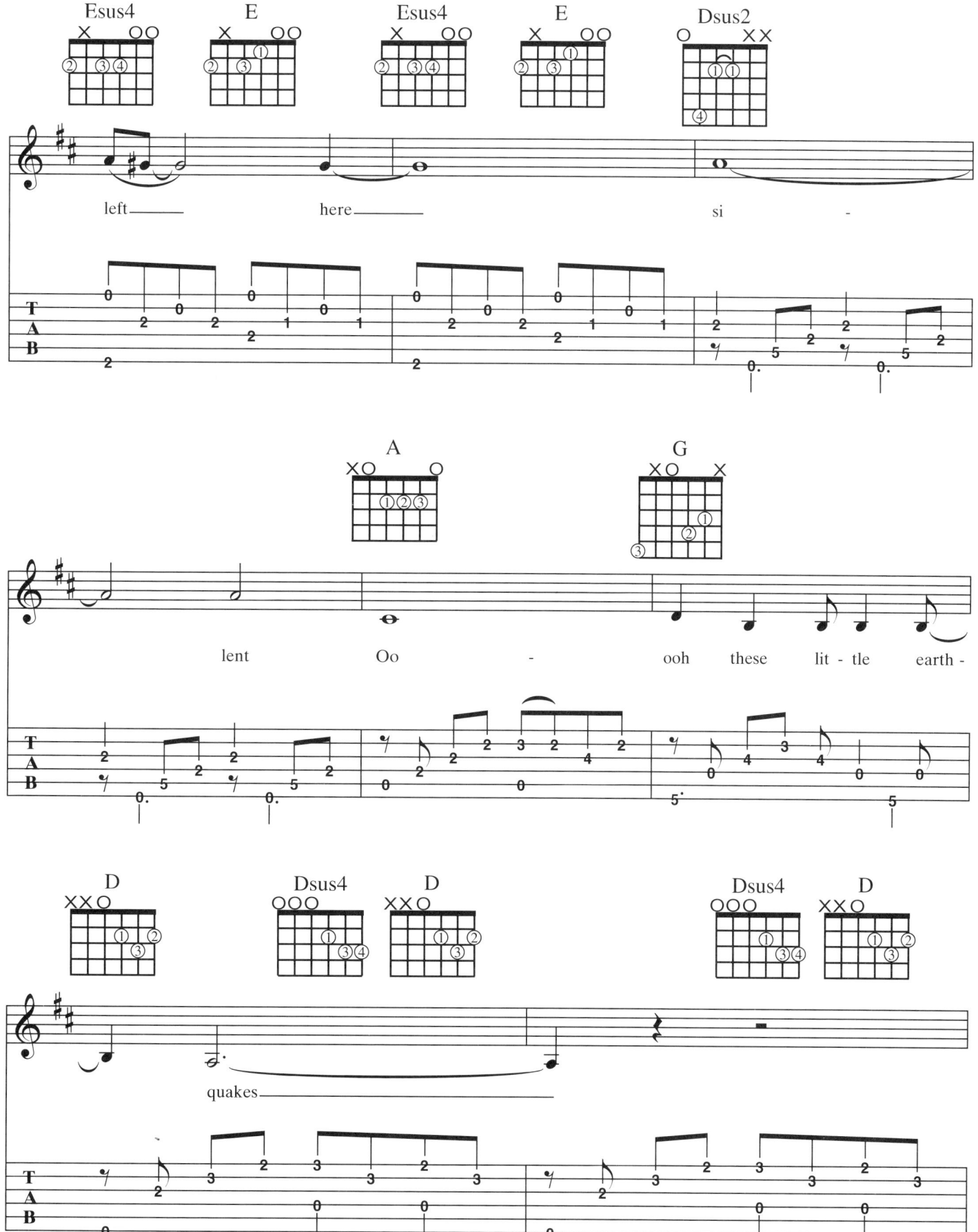

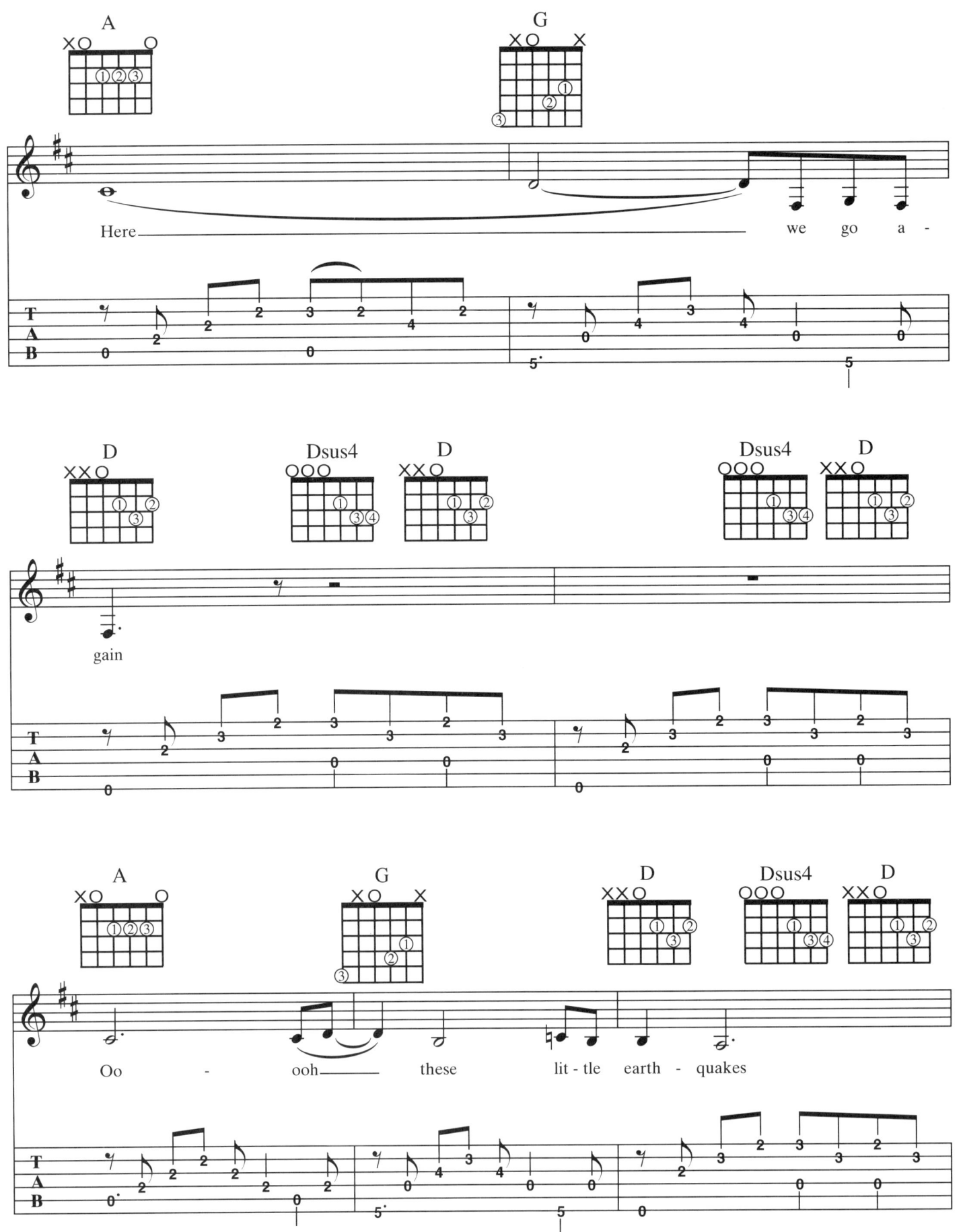

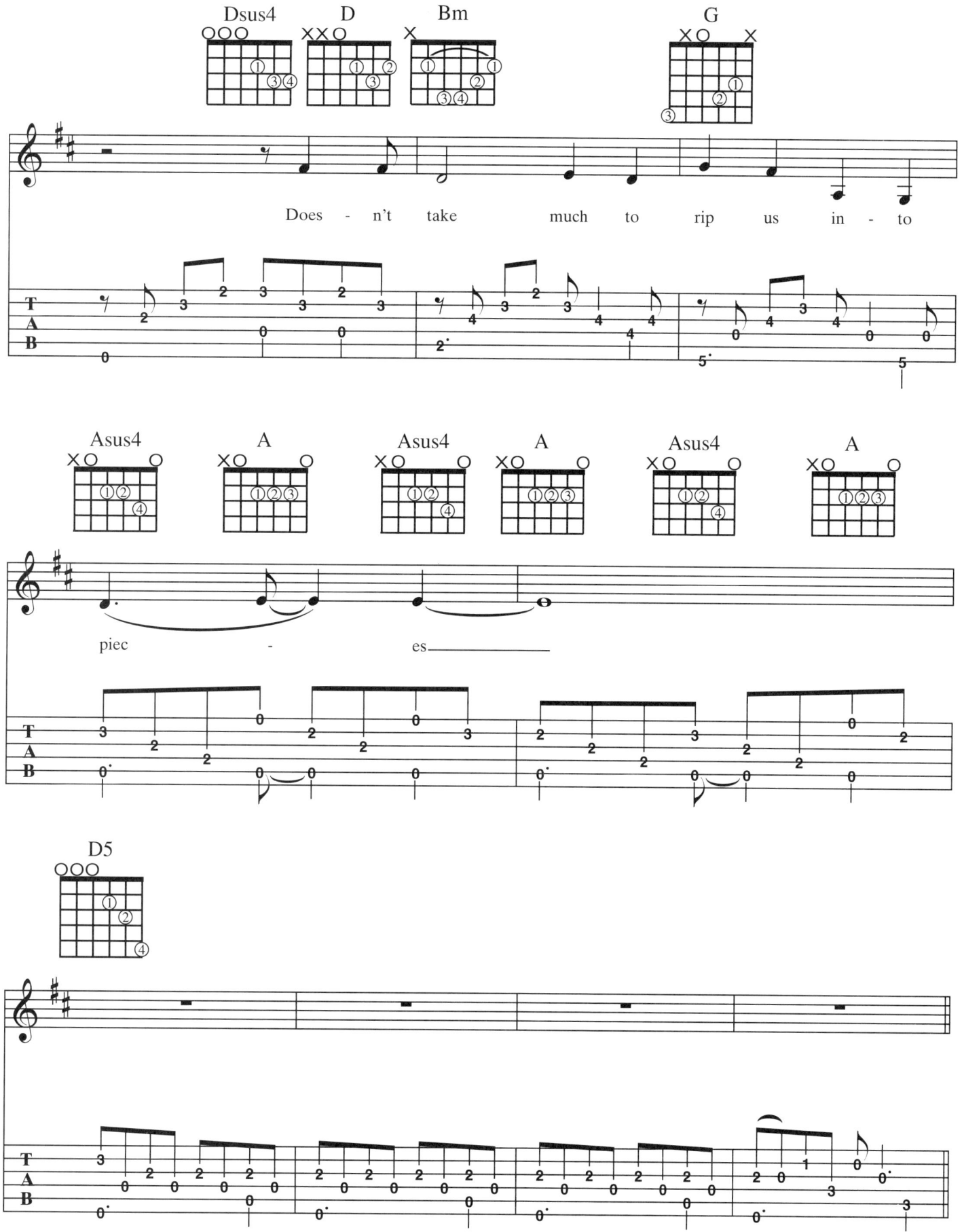

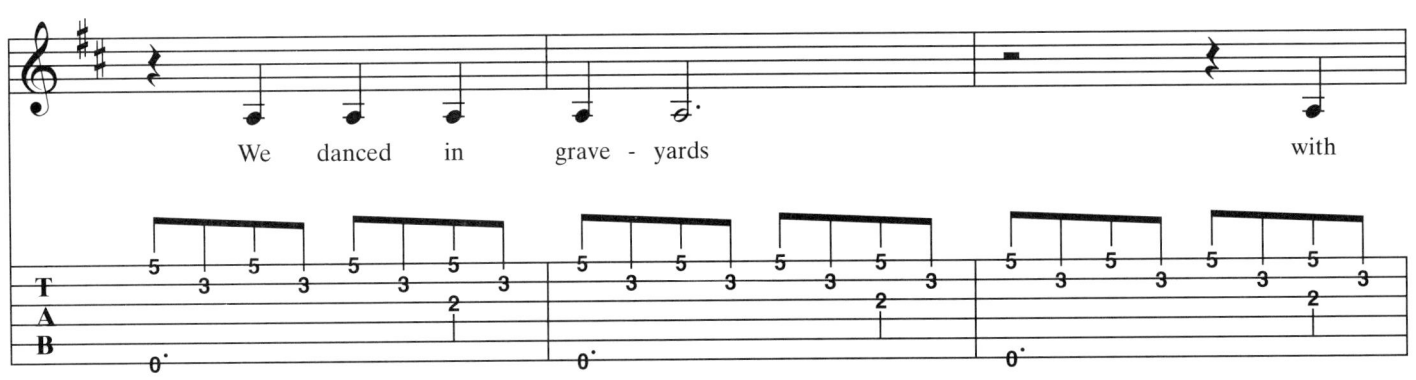
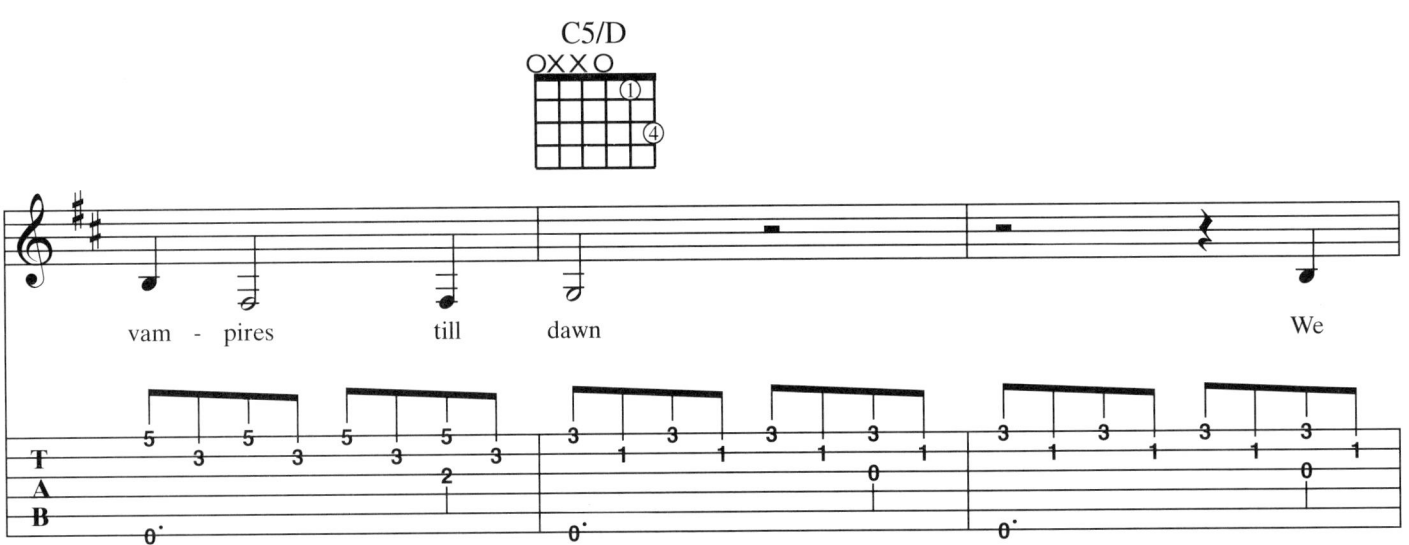
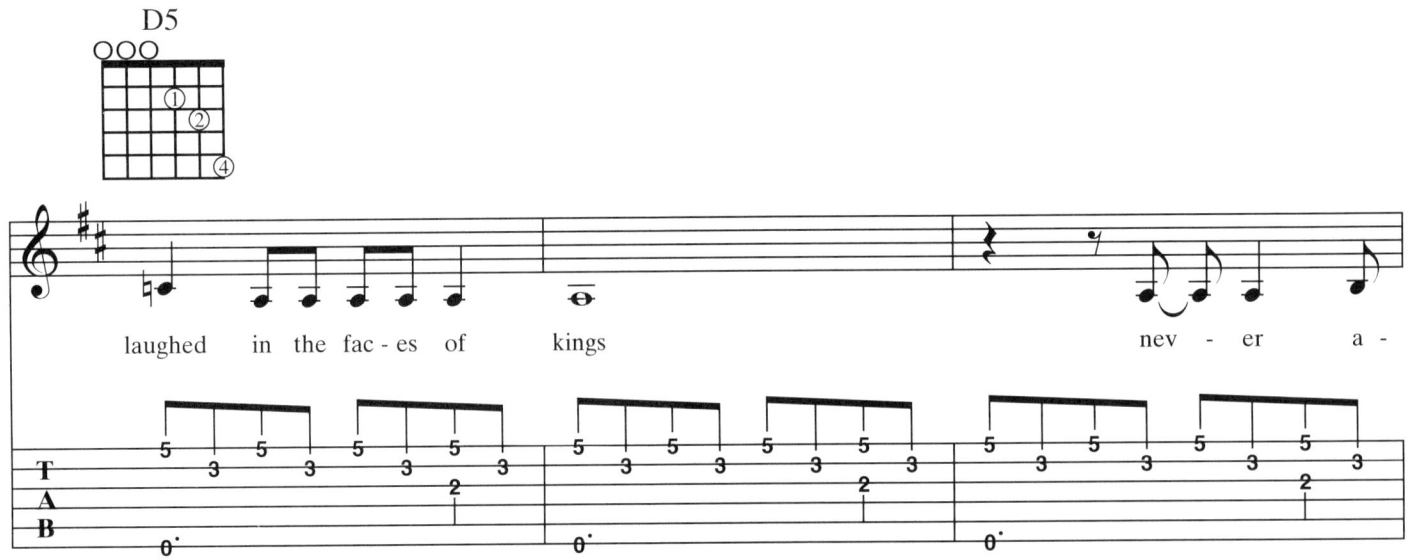

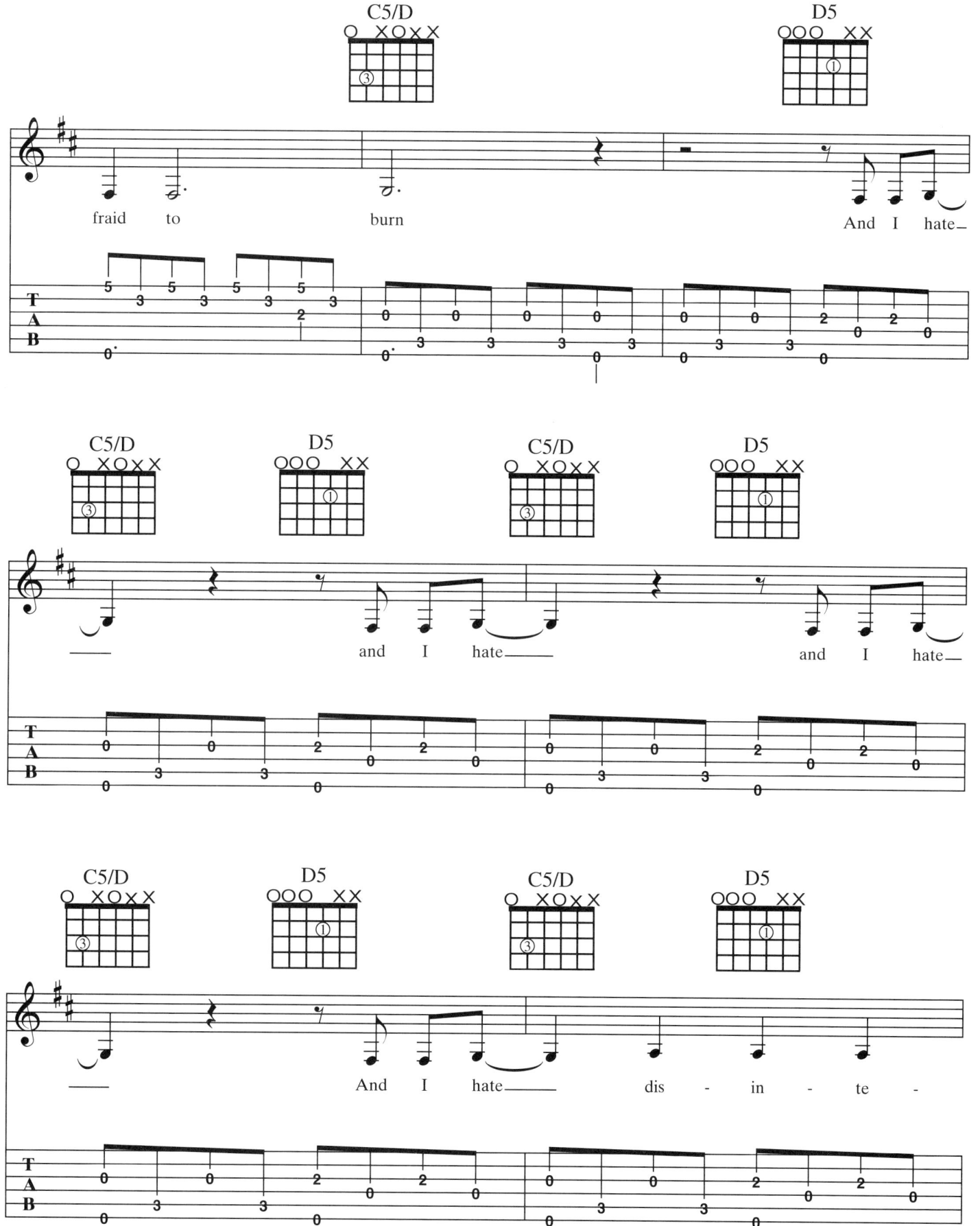

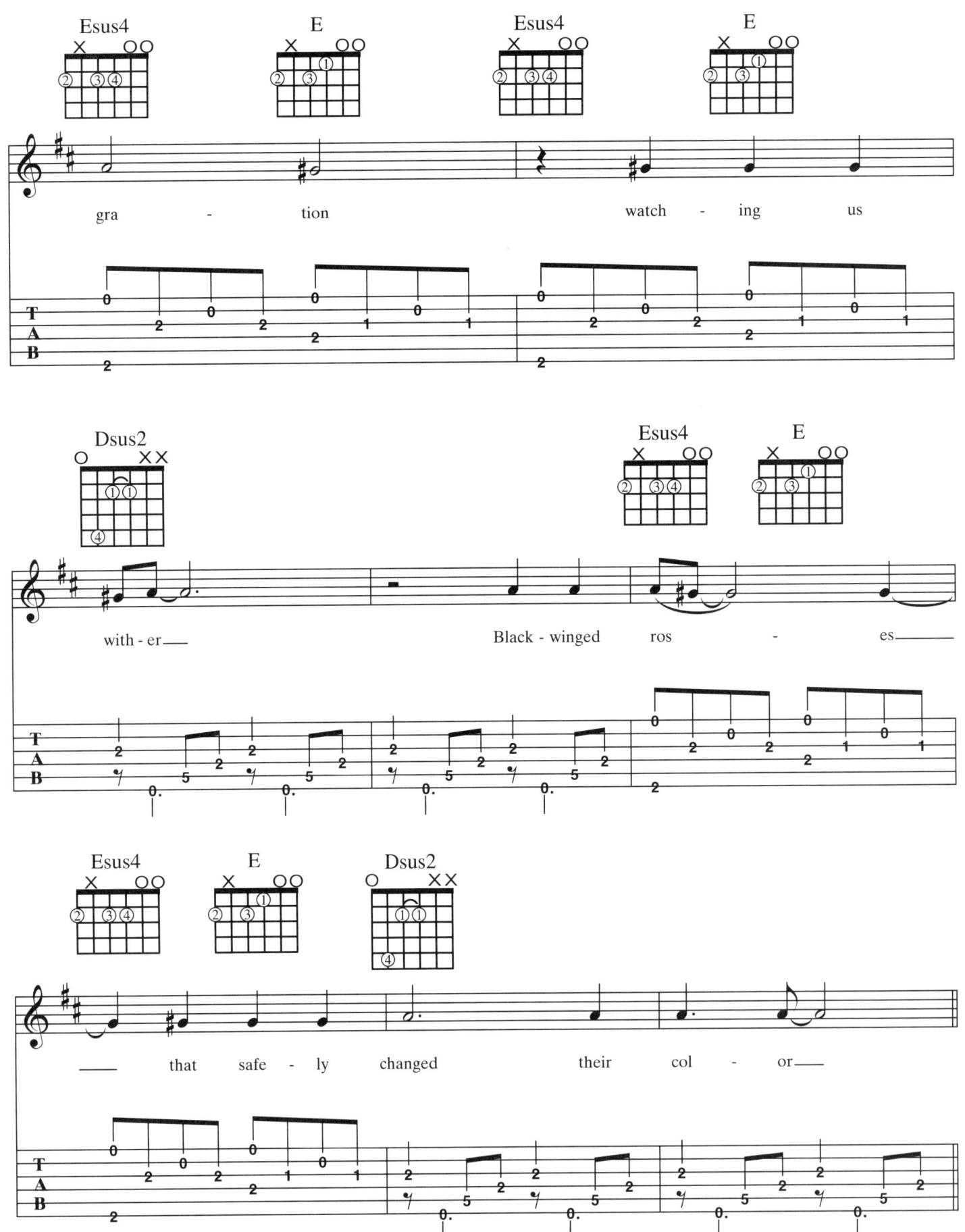

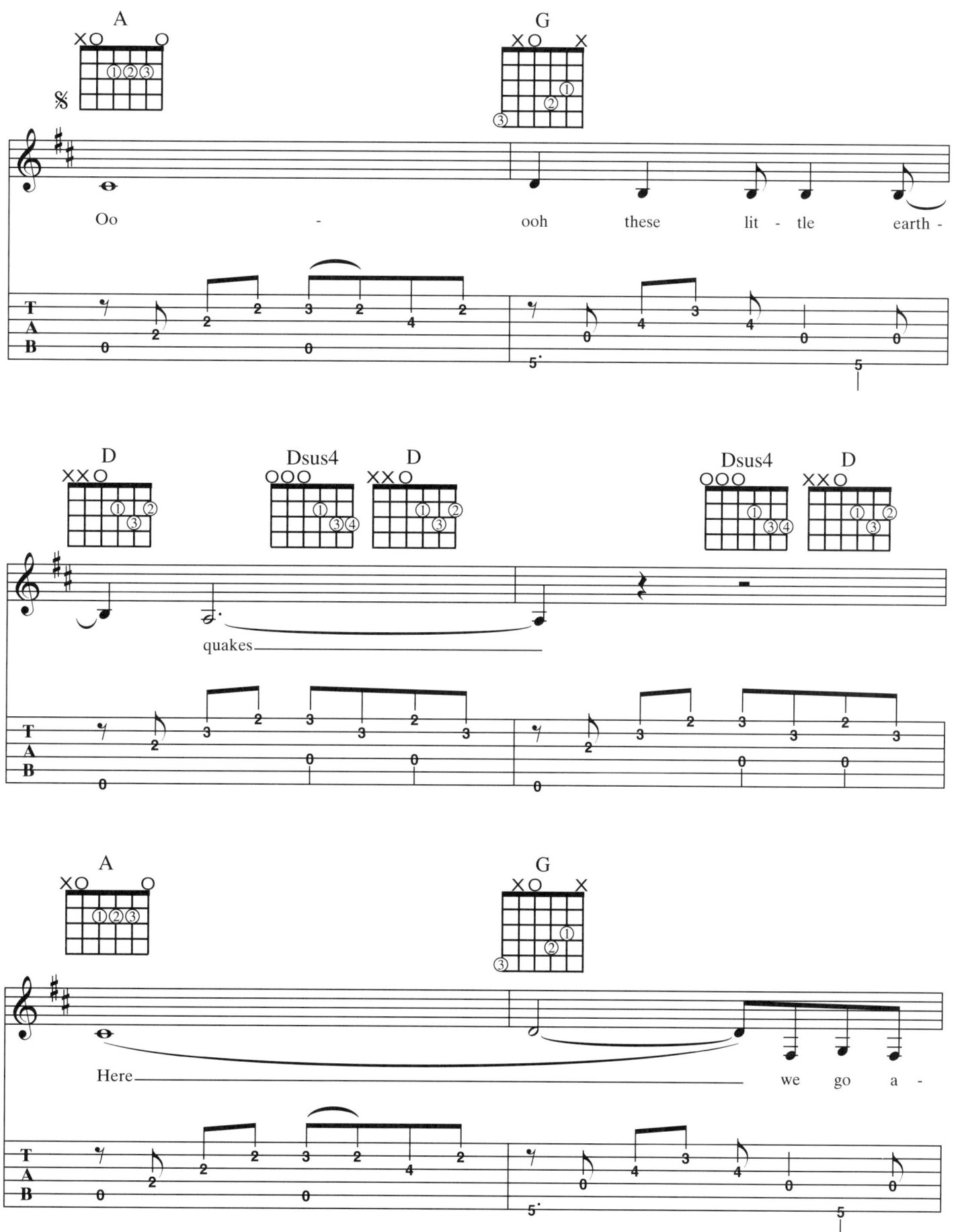

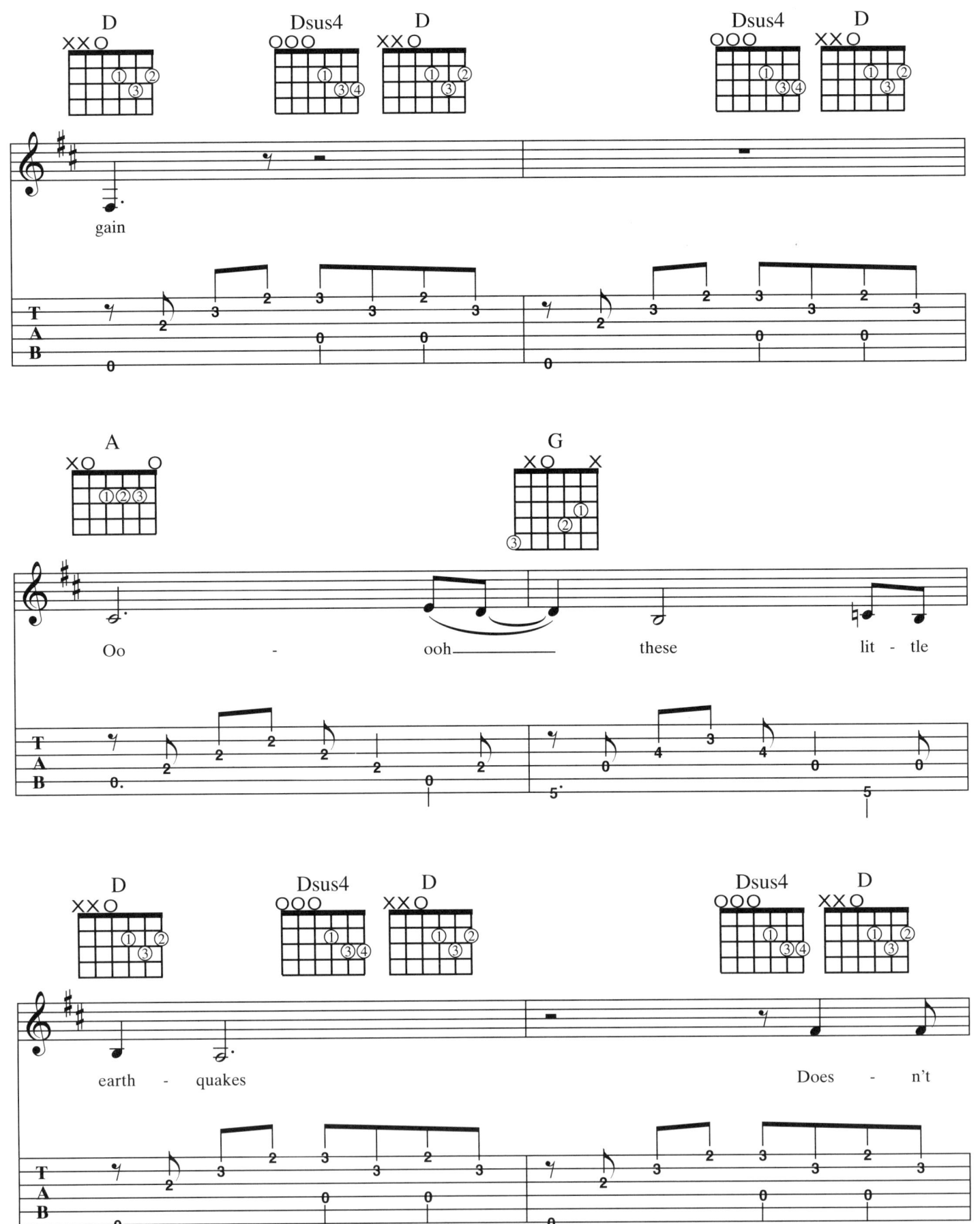

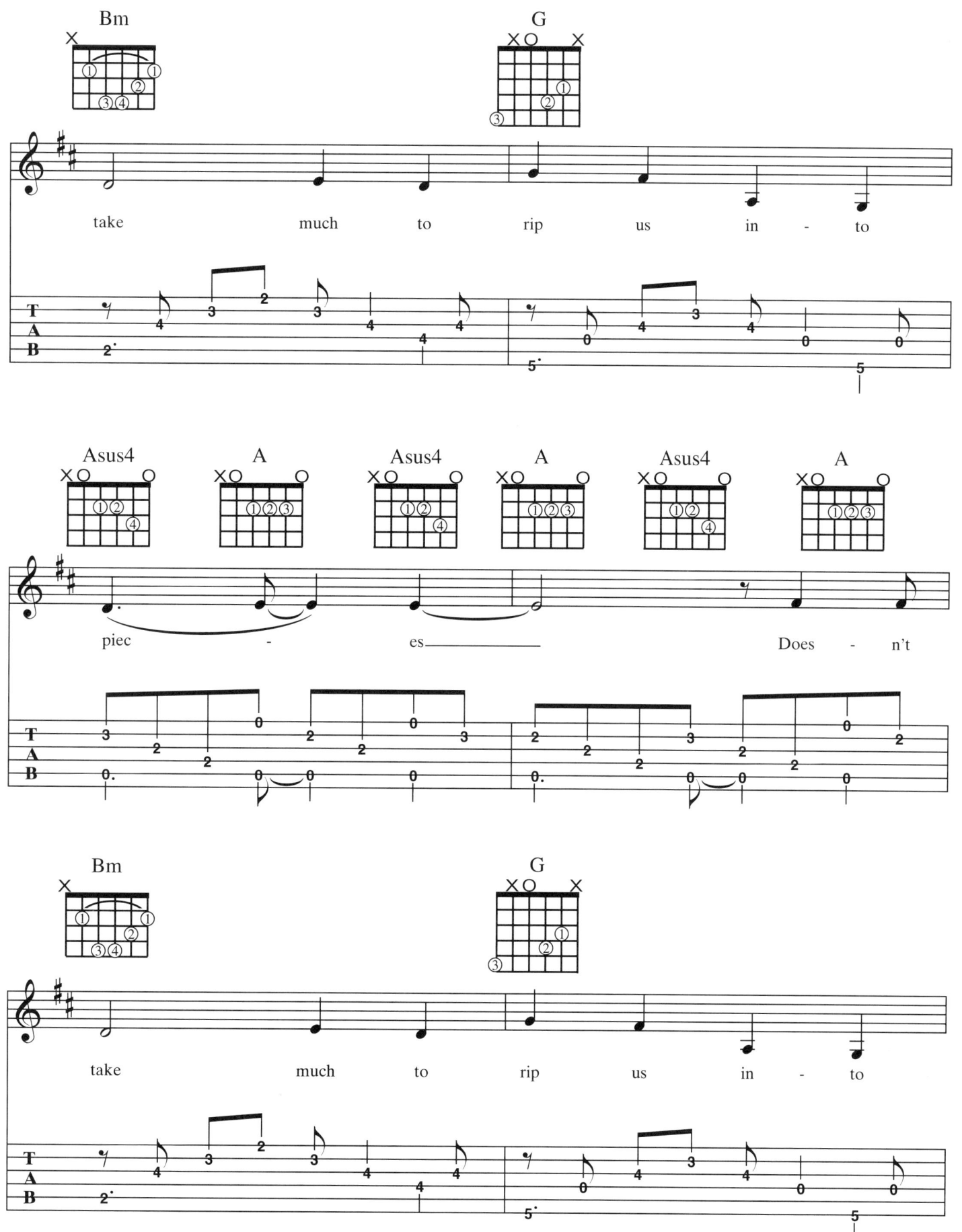

78

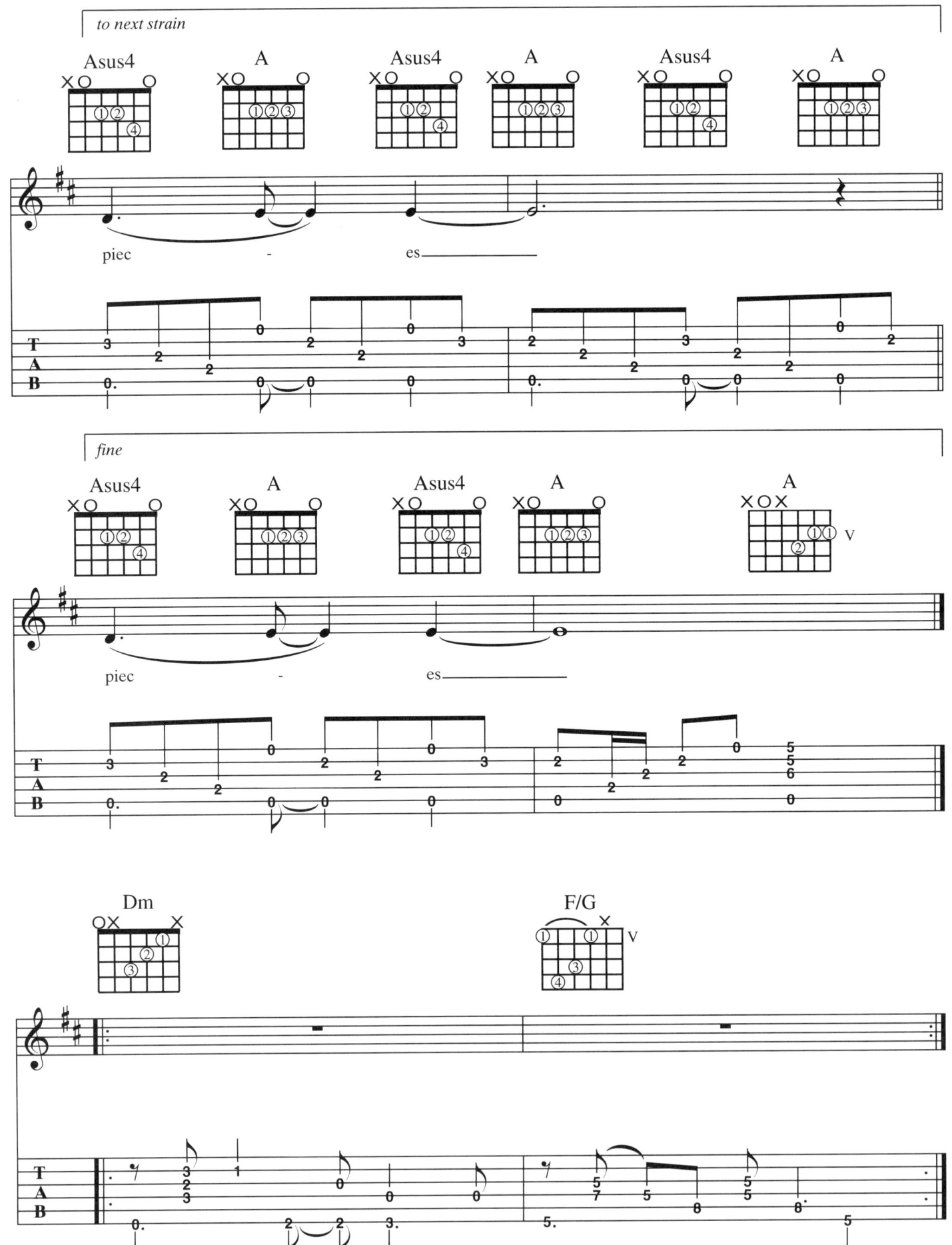

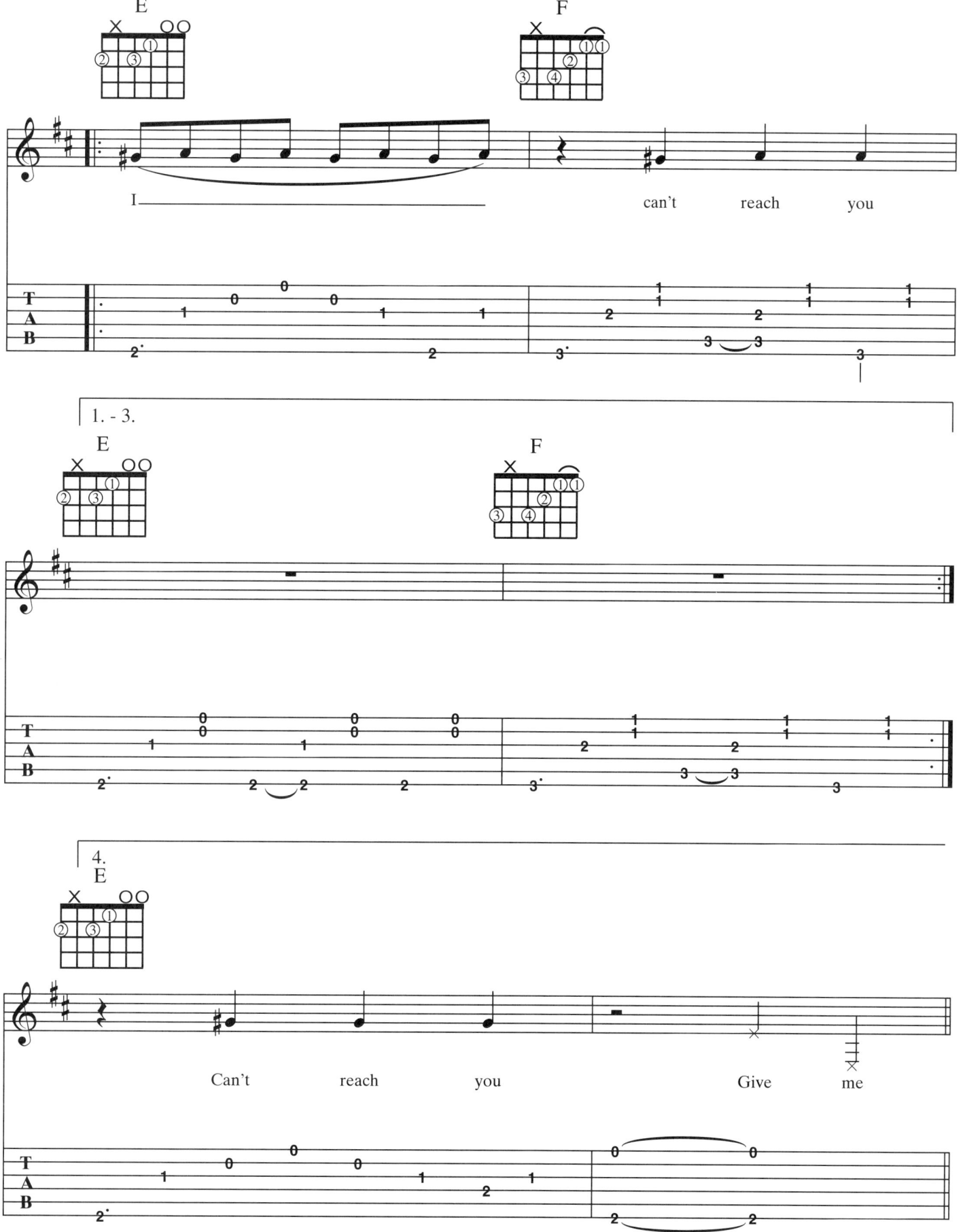

D5
F5
C5
life give me pain Give me my - self a -
T
A
B
1. - 3.
G5
4.
Gm6
E
gain Give me gain
Ee
D.S. al Fine
Ee
T
A
B

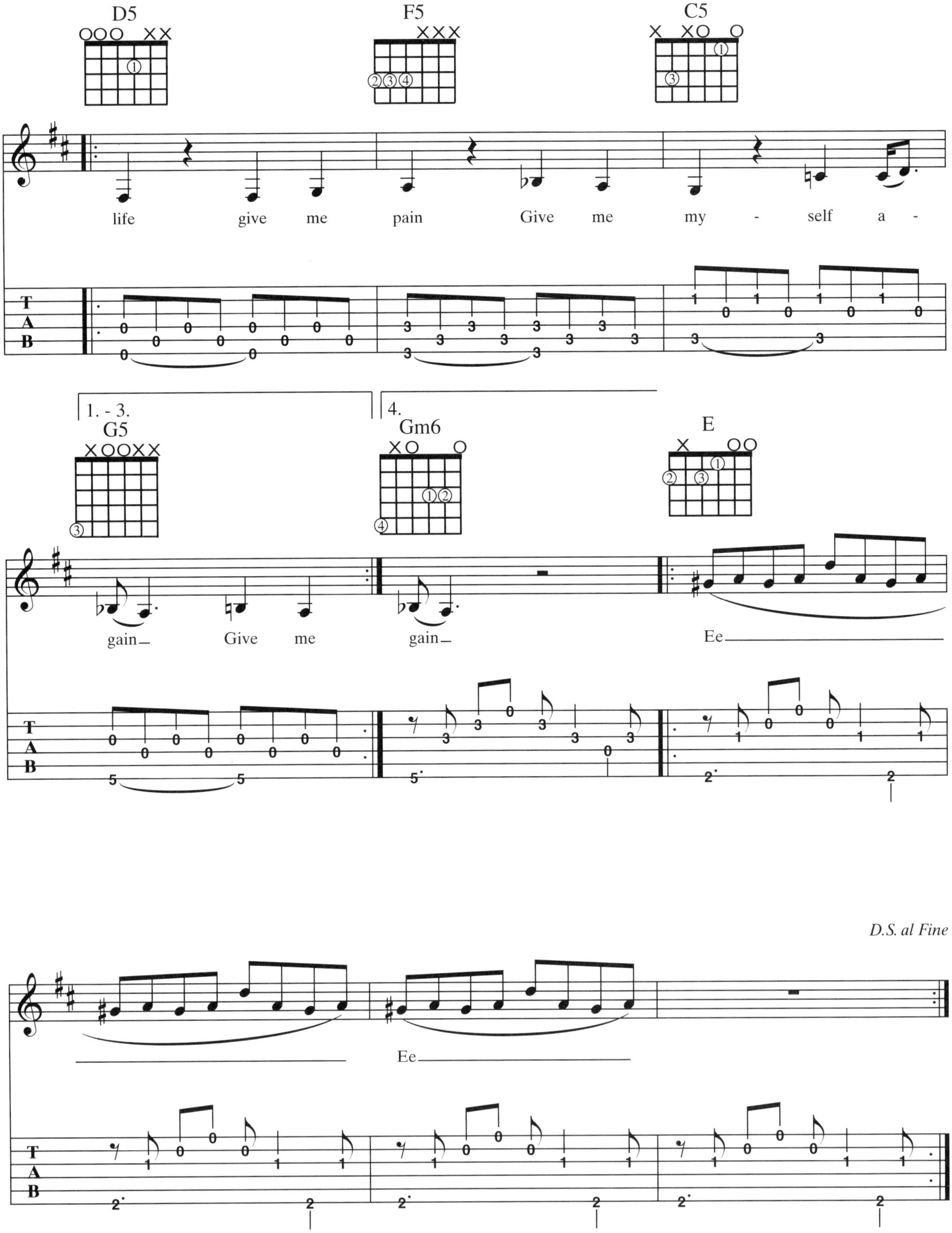

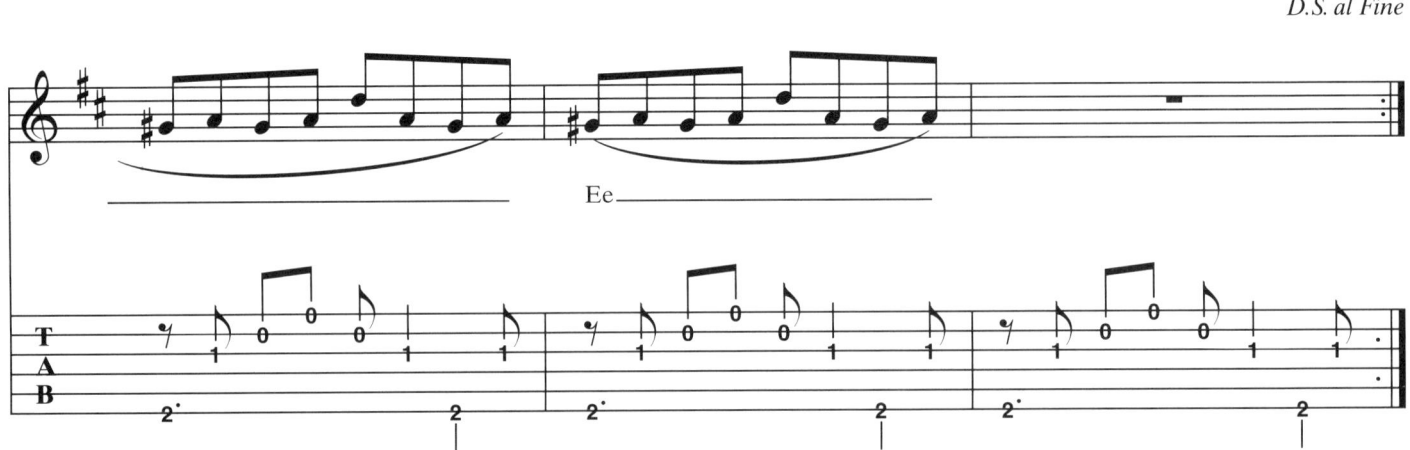

In the Springtime of His Voodoo
Words and Music by Tori Amos

melody note for voice

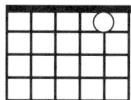

Moderate shuffle (triplet feel)

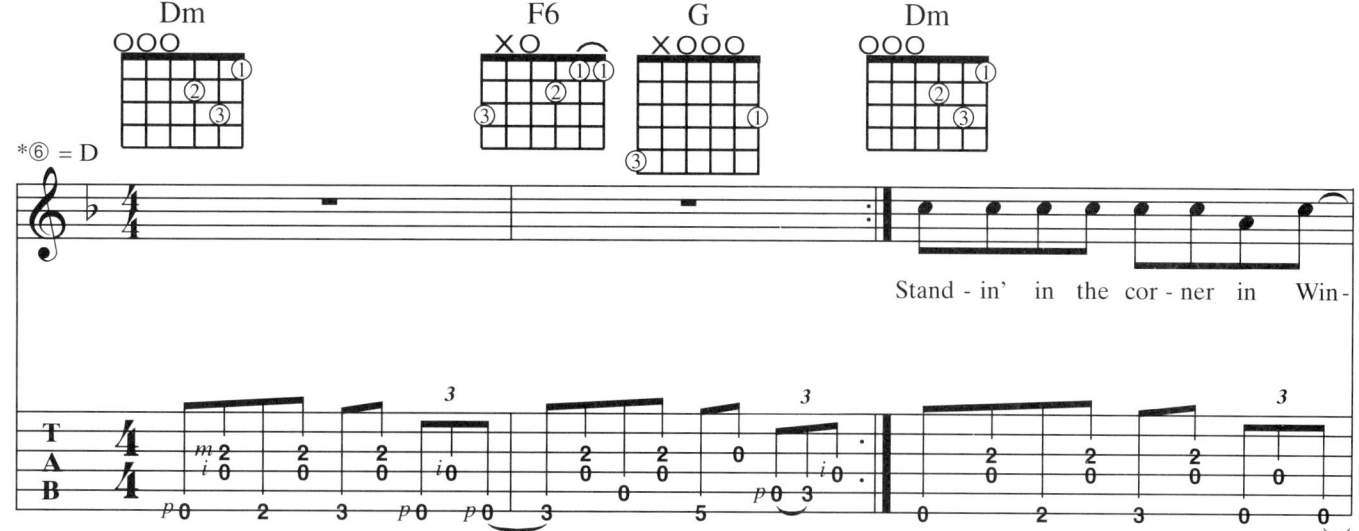

Standin' in the corner in Win-

*Drop D tuning: ⑥ D ⑤ A ④ D ③ G ② B ① E

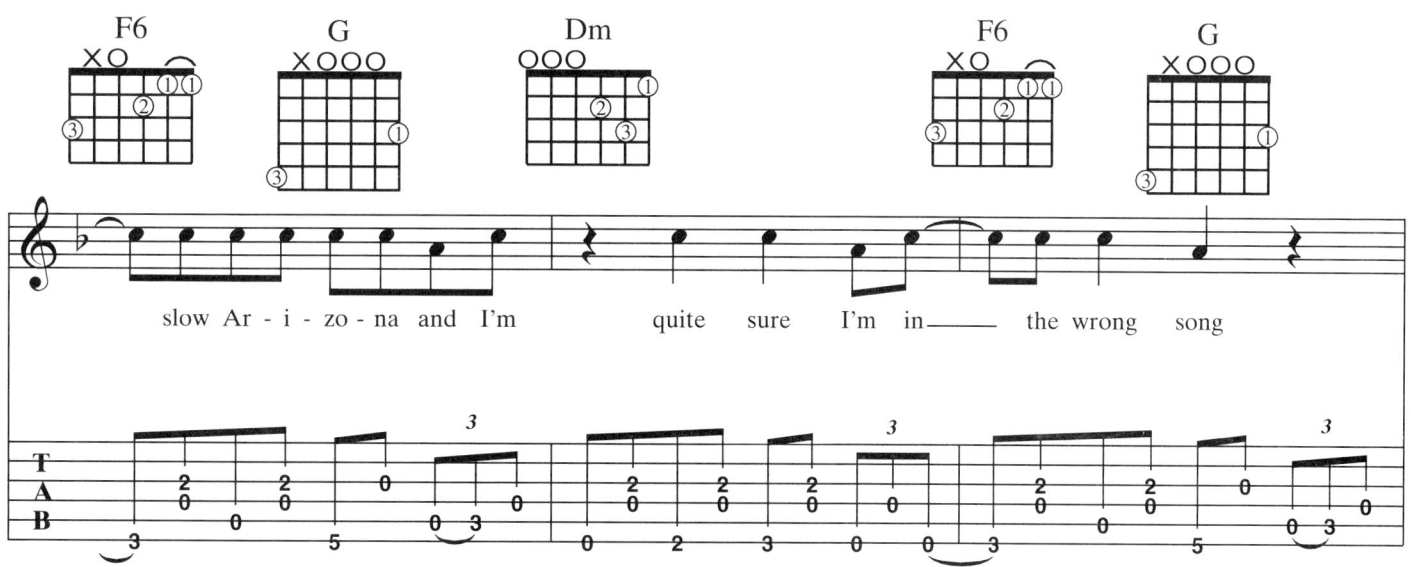

slow Arizona and I'm quite sure I'm in the wrong song

Copyright © 1995 Sword and Stone Publishing Inc. (ASCAP)
International Copyright Secured. All Rights Reserved.

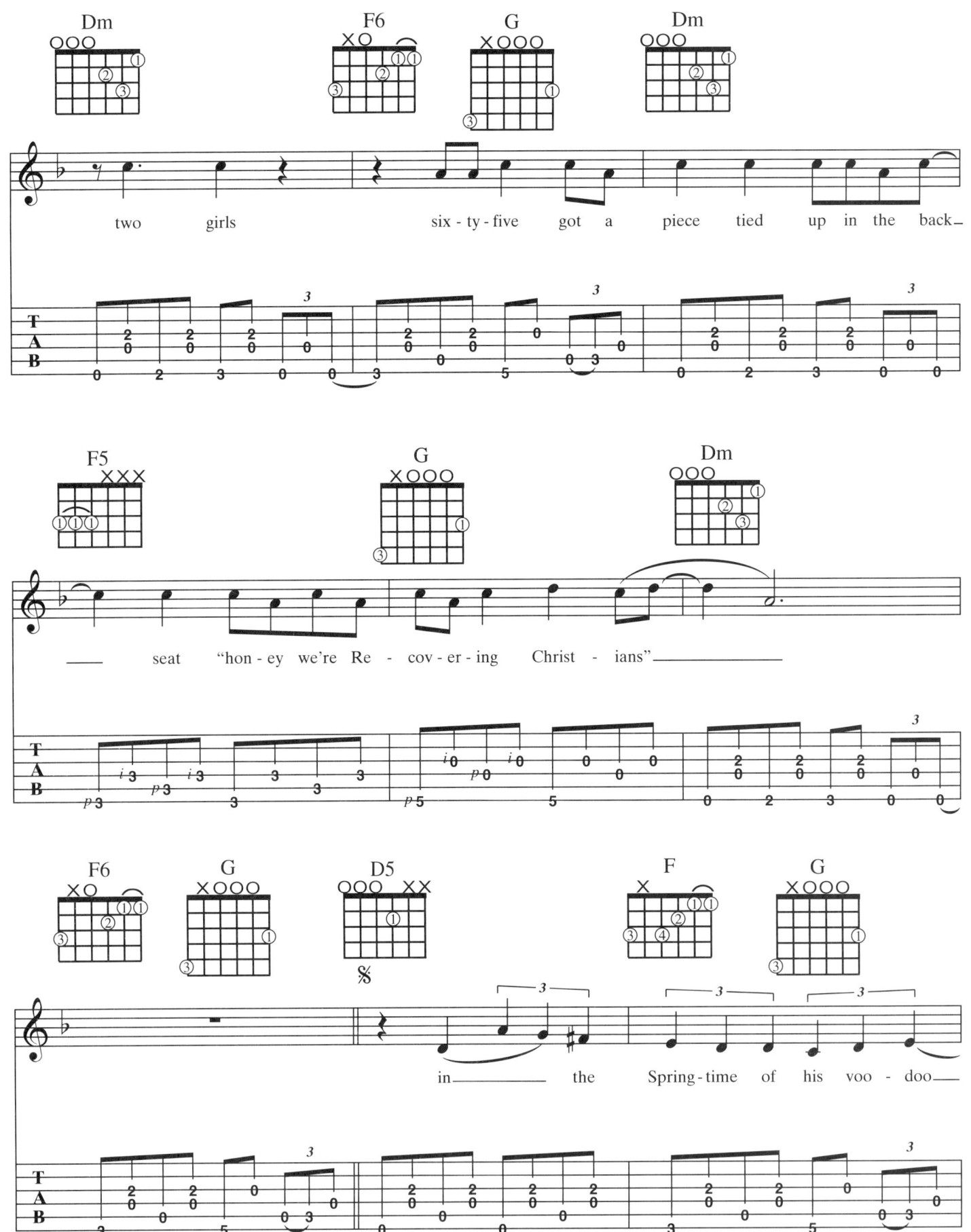

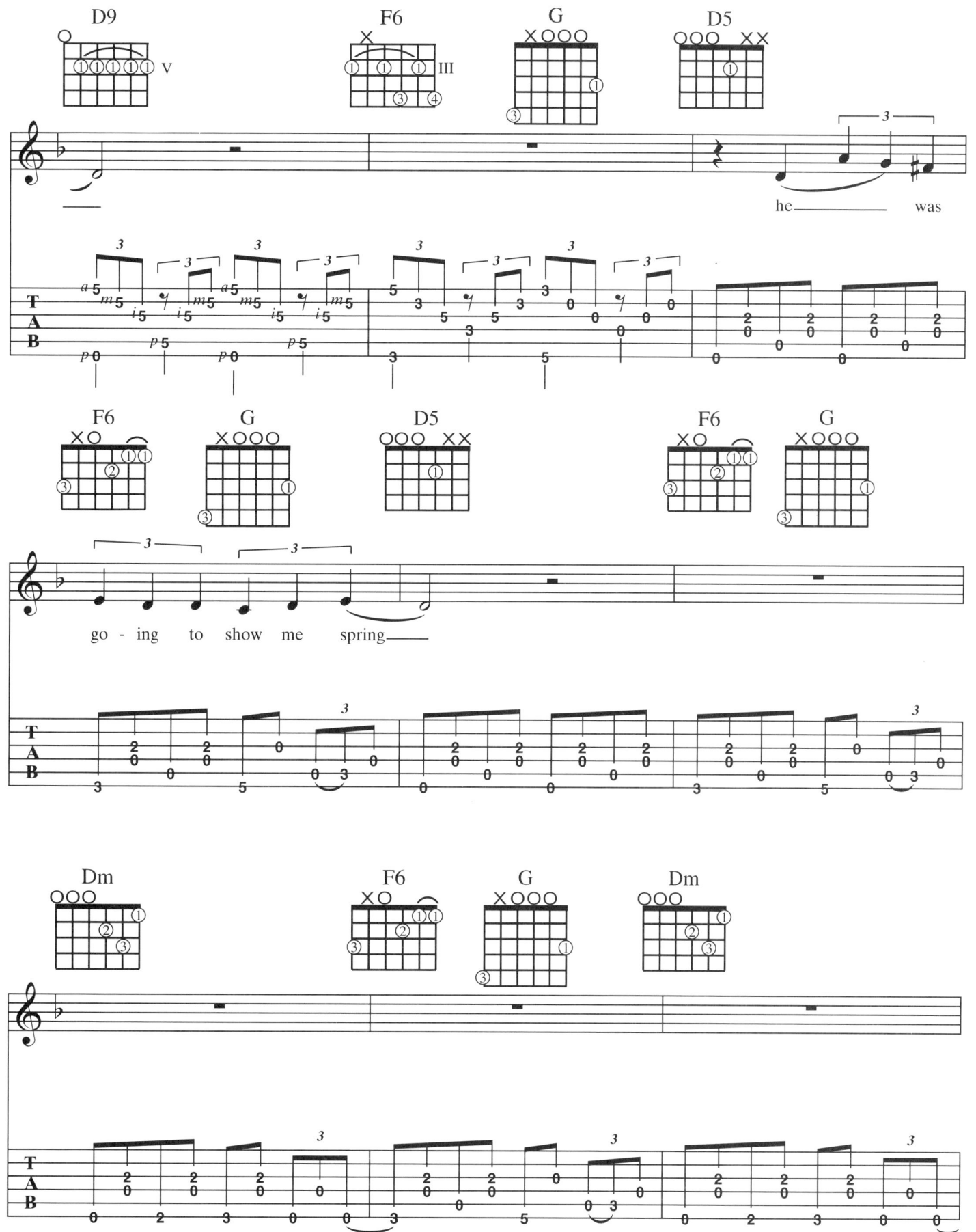

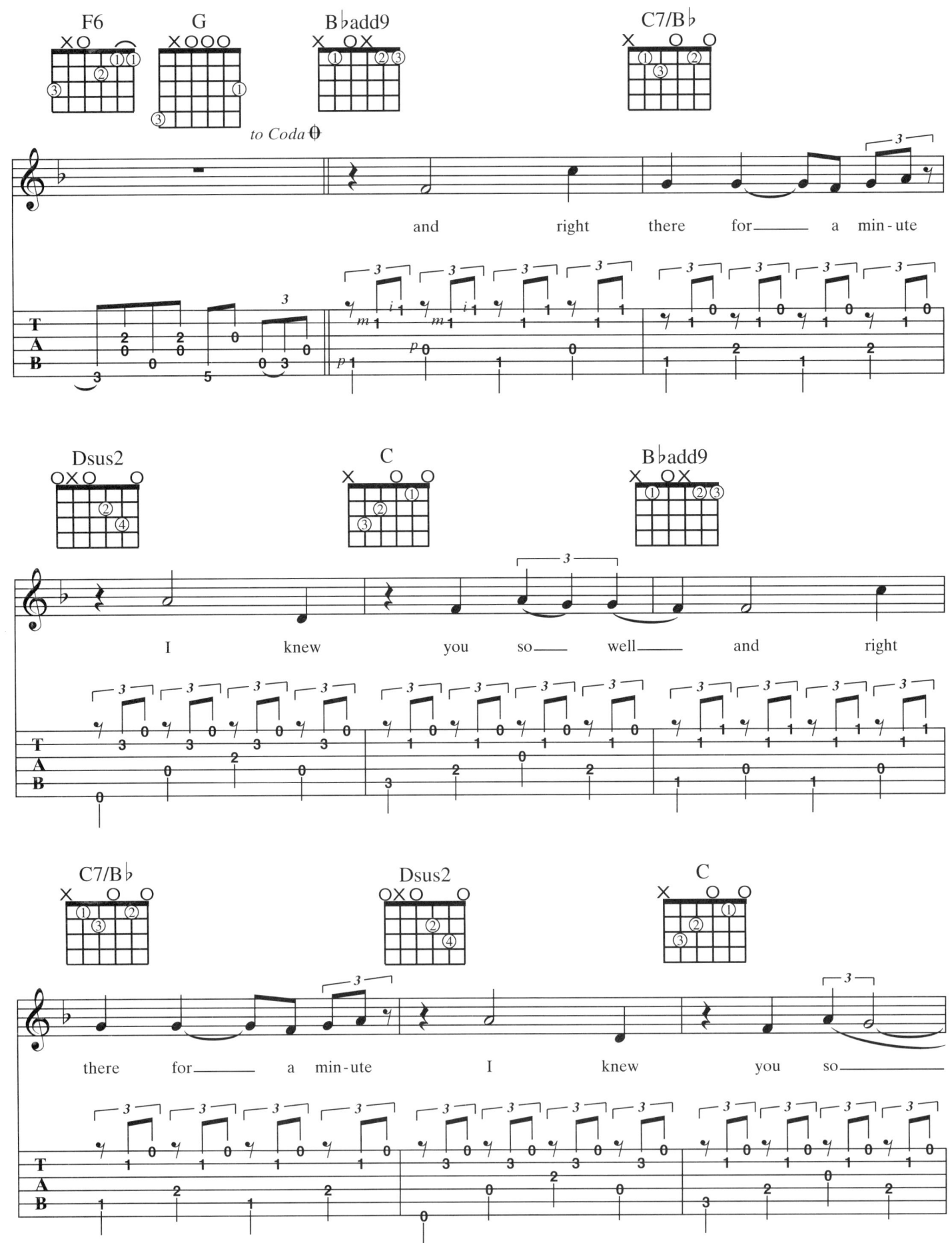

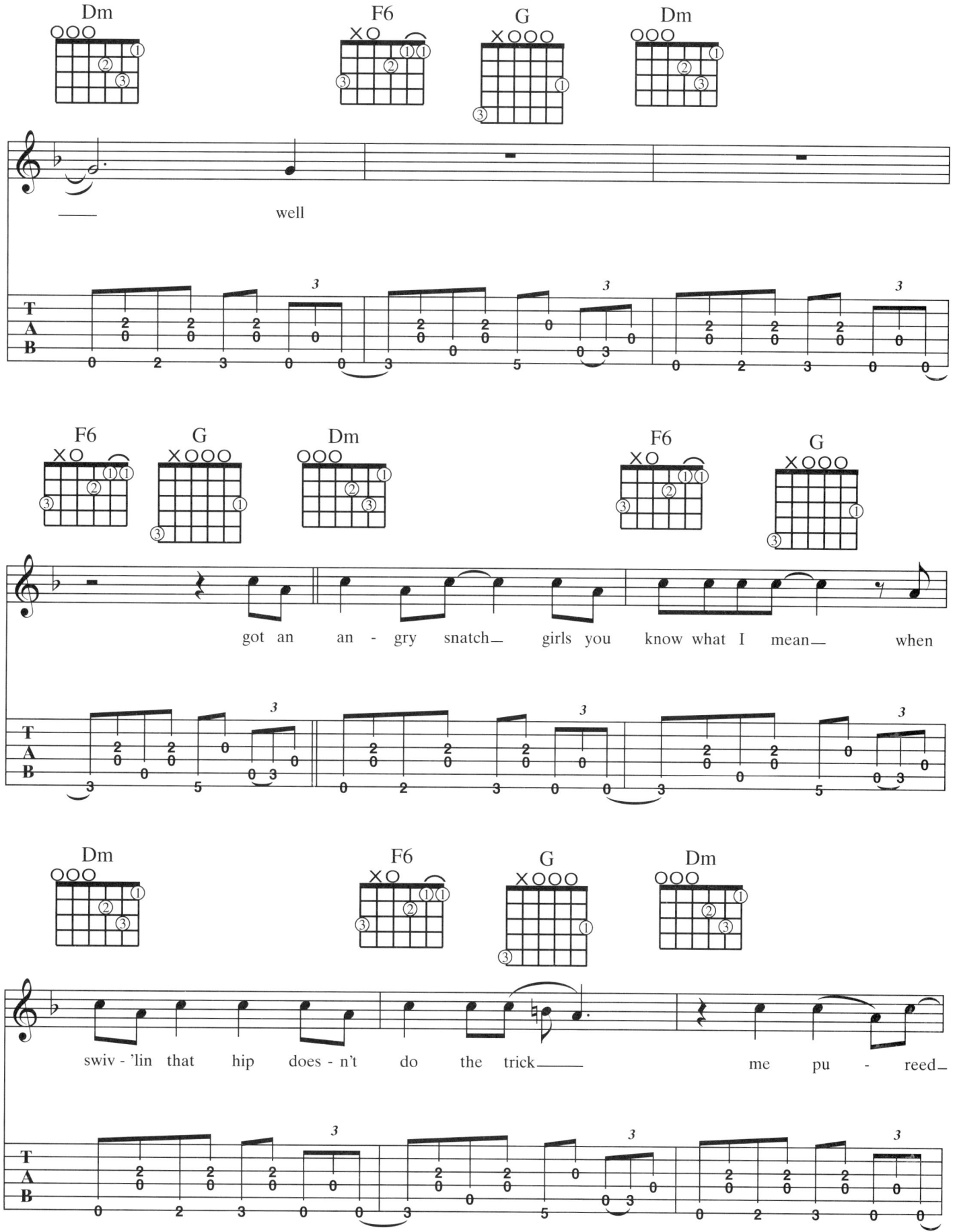

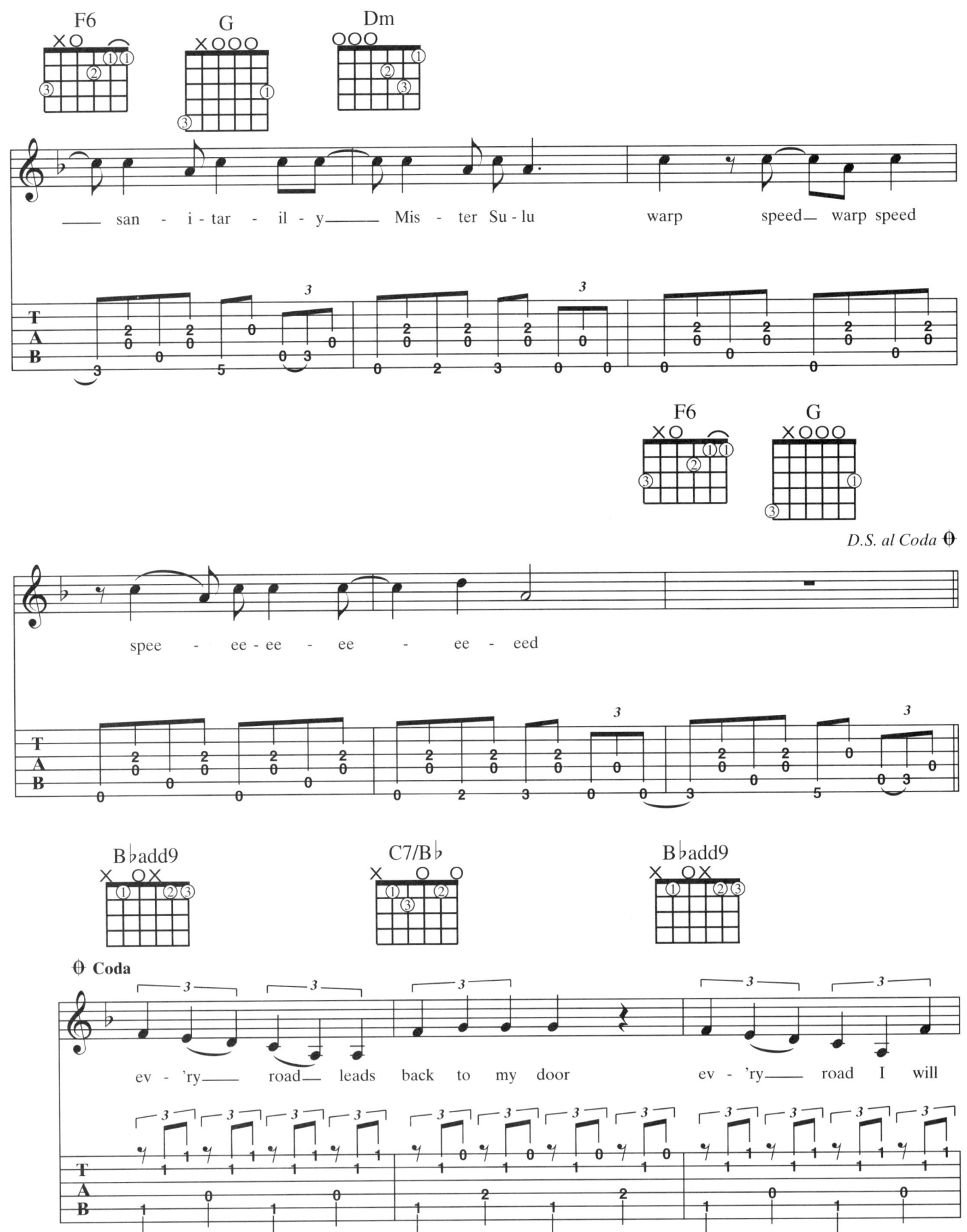

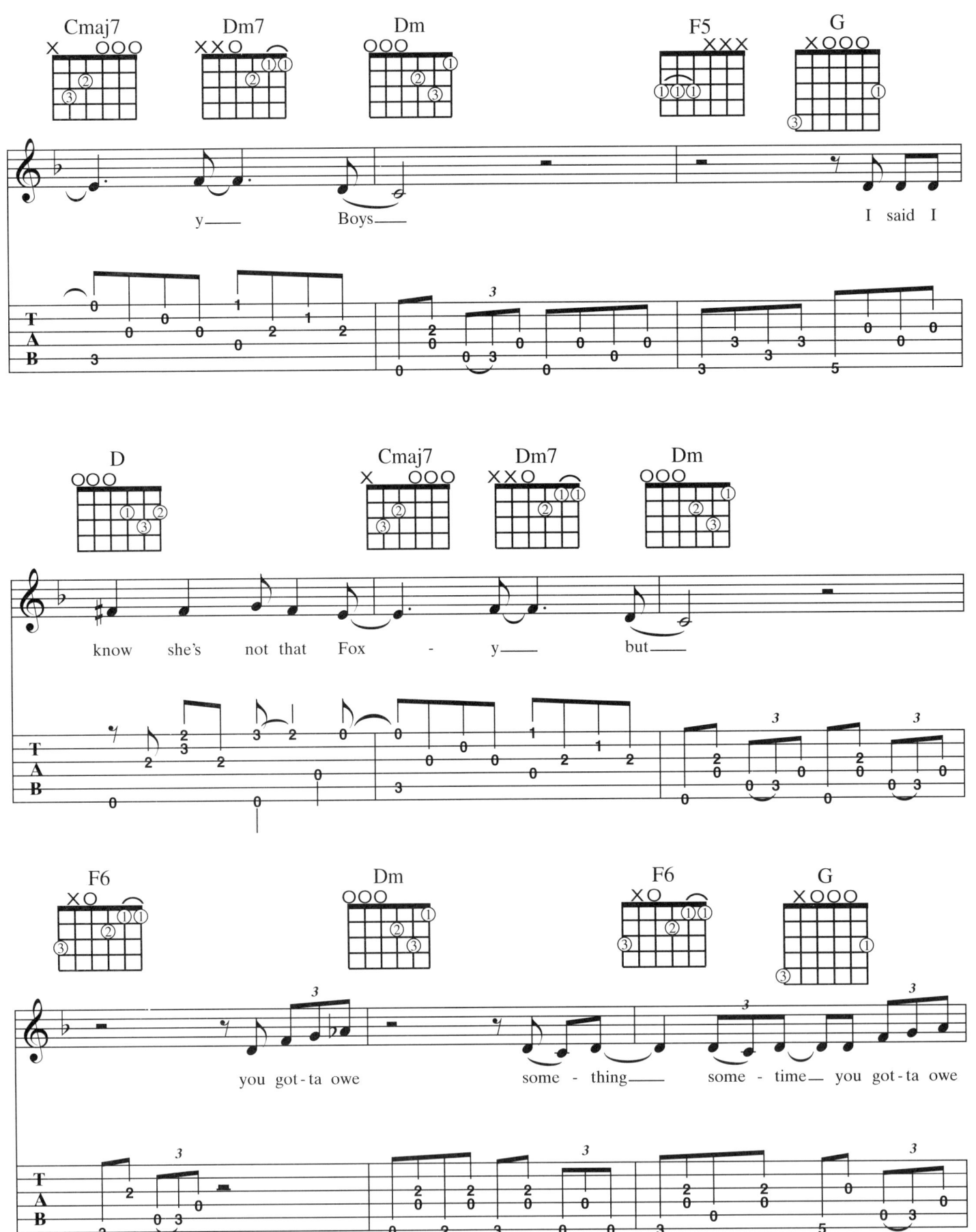

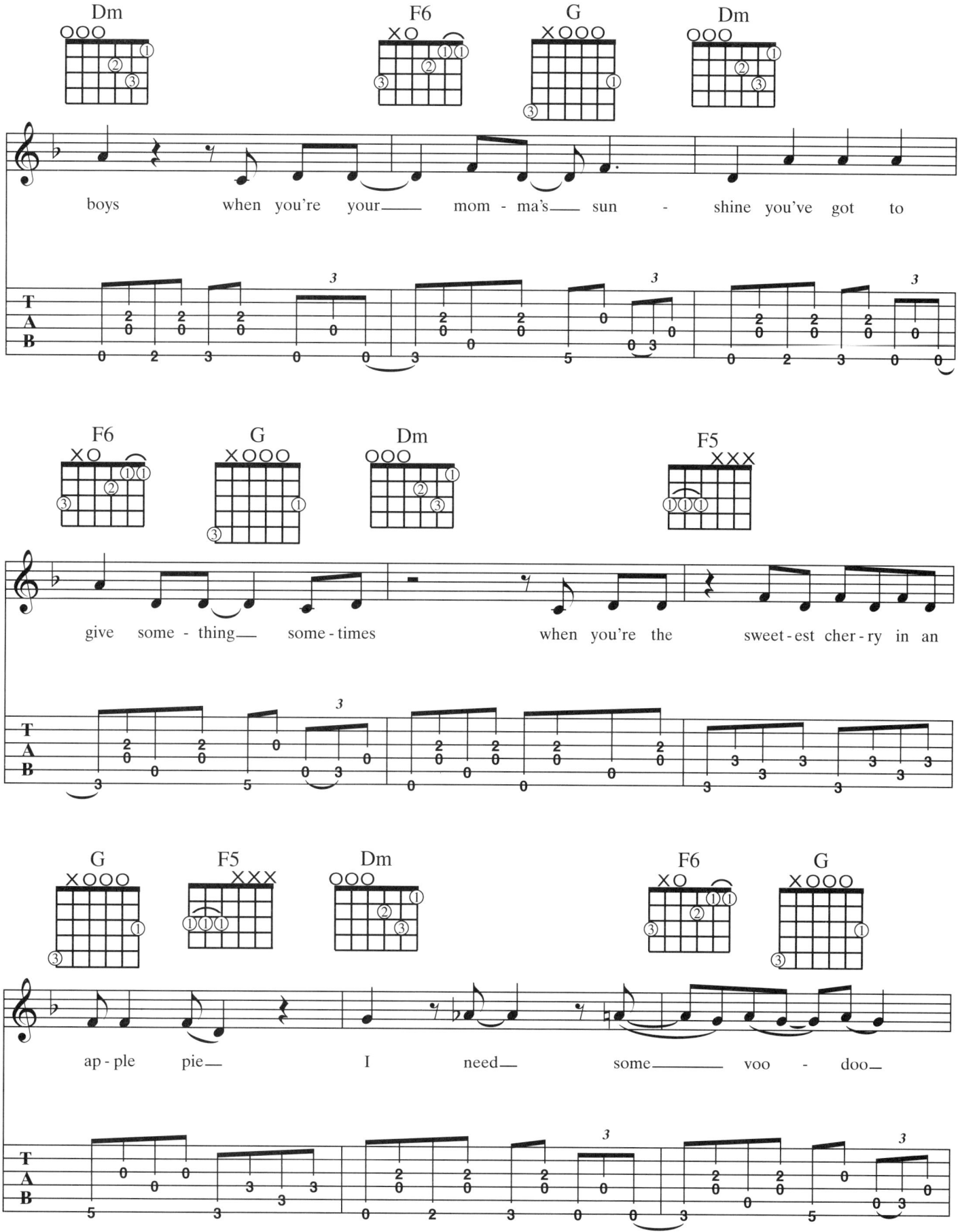

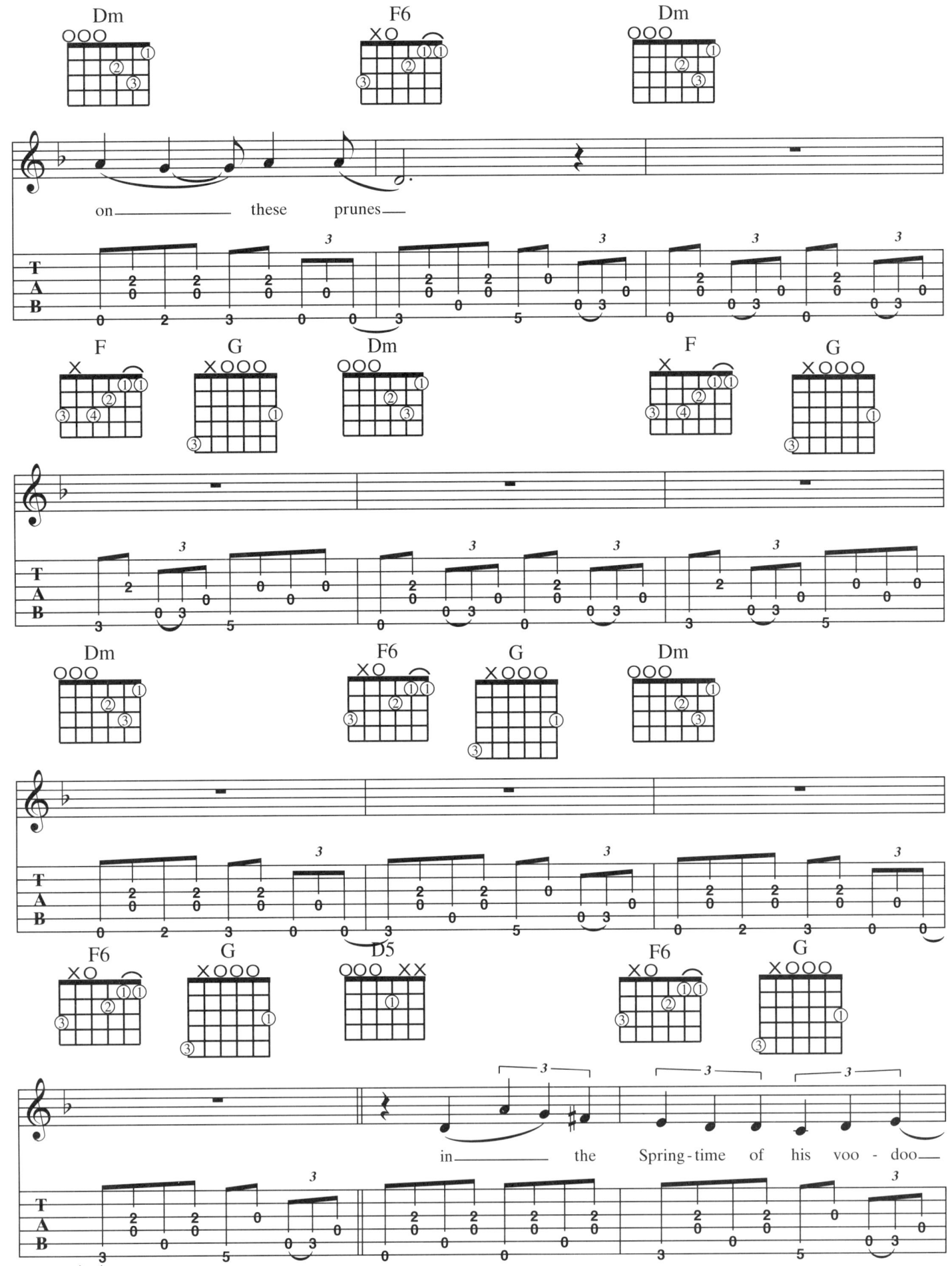

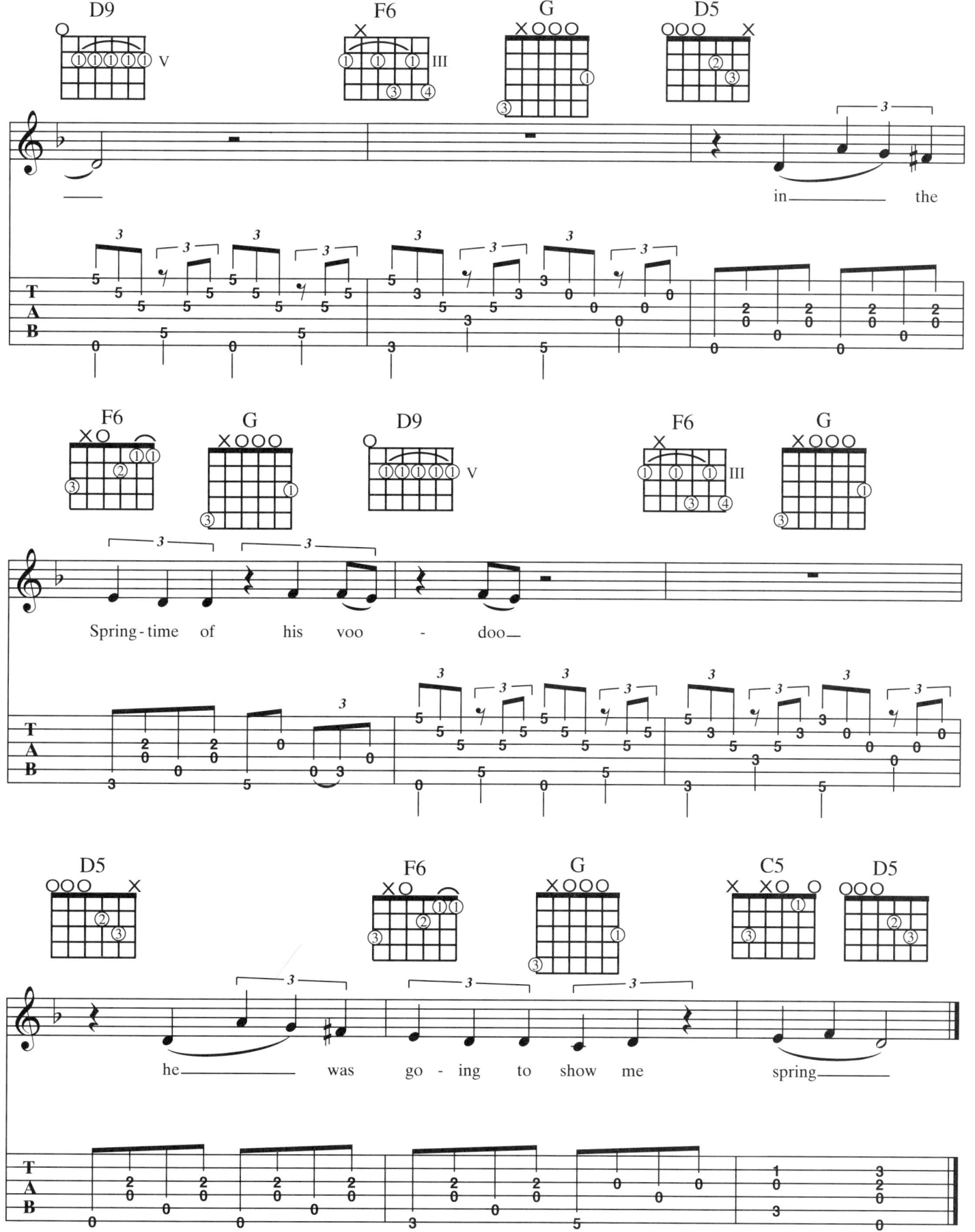

Past the Mission
Words and Music by Tori Amos

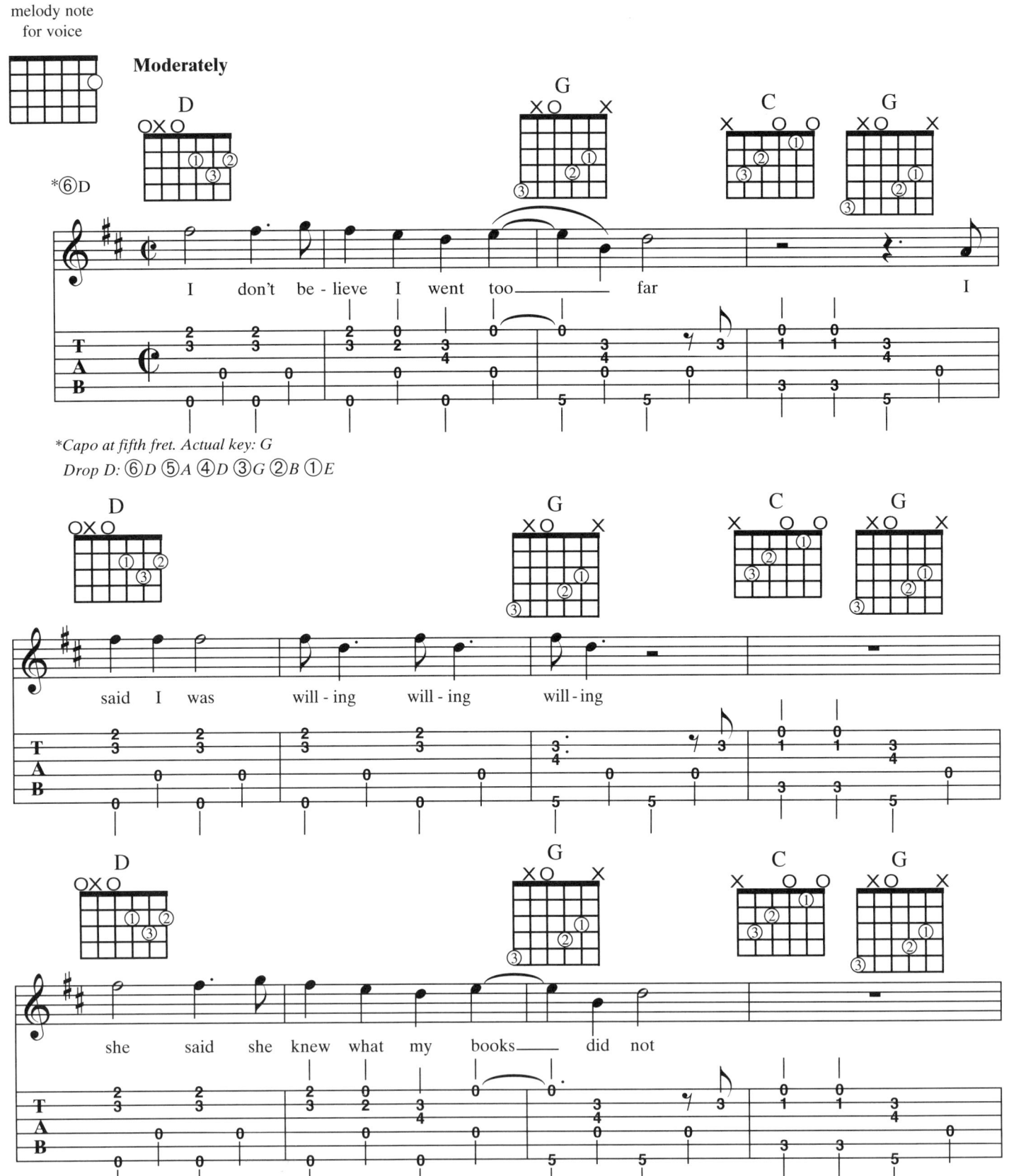

*Capo at fifth fret. Actual key: G
Drop D: ⑥D ⑤A ④D ③G ②B ①E

Lyrics:
I don't believe I went too far
I said I was willing willing willing
she said she knew what my books did not

Copyright © 1993 Sword and Stone Publishing Inc. (ASCAP)
International Copyright Secured. All Rights Reserved.

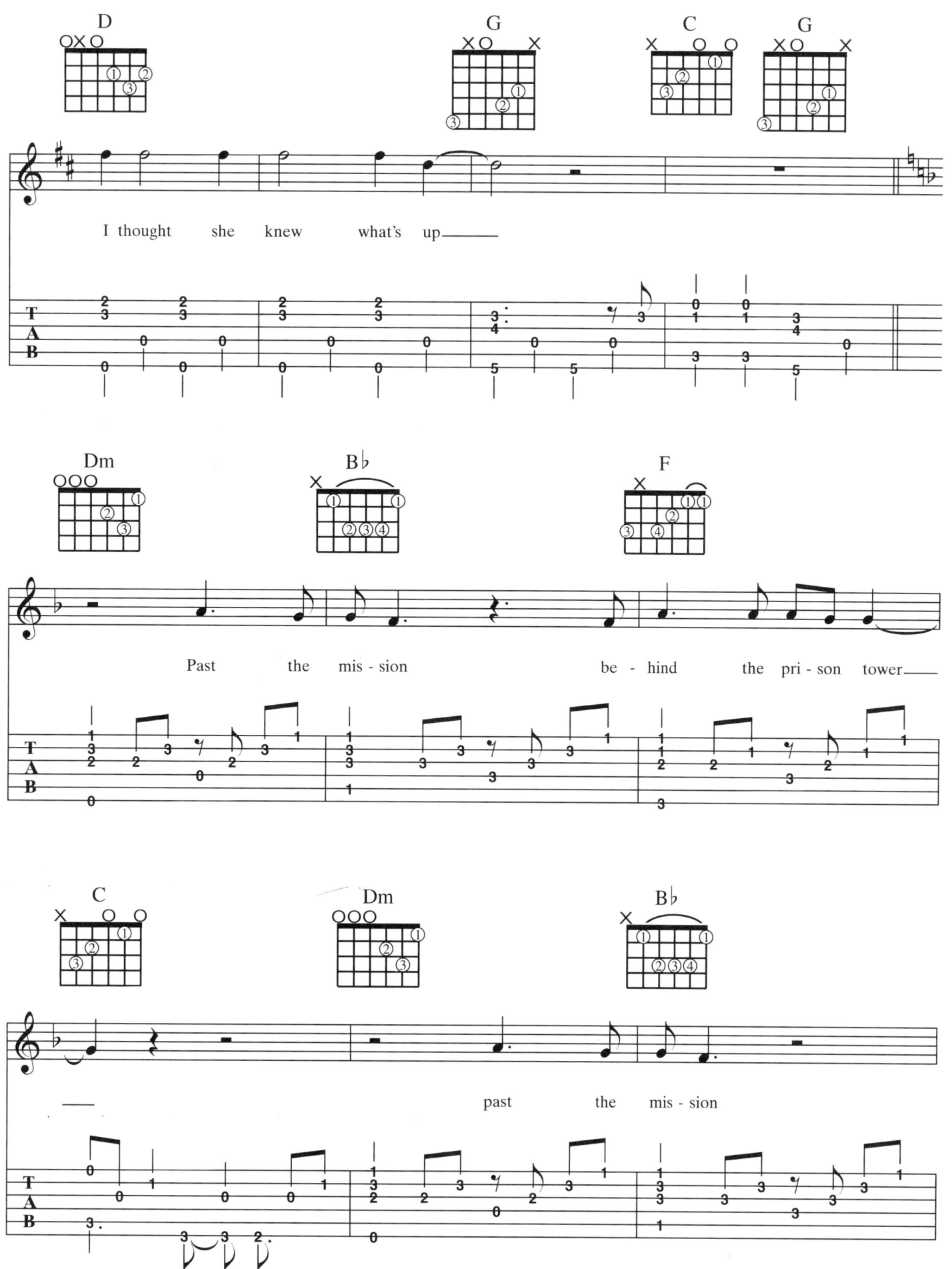

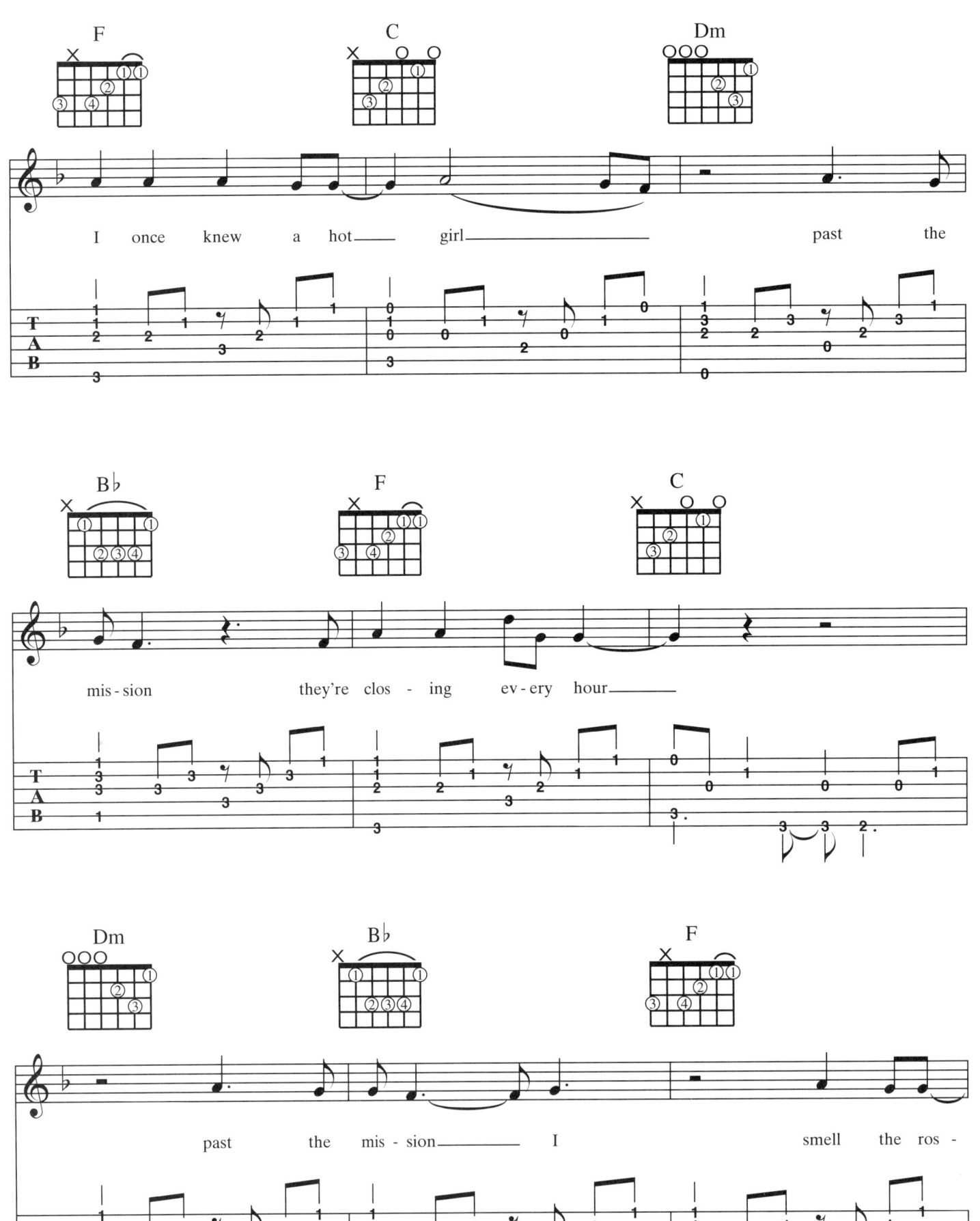

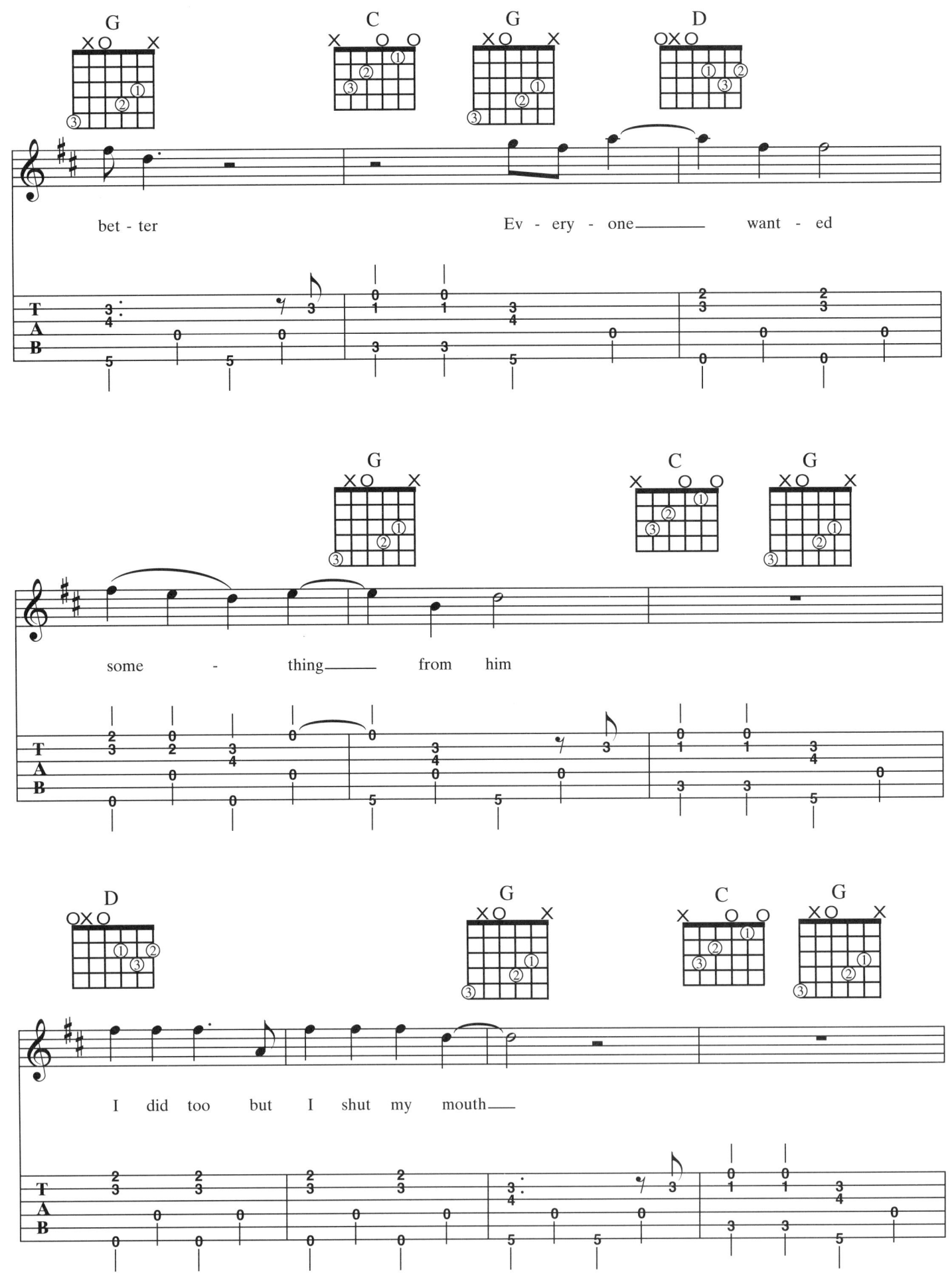

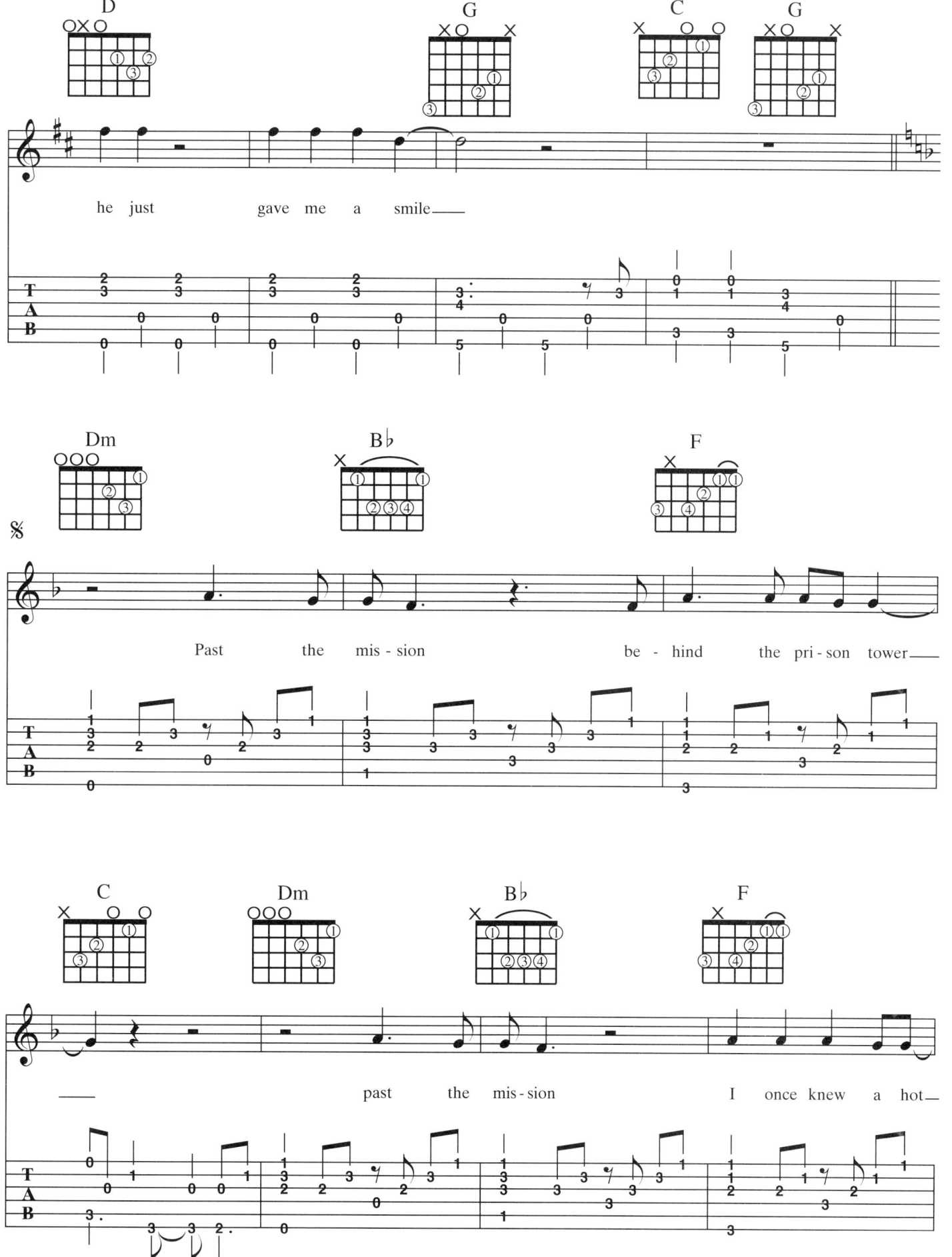

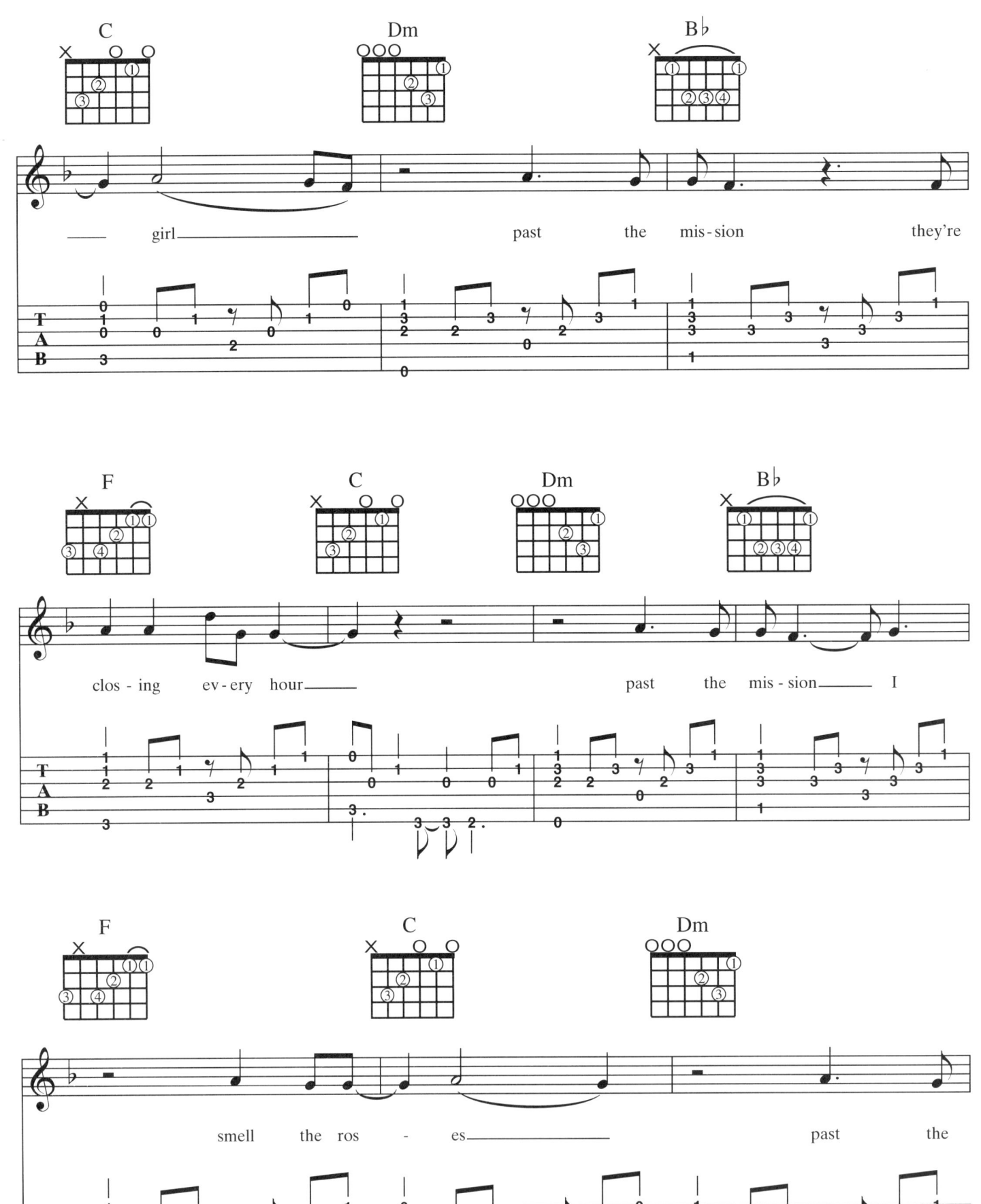

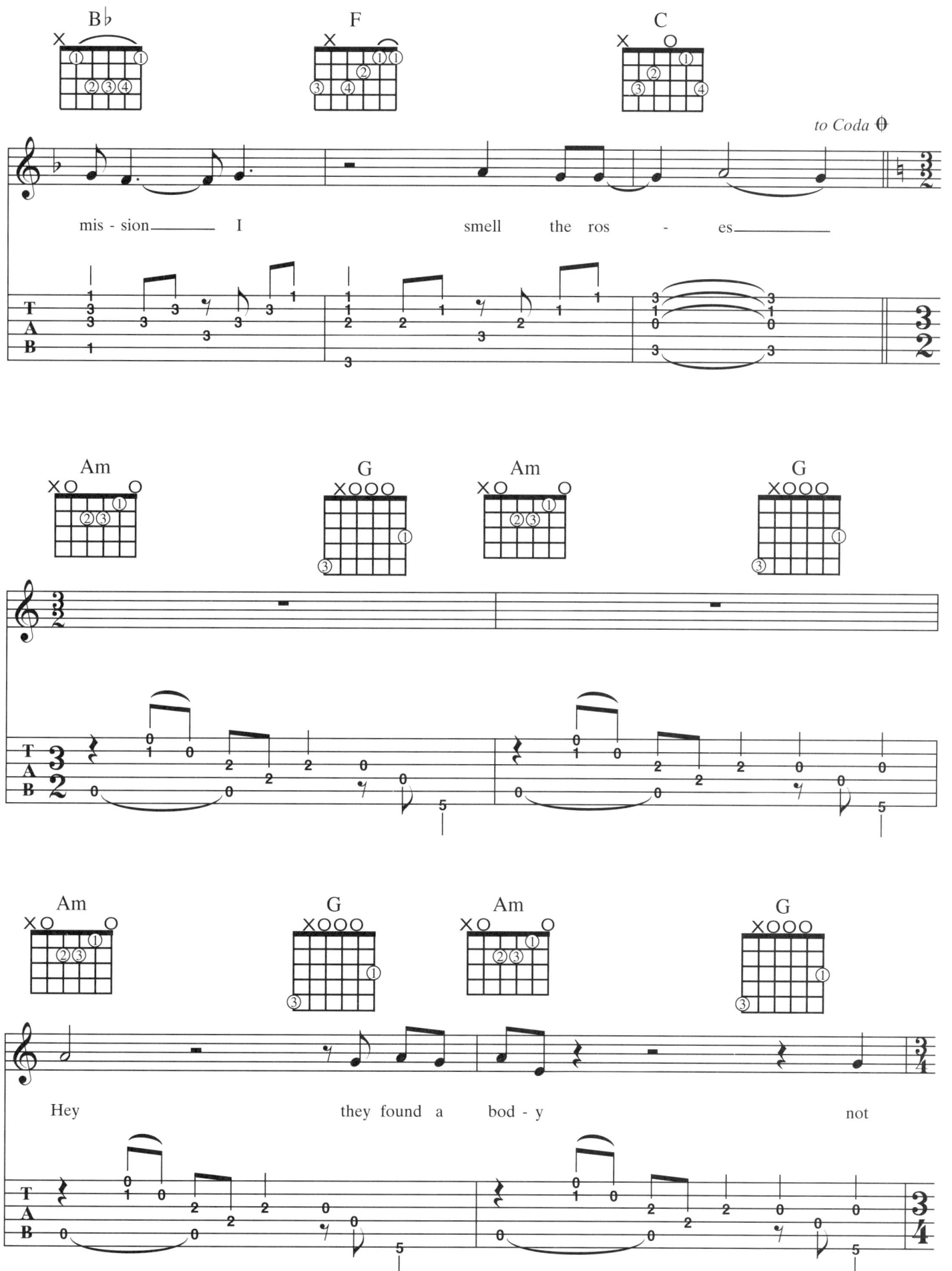

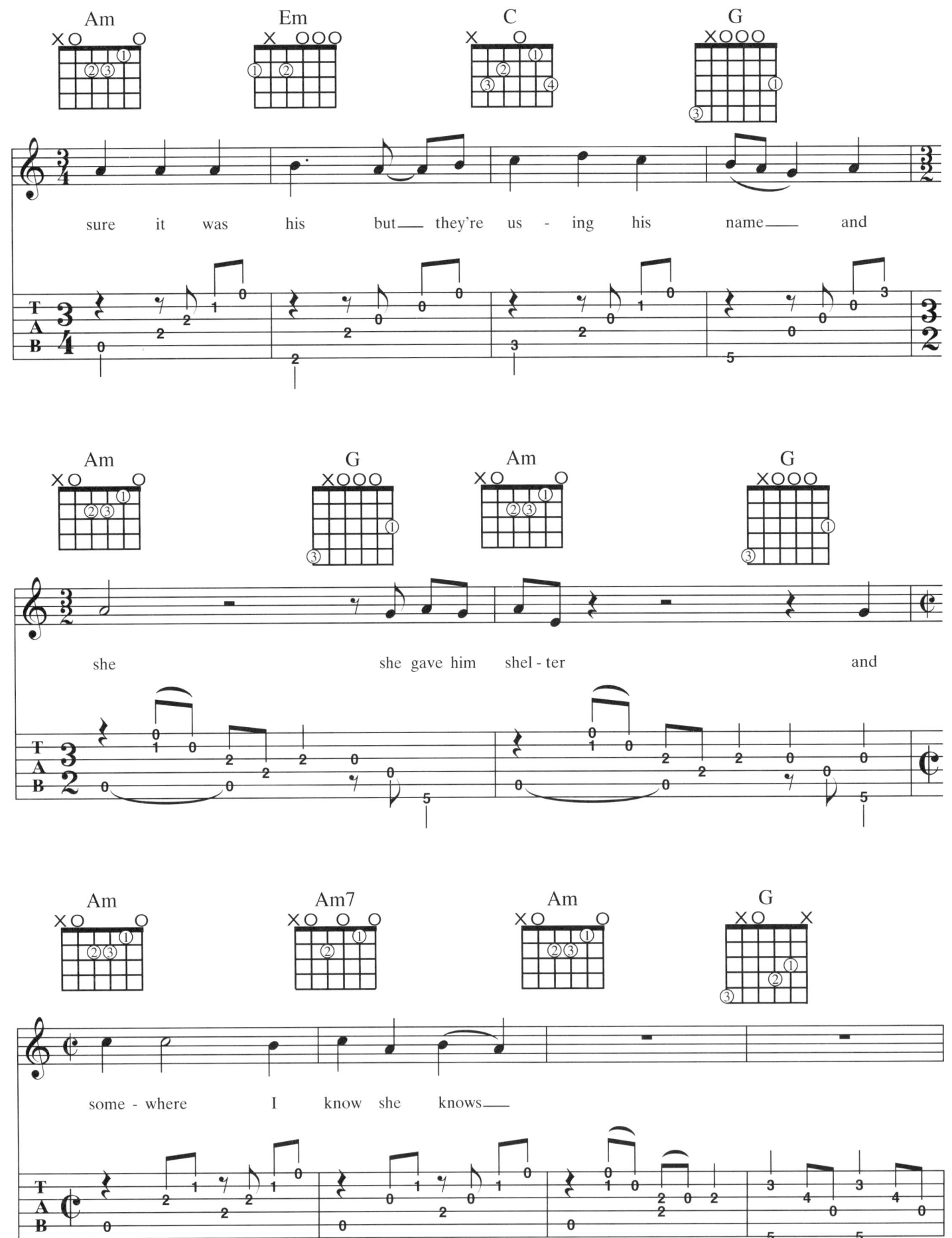

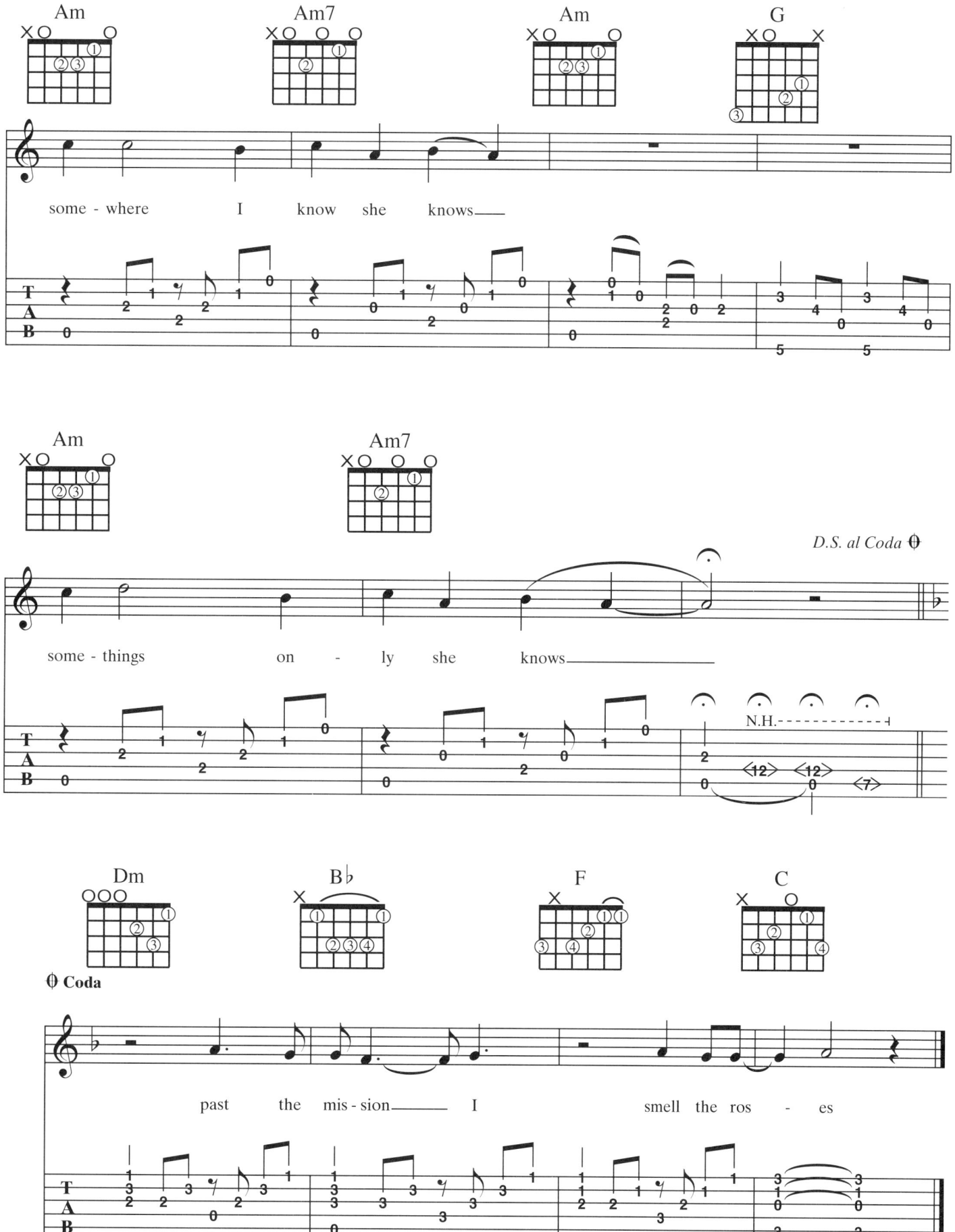

Blood Roses
Words and Music by Tori Amos

Moderately

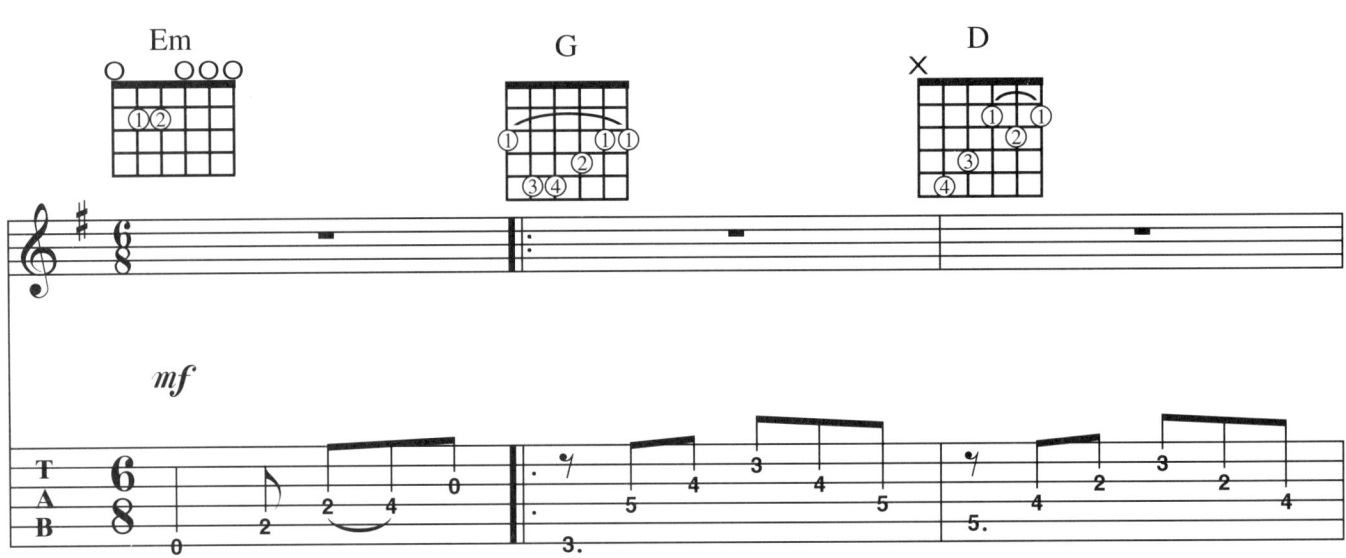

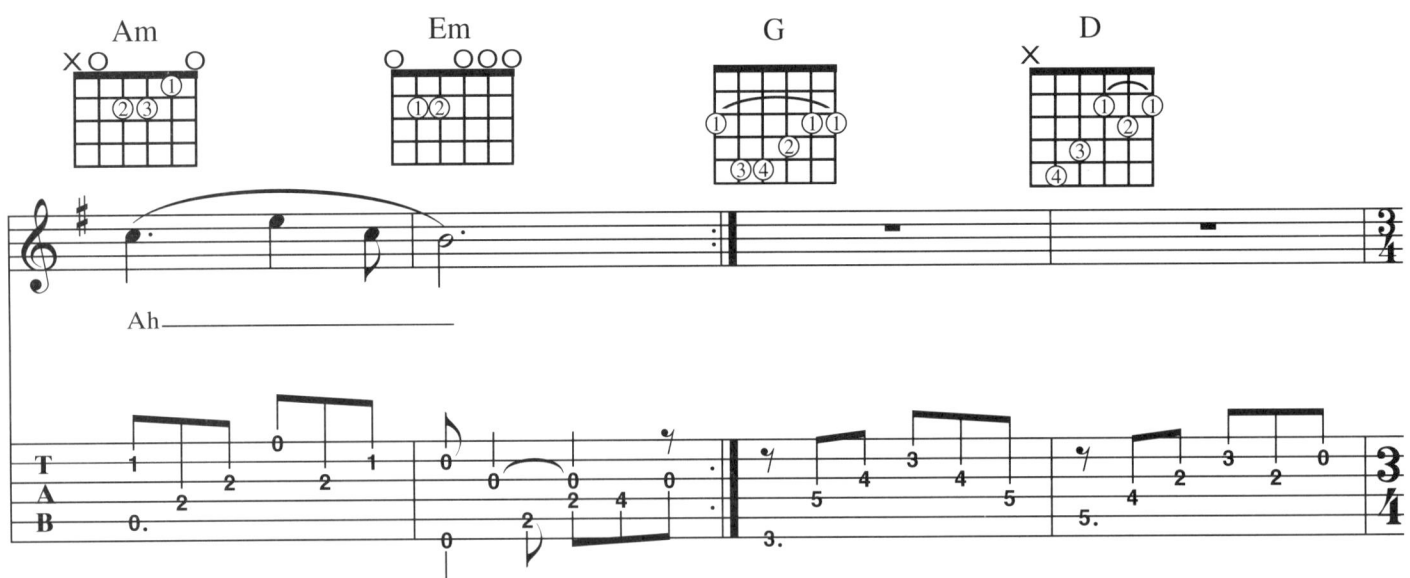

Copyright © 1995 Sword and Stone Publishing Inc. (ASCAP)
International Copyright Secured. All Rights Reserved.

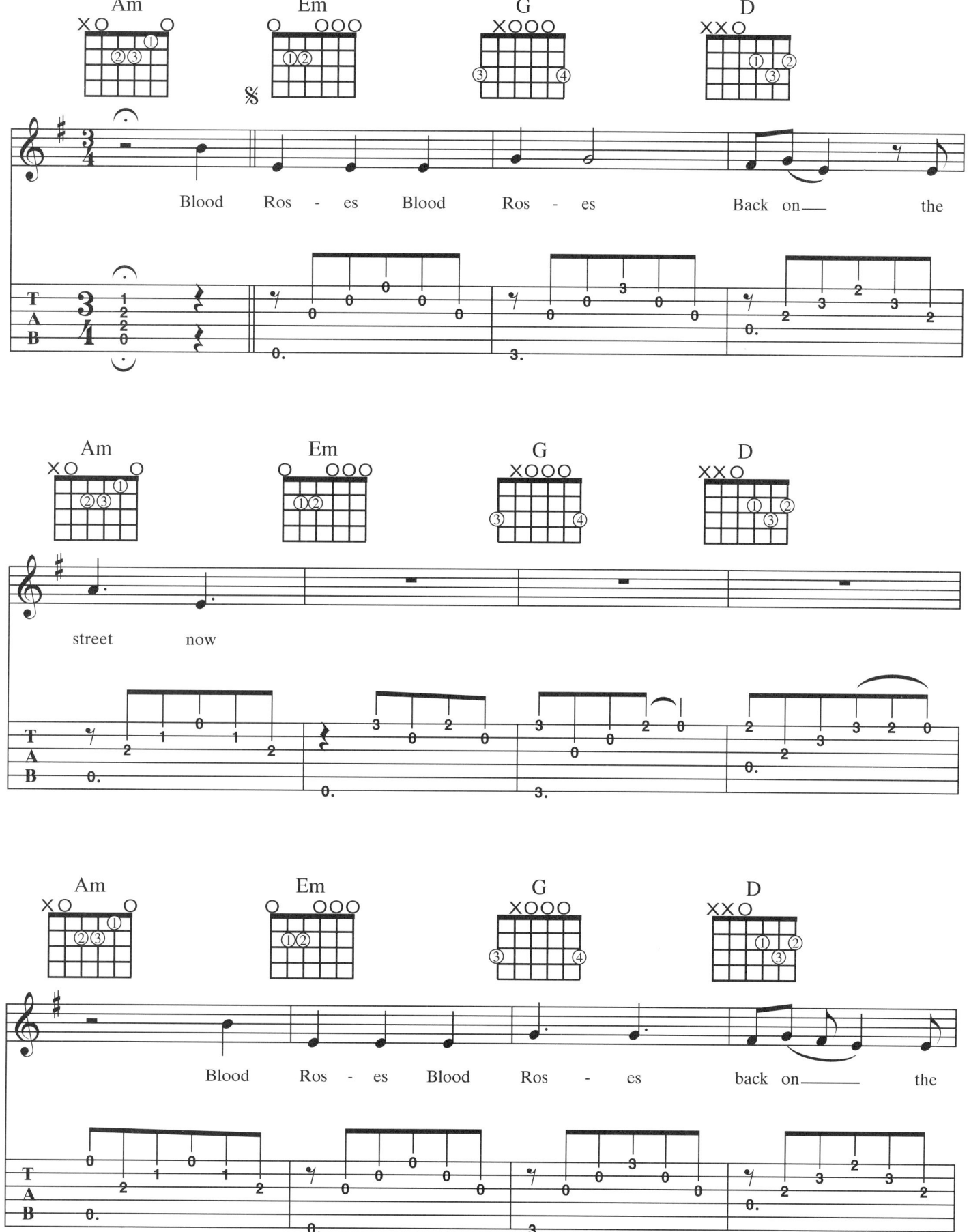

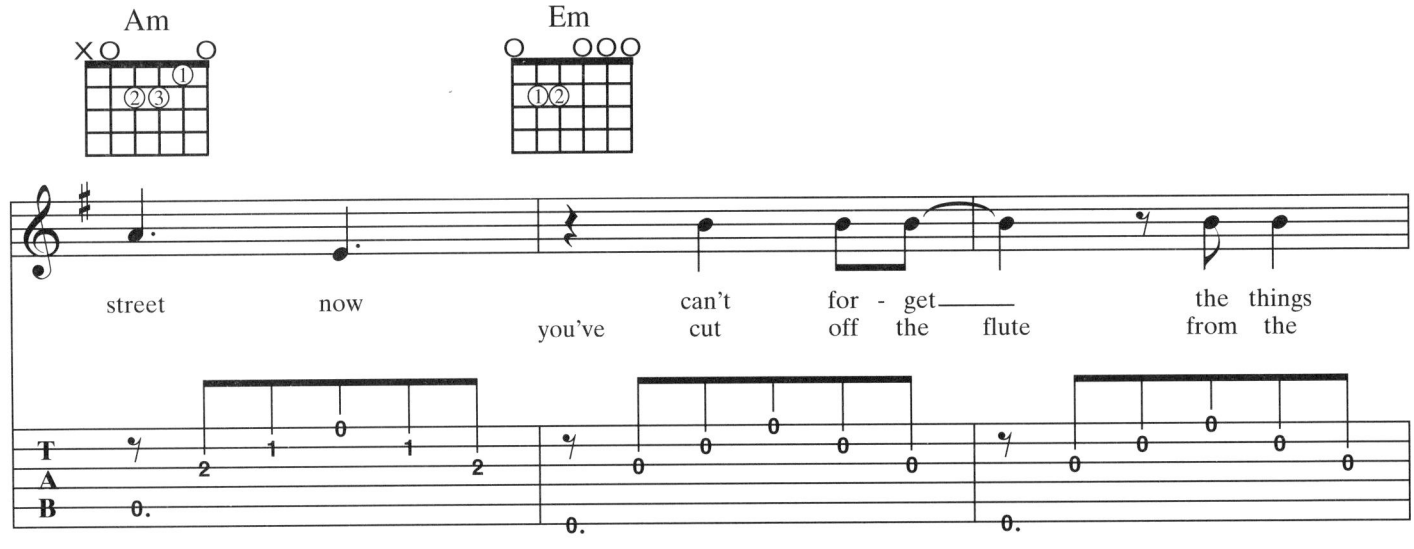
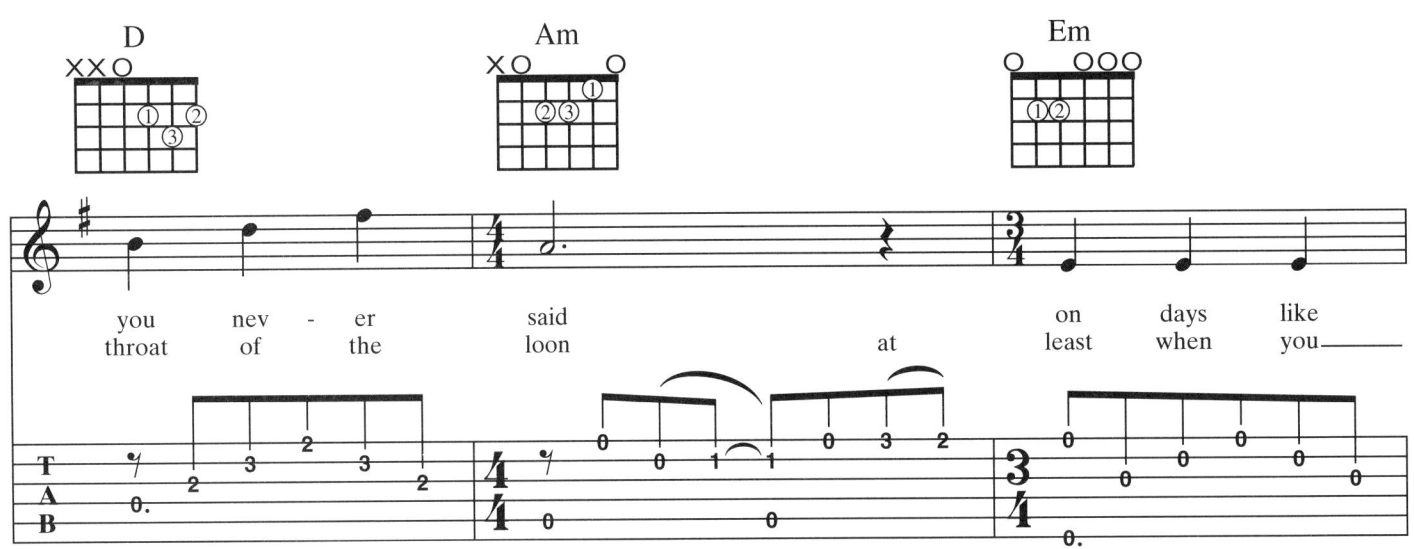
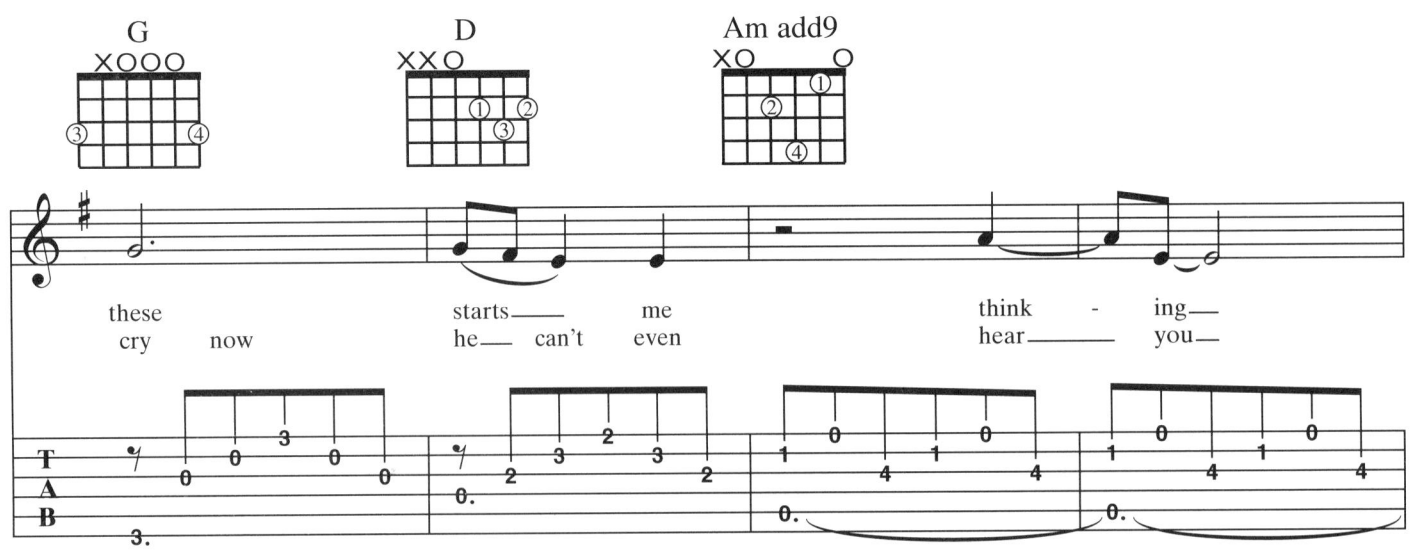

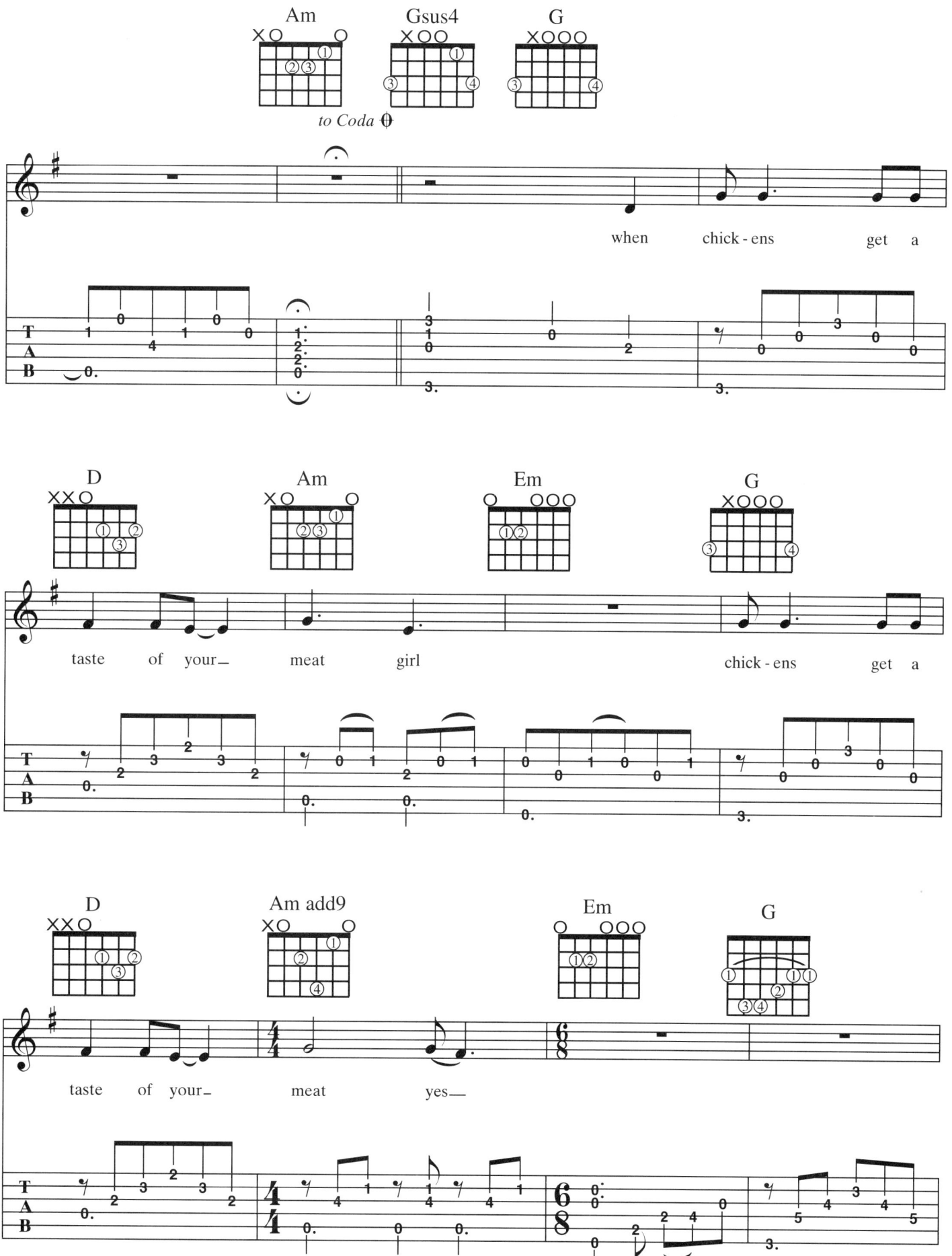

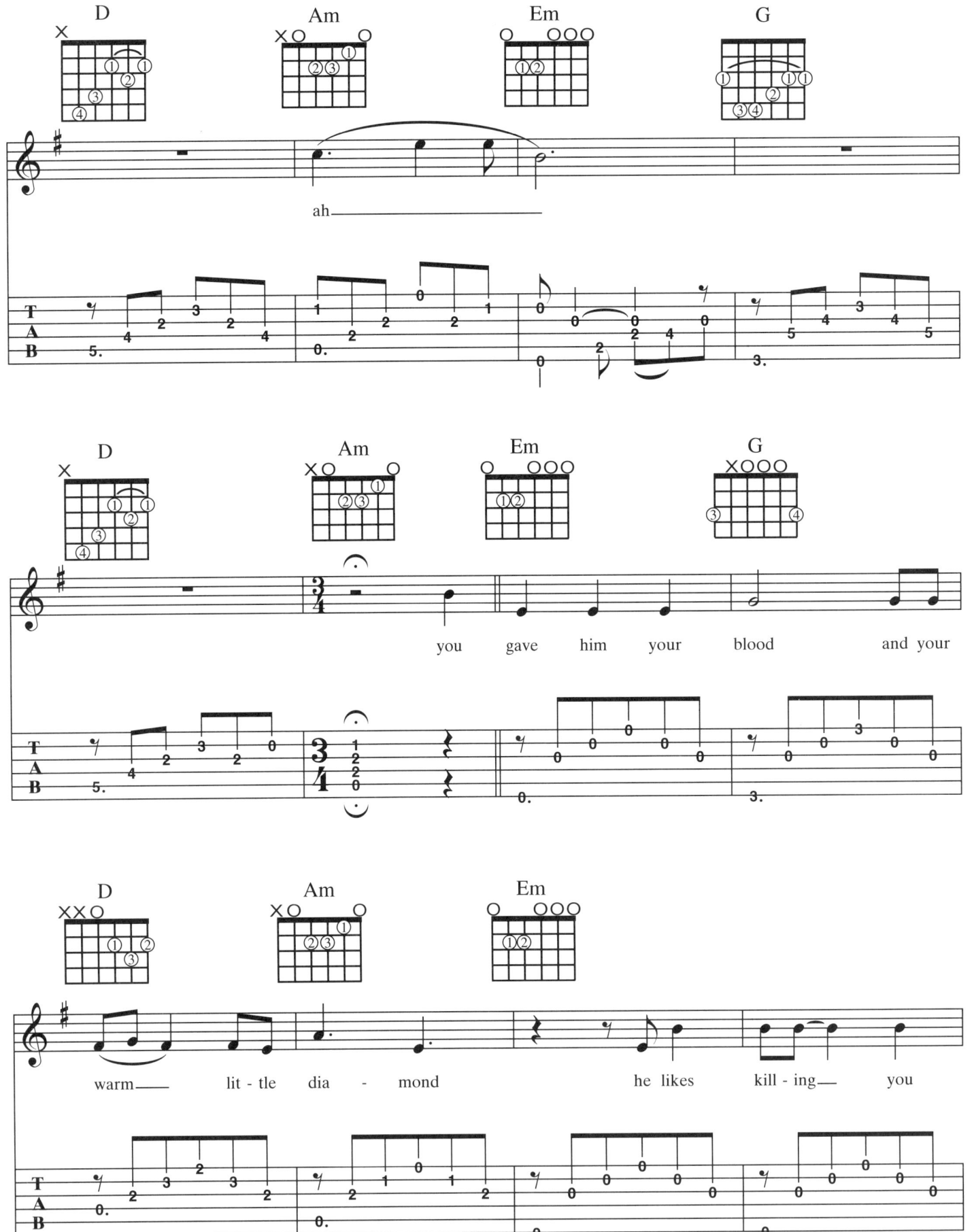

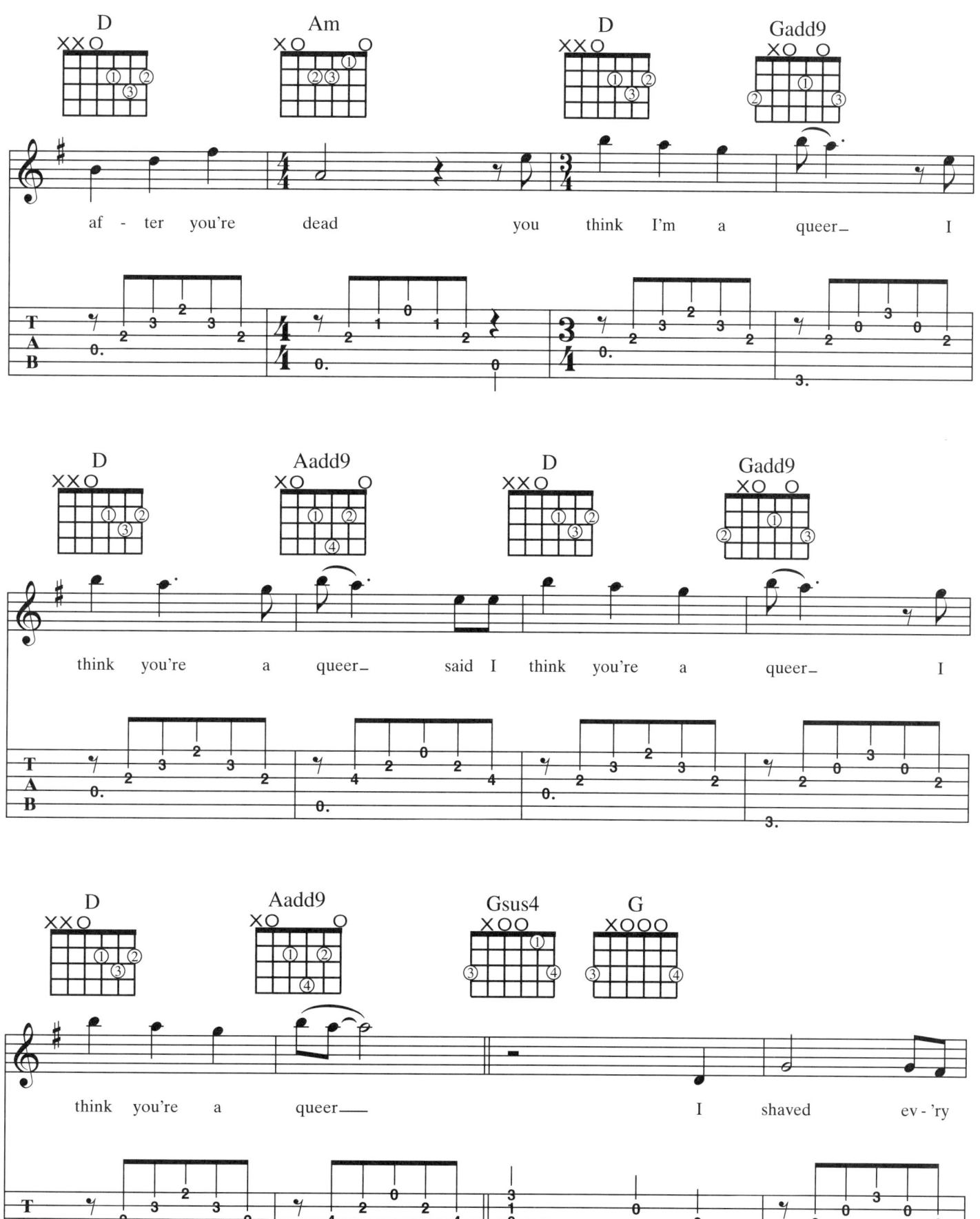

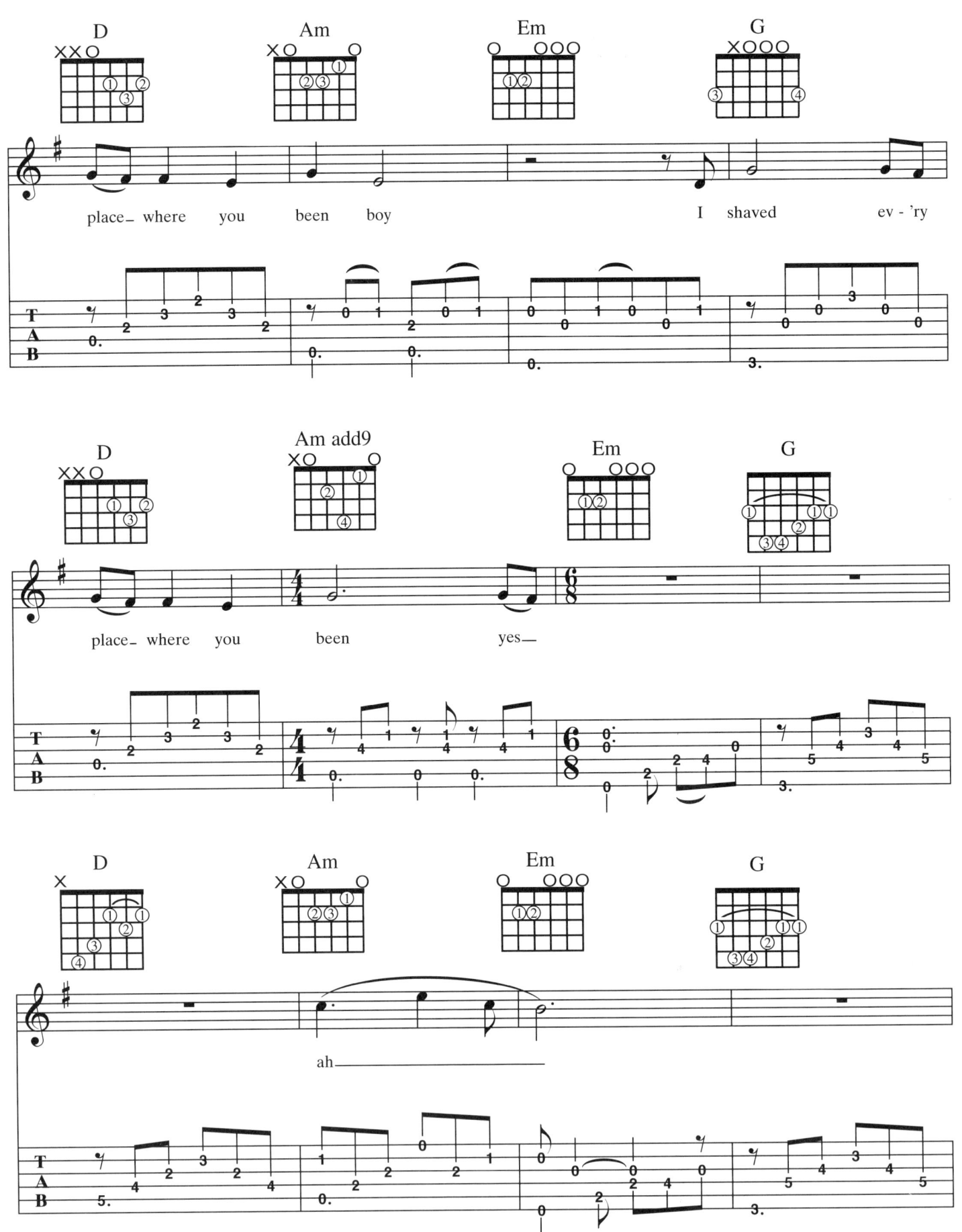

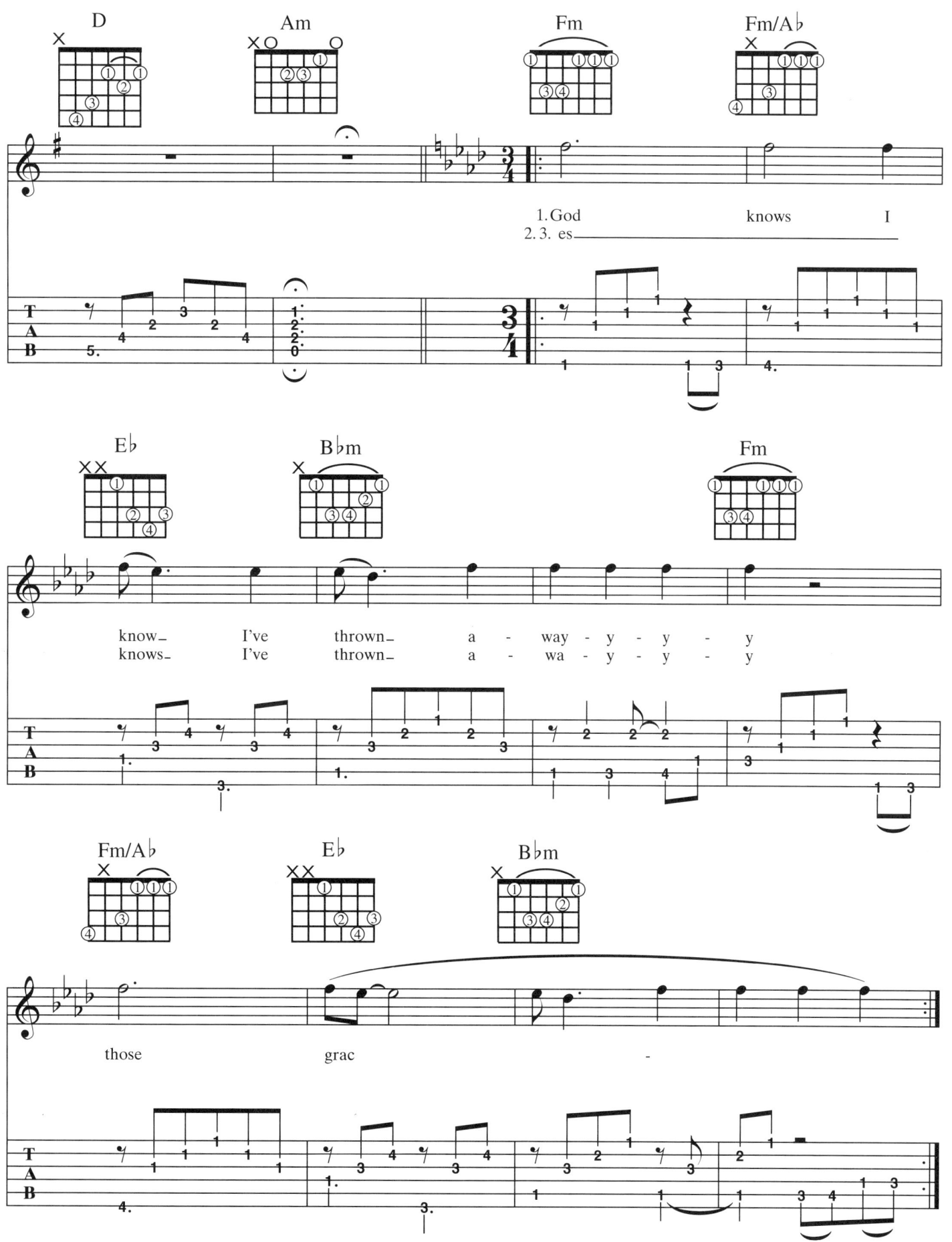

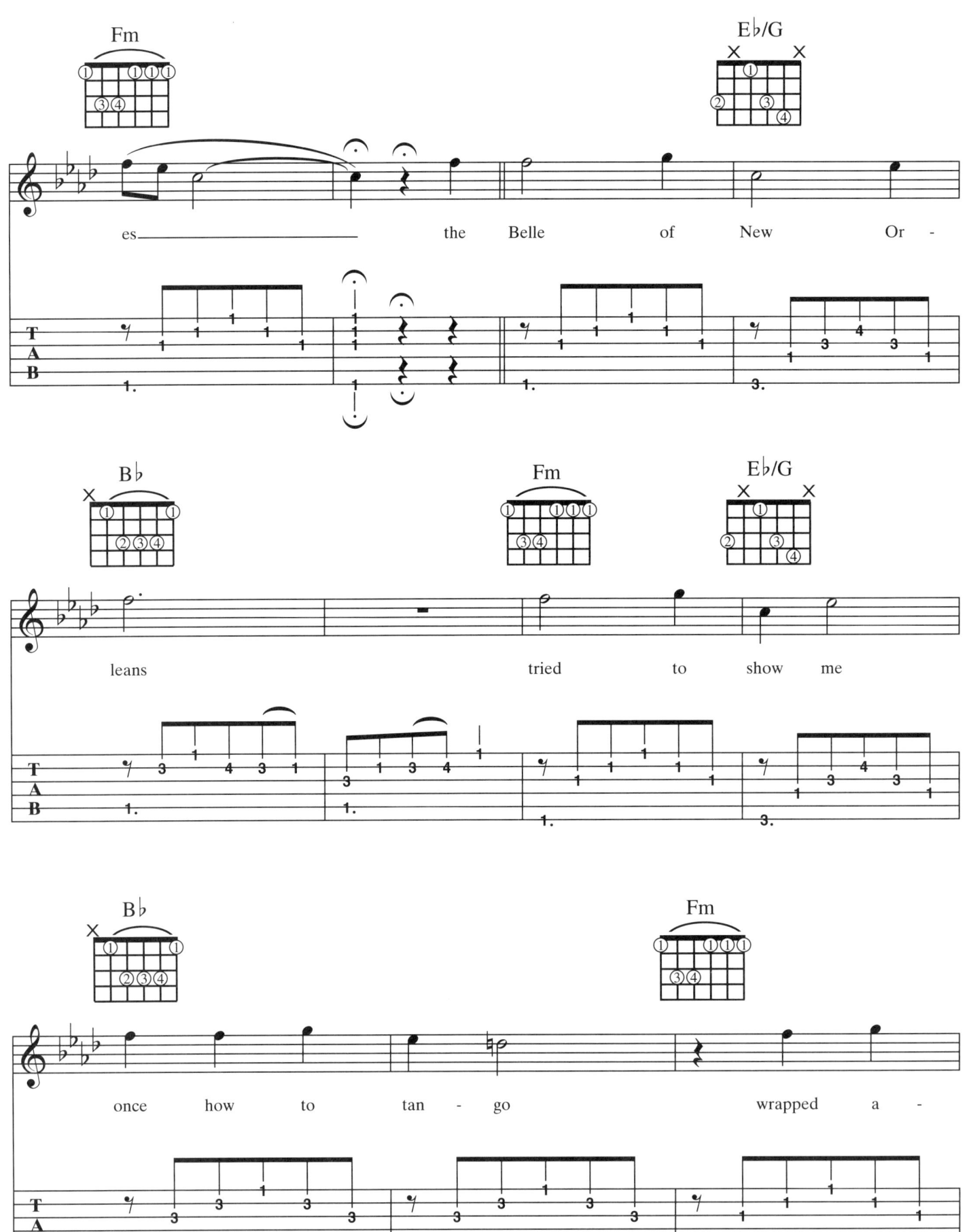

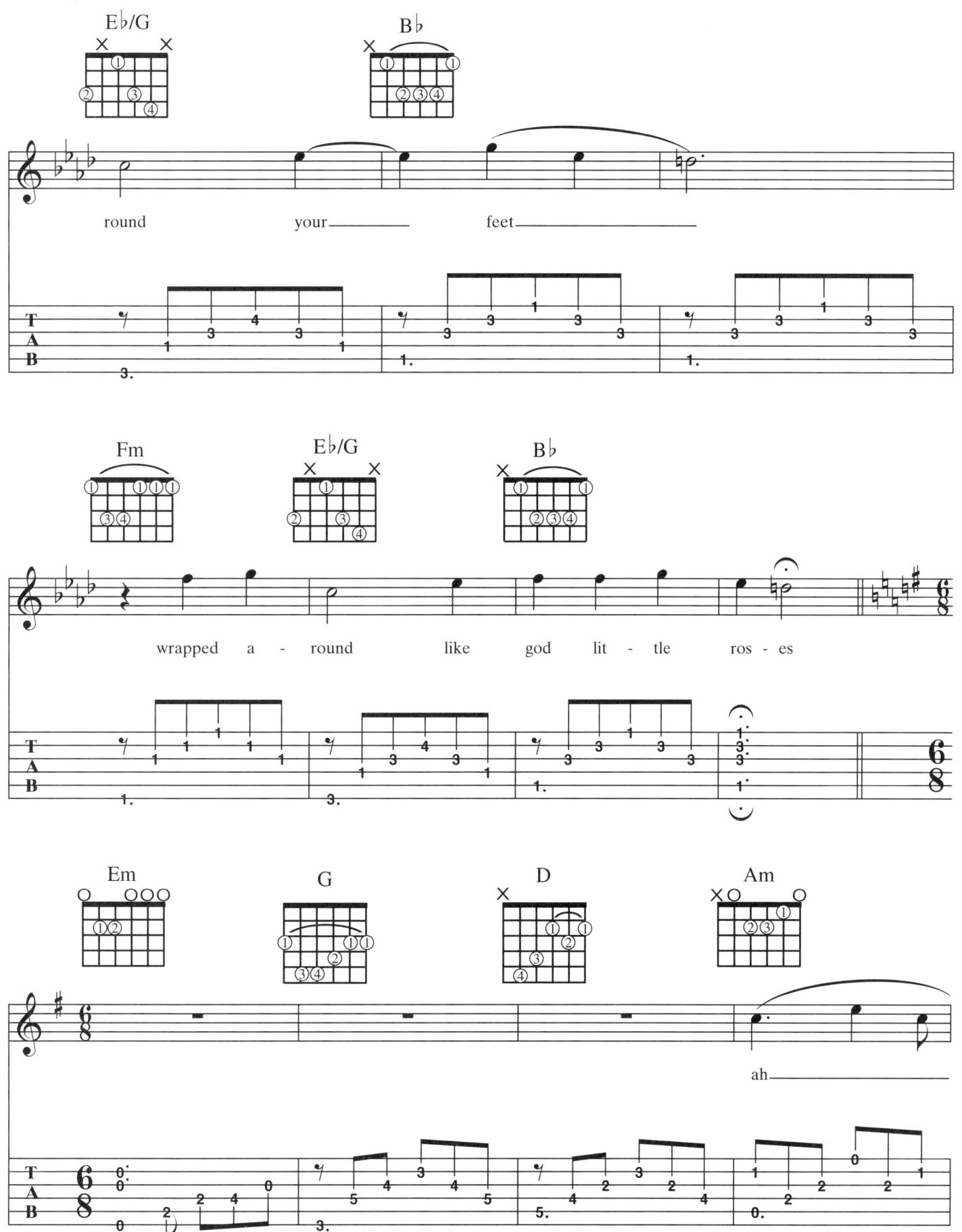

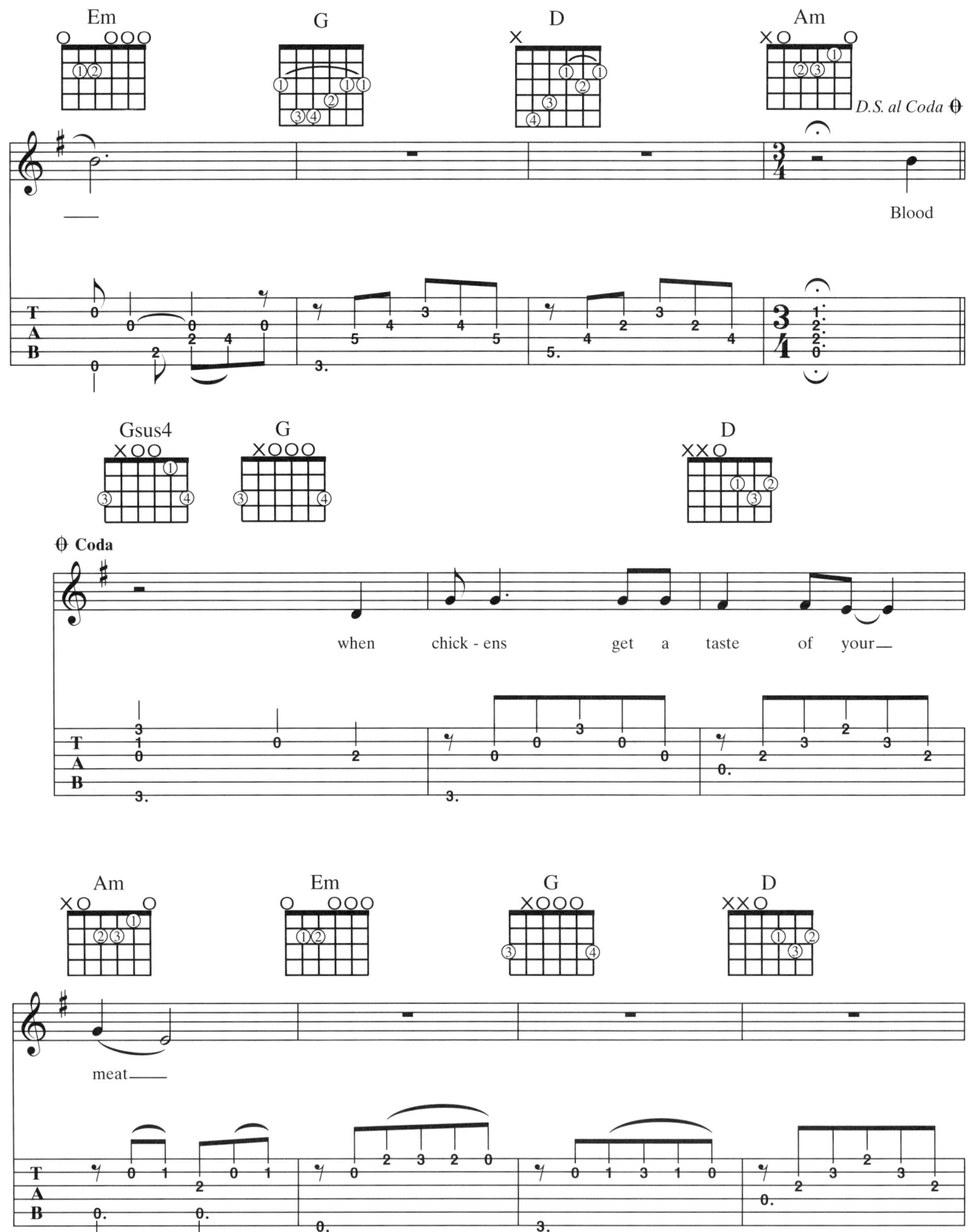

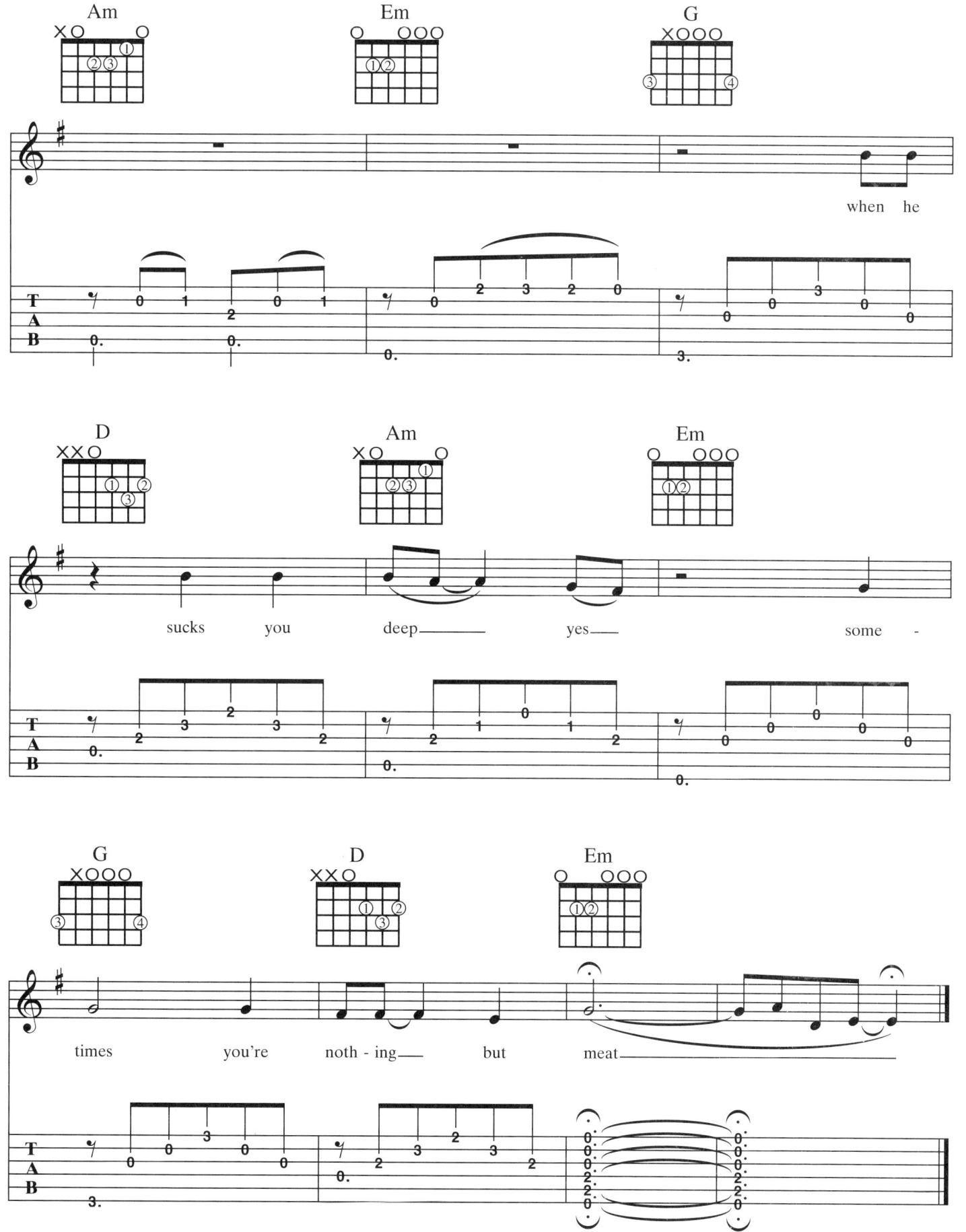

Black Swan
Words and Music by Tori Amos

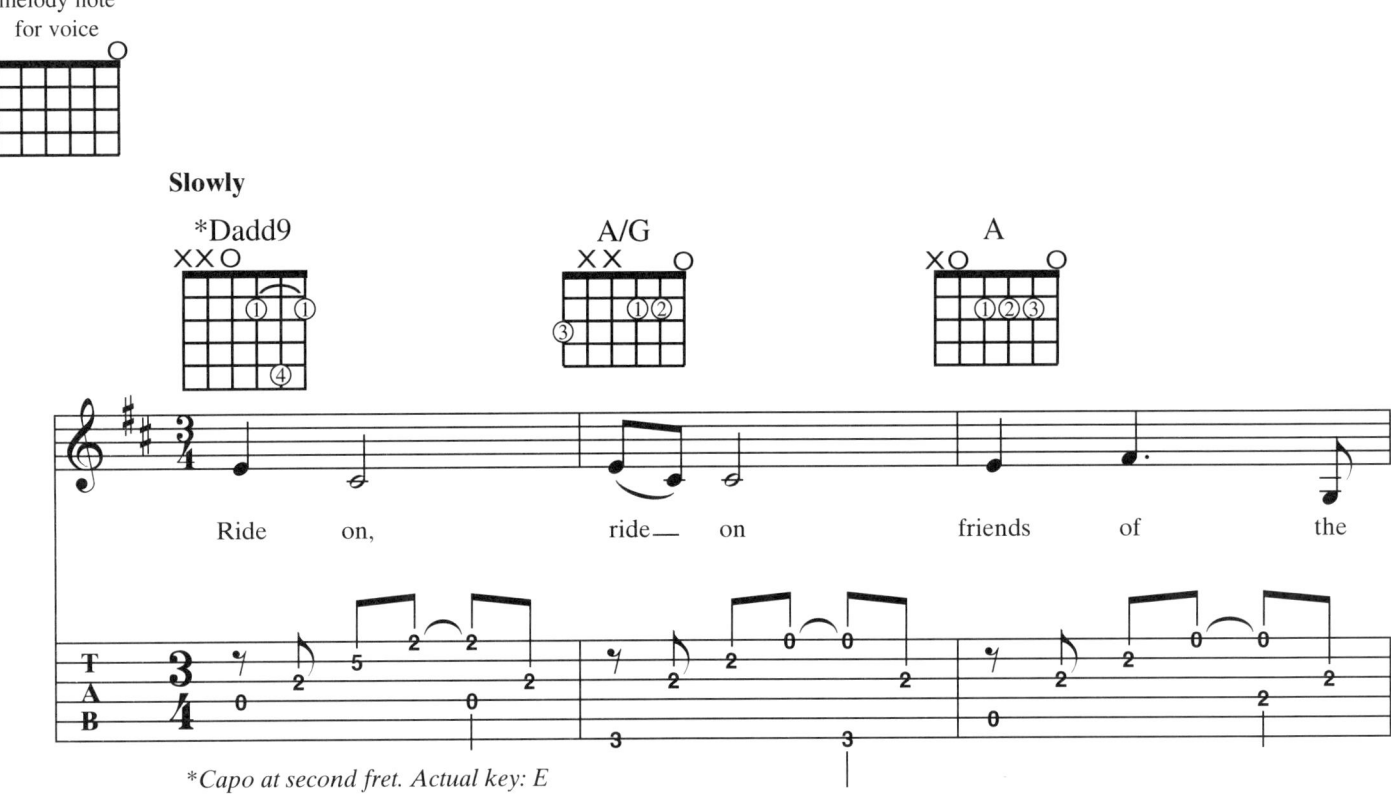

*Capo at second fret. Actual key: E

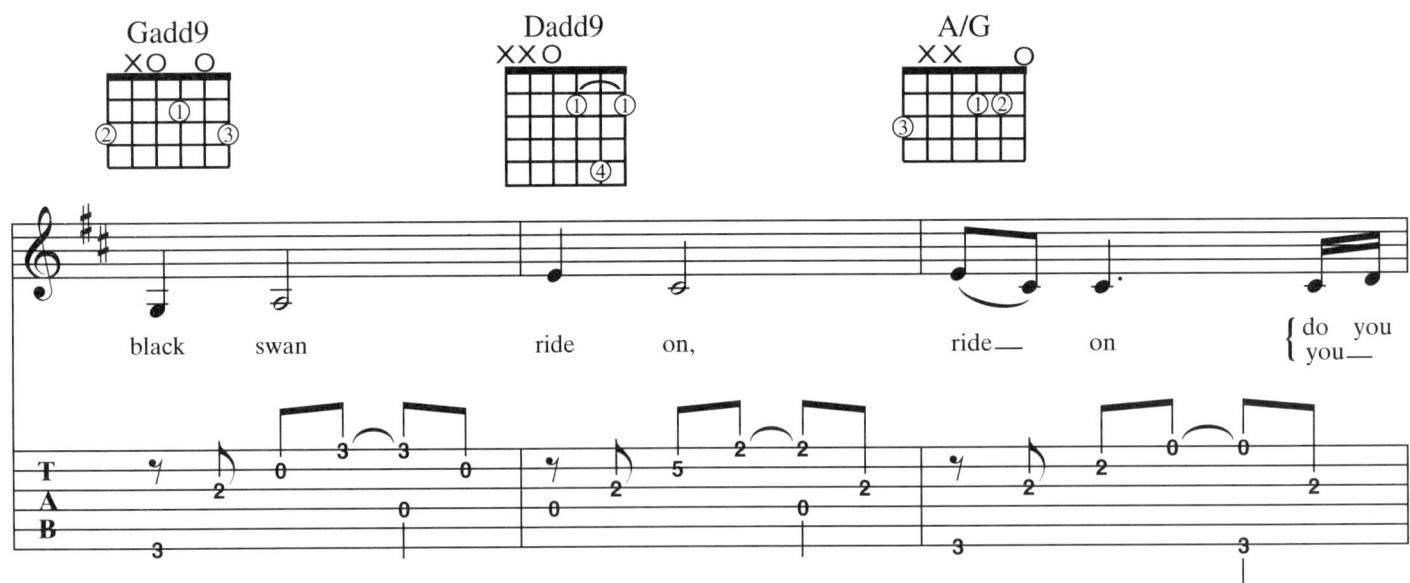

Copyright © 1993 Sword and Stone Publishing Inc. (ASCAP)
International Copyright Secured. All Rights Reserved.

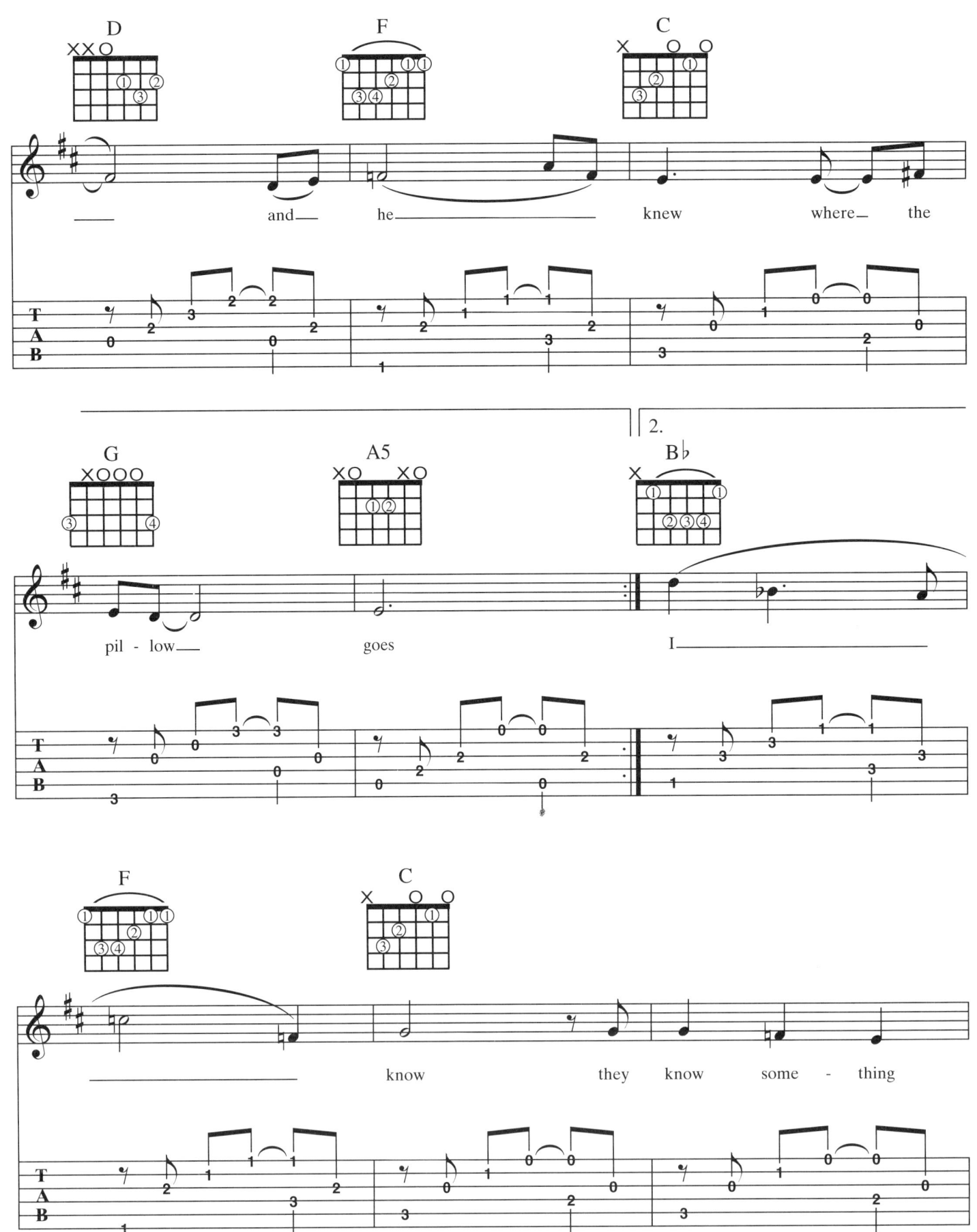

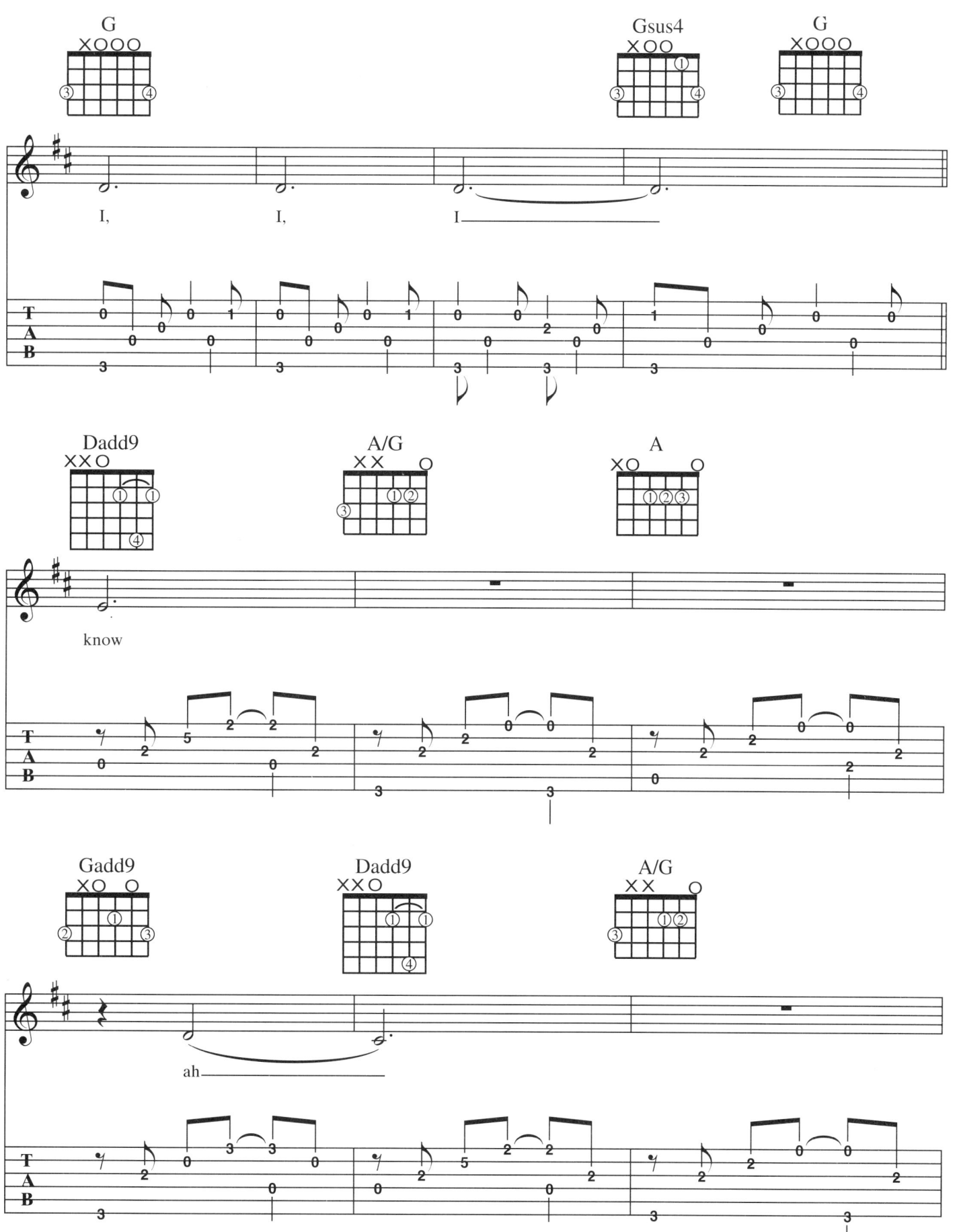

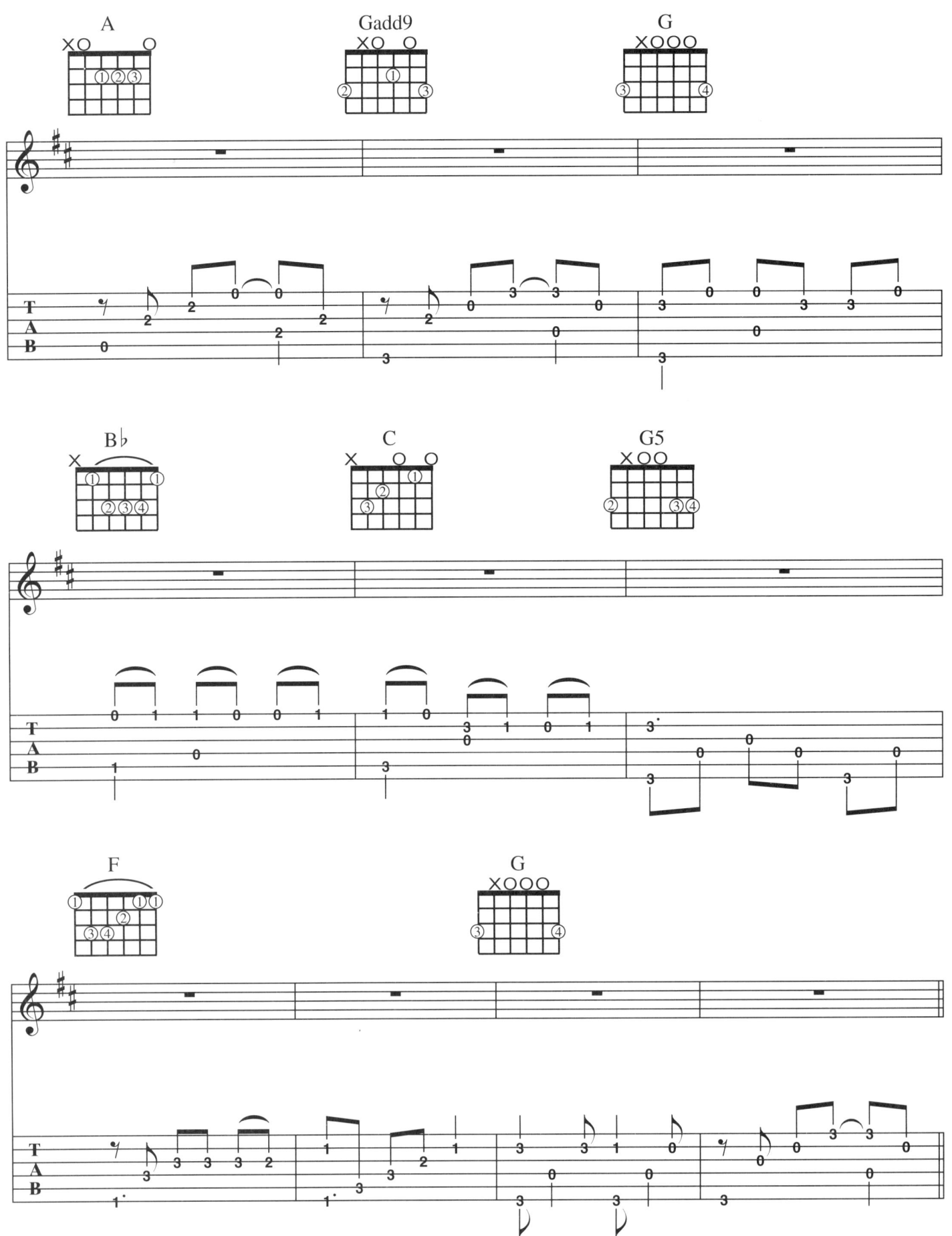

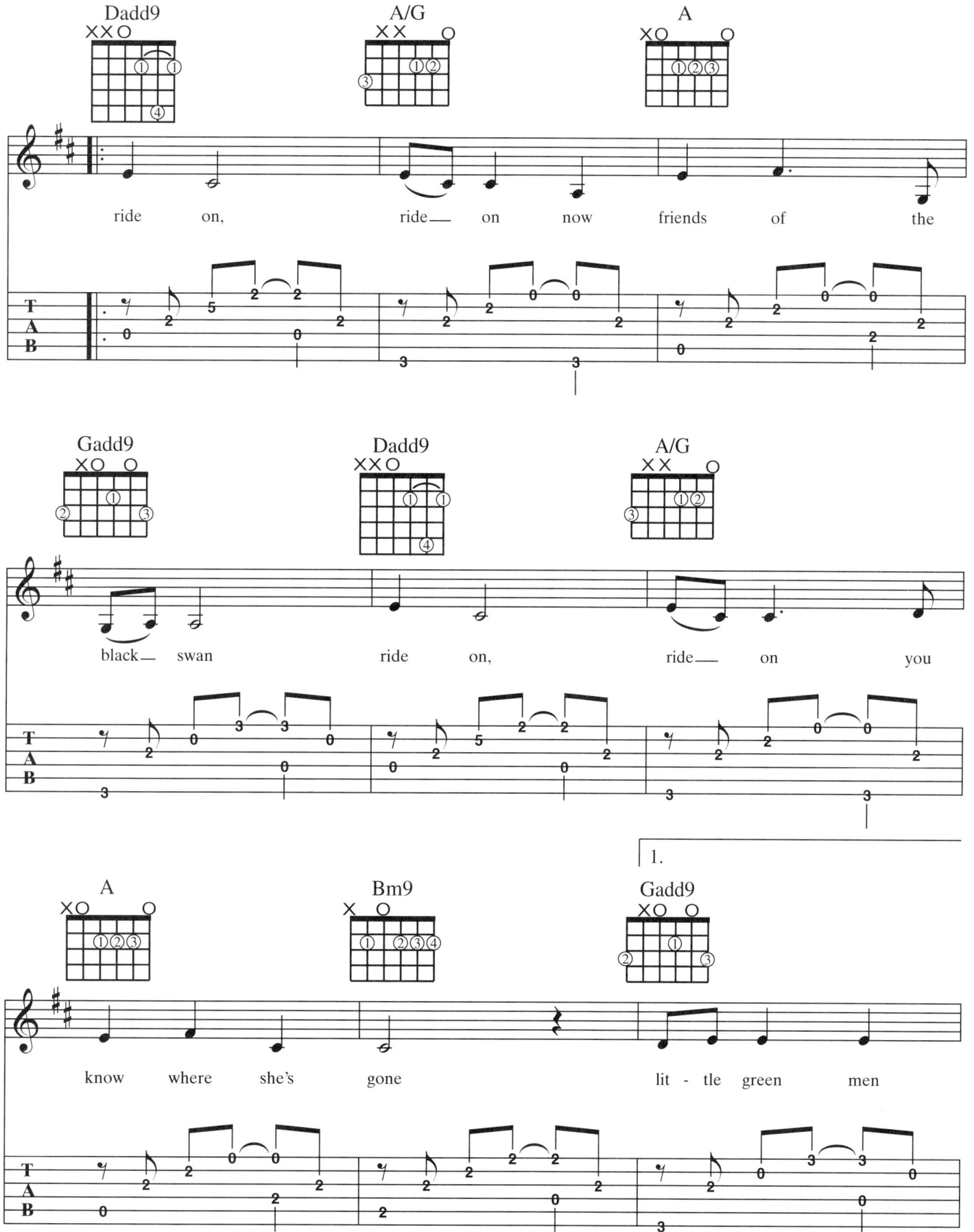

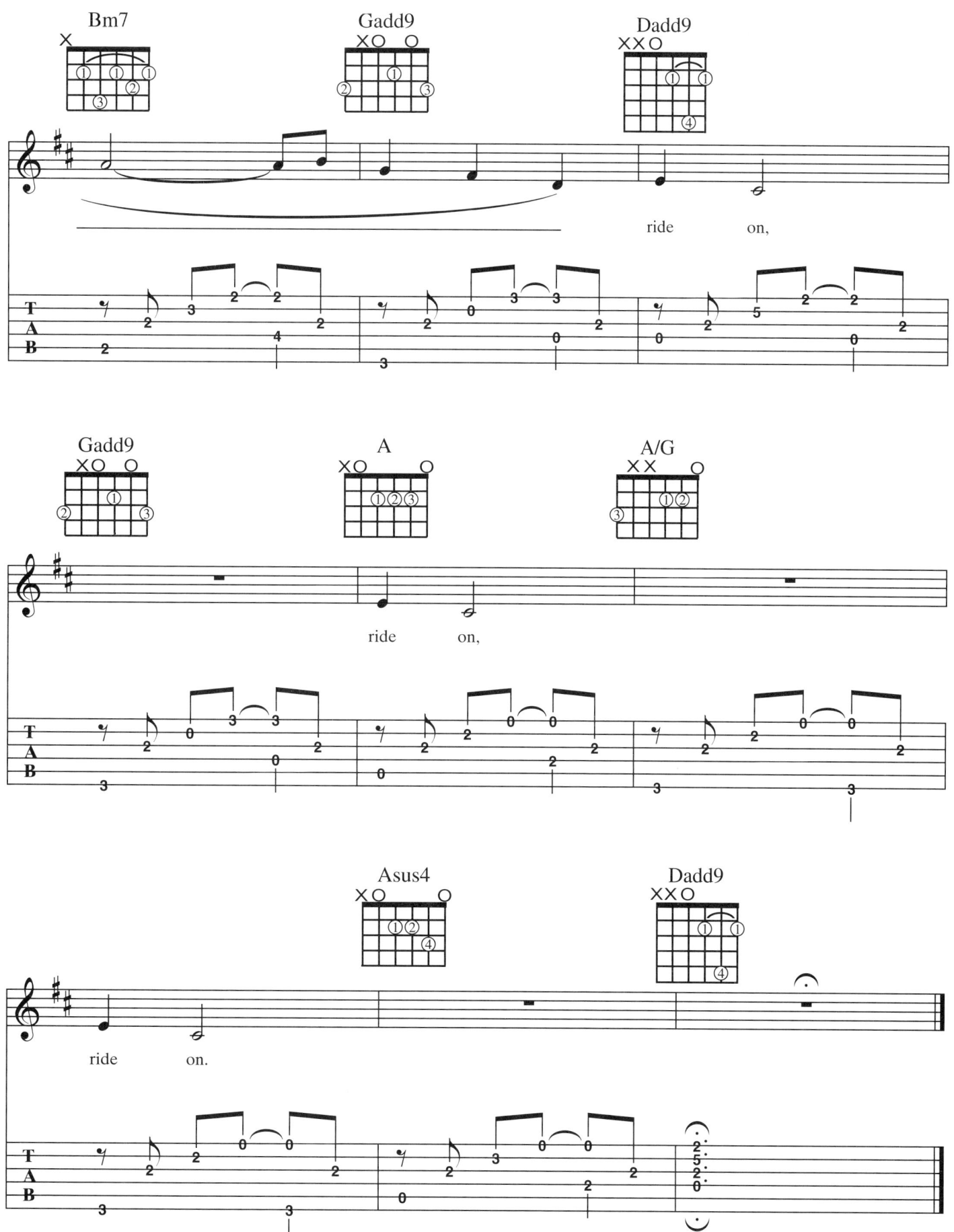

Jackie's Strength
Words and Music by Tori Amos

melody note for voice

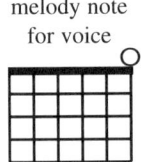

Moderately flowing

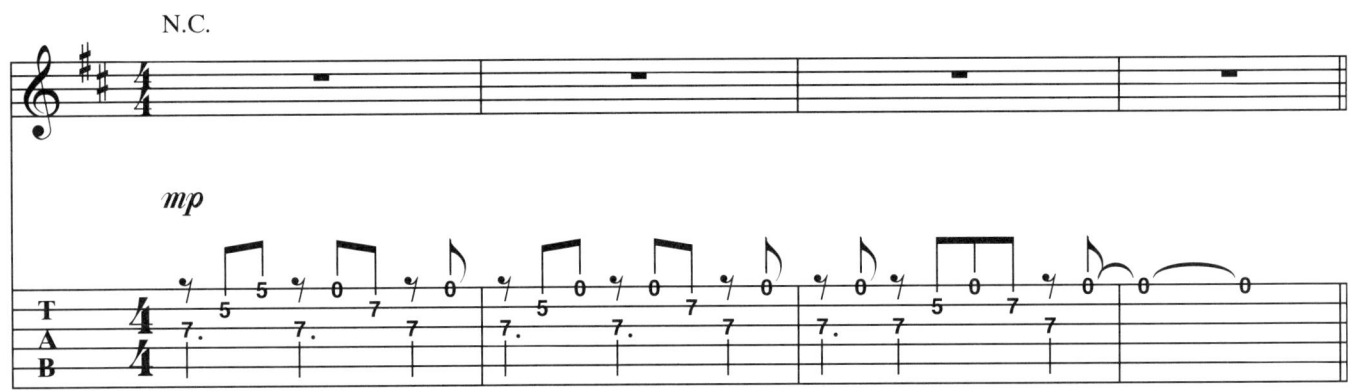

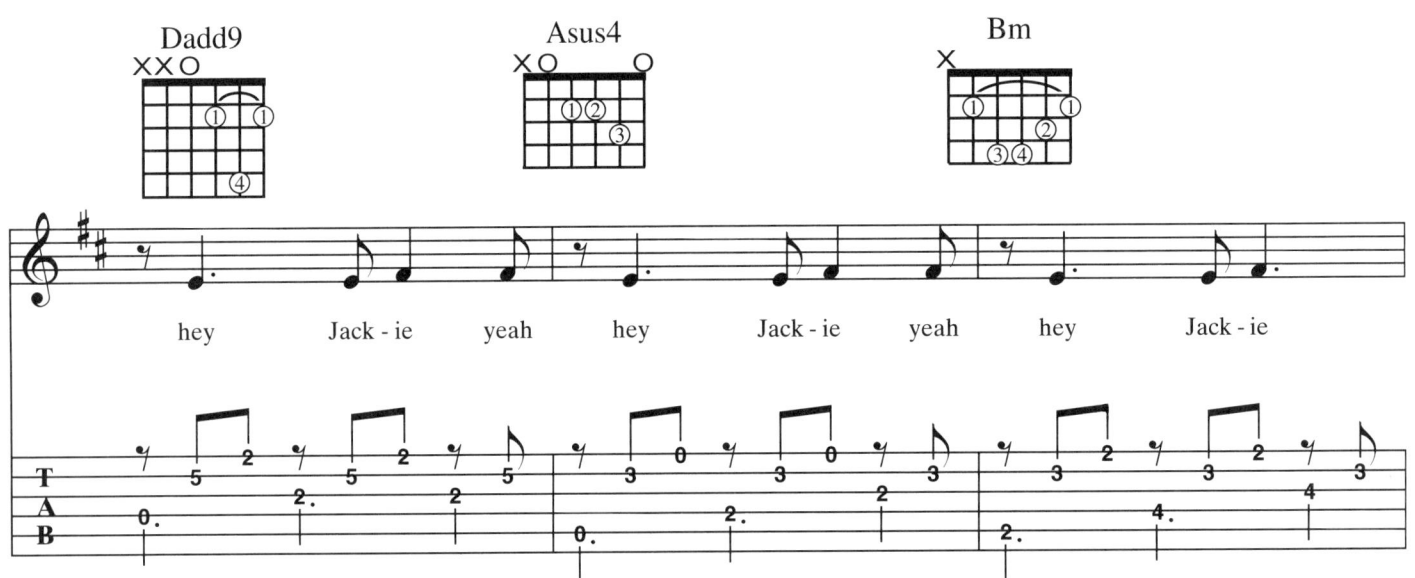

hey   Jack-ie   yeah   hey   Jack-ie   yeah   hey   Jack-ie

Copyright © 1997 Sword and Stone Publishing Inc. (ASCAP)
International Copyright Secured. All Rights Reserved.

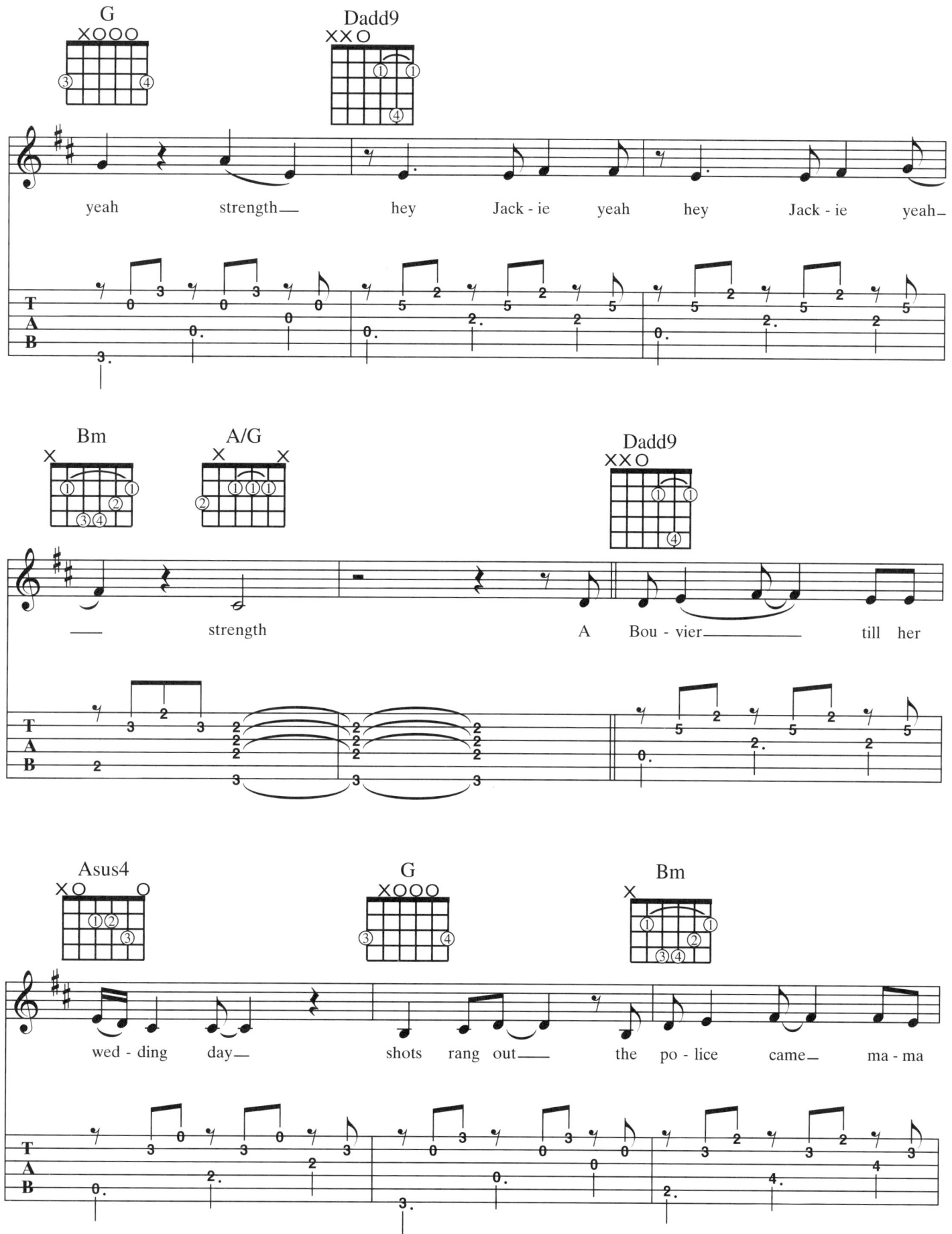

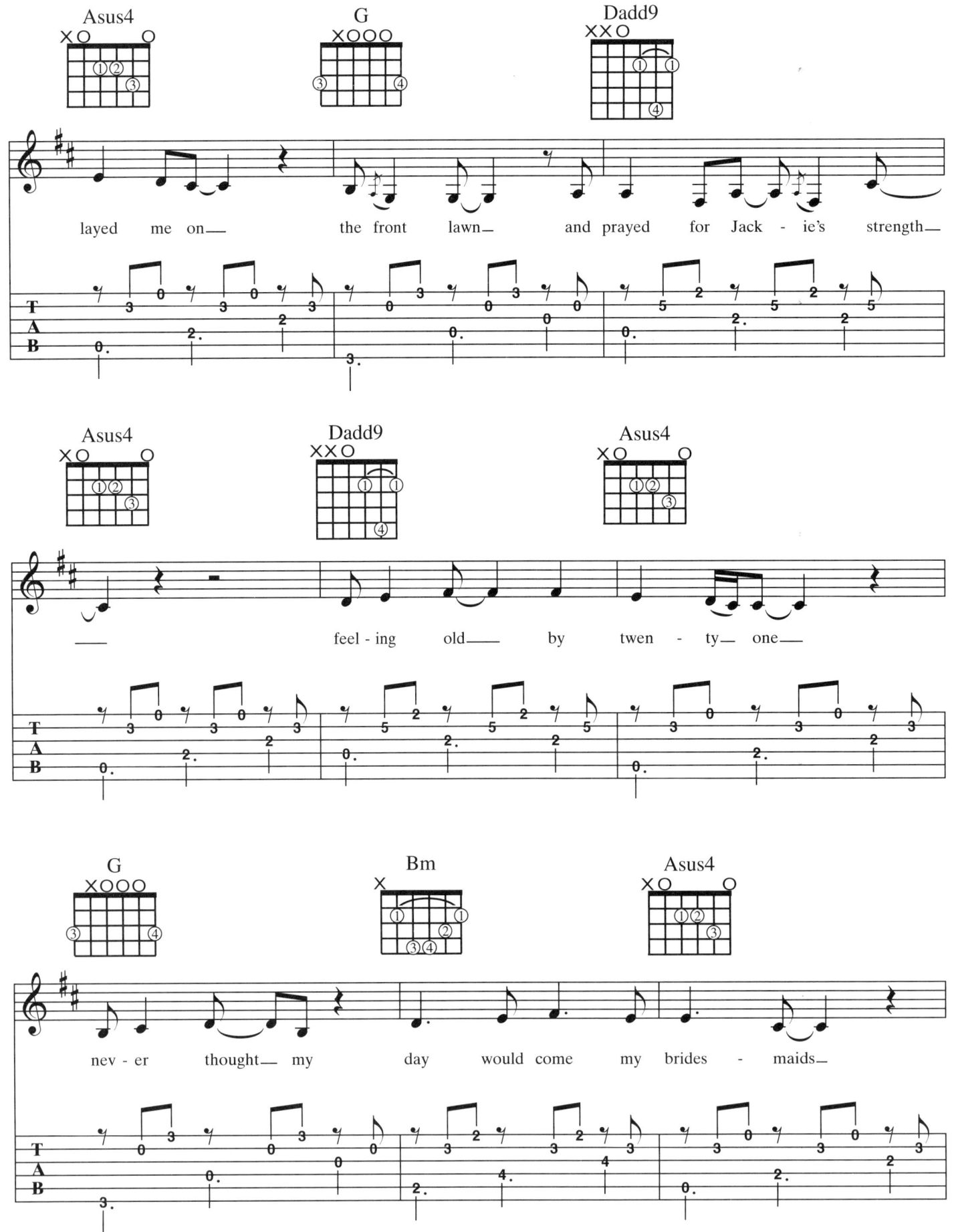

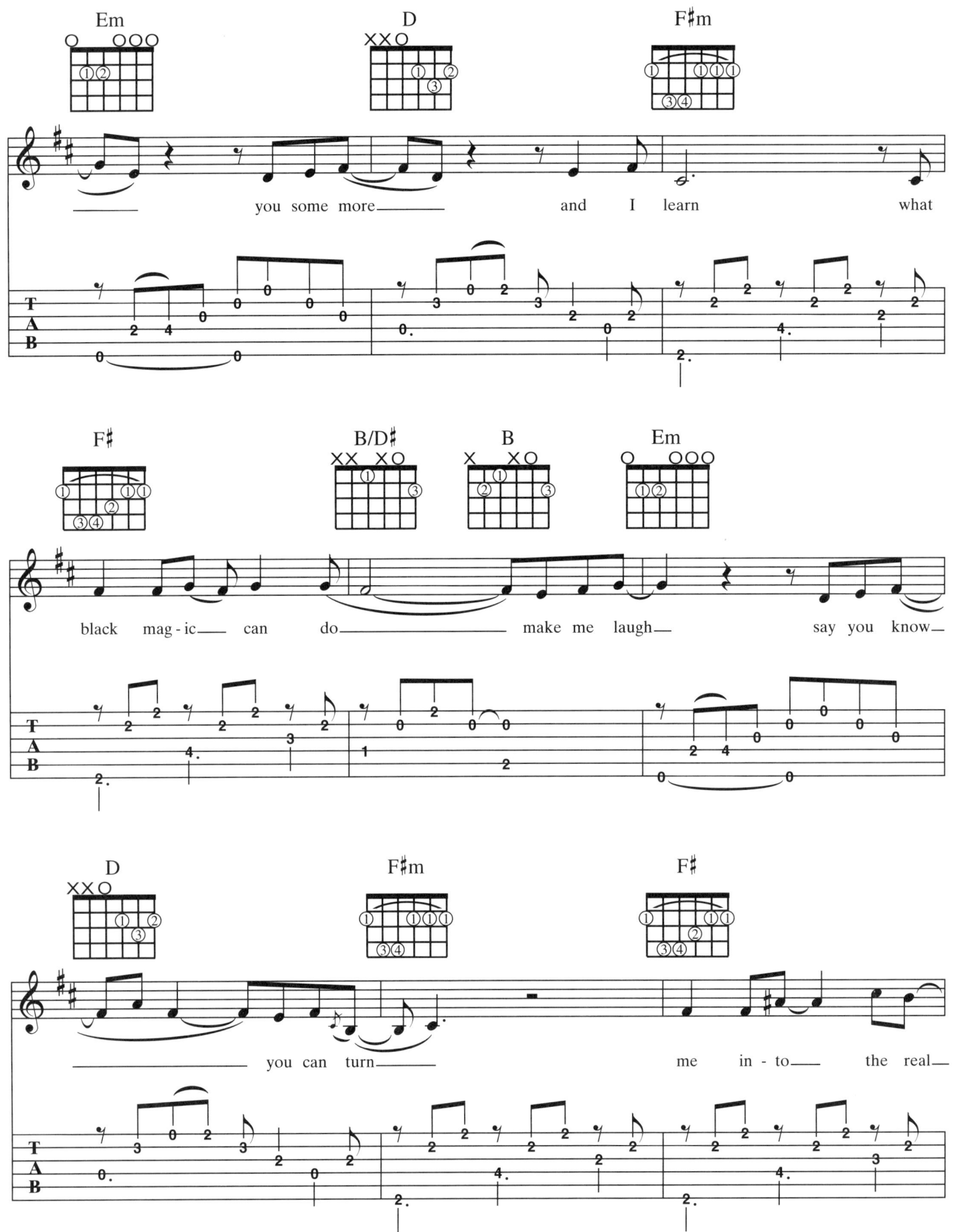

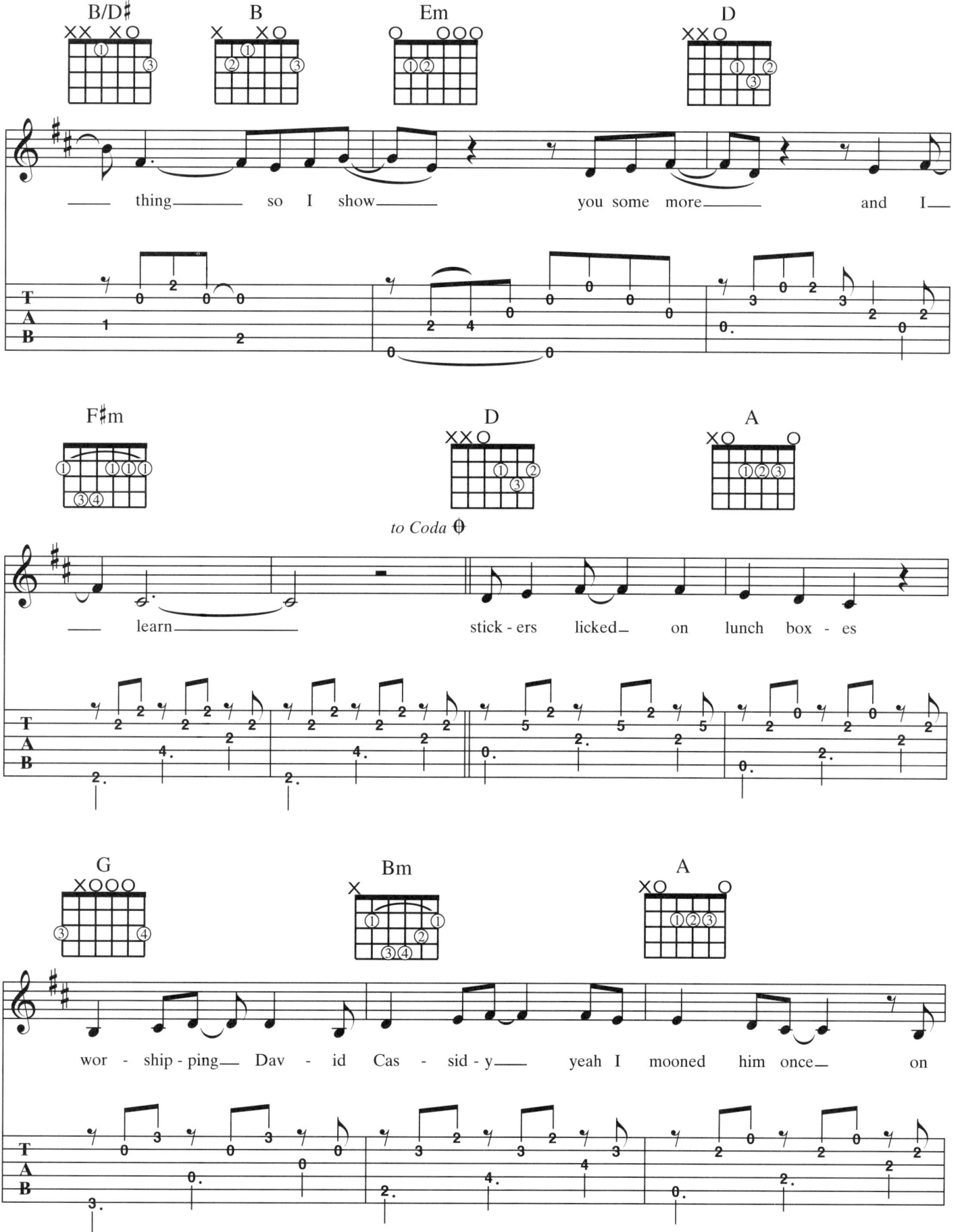

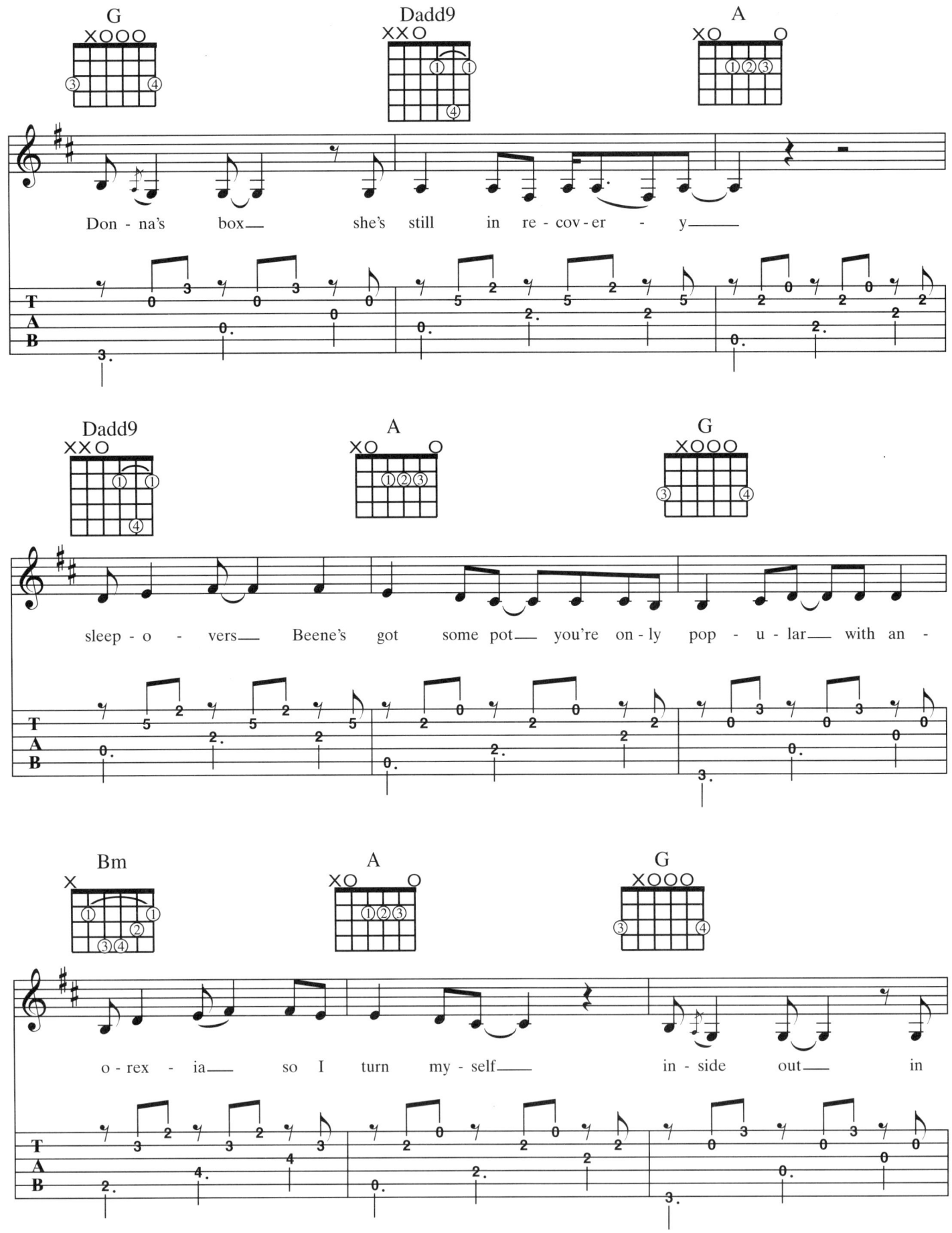

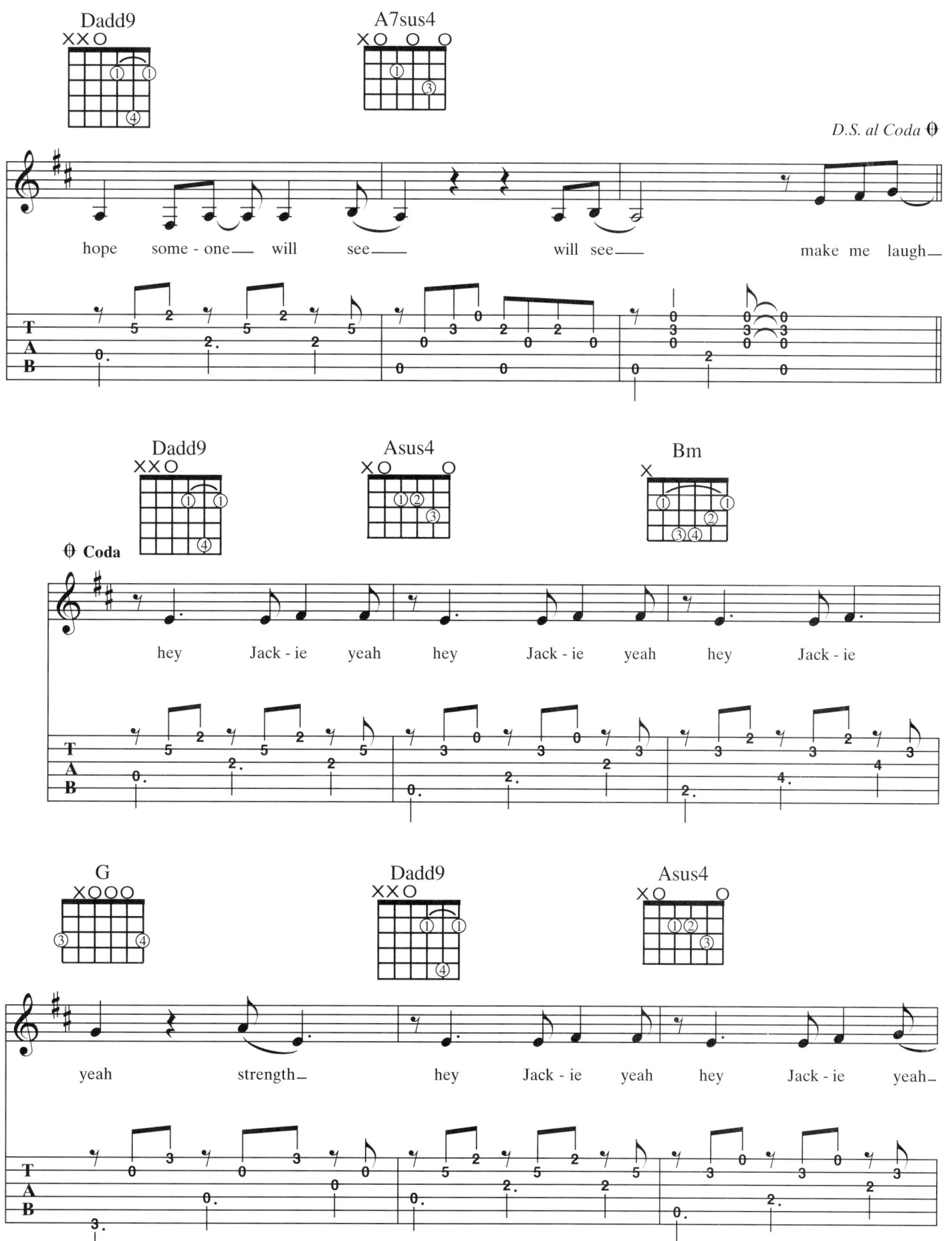

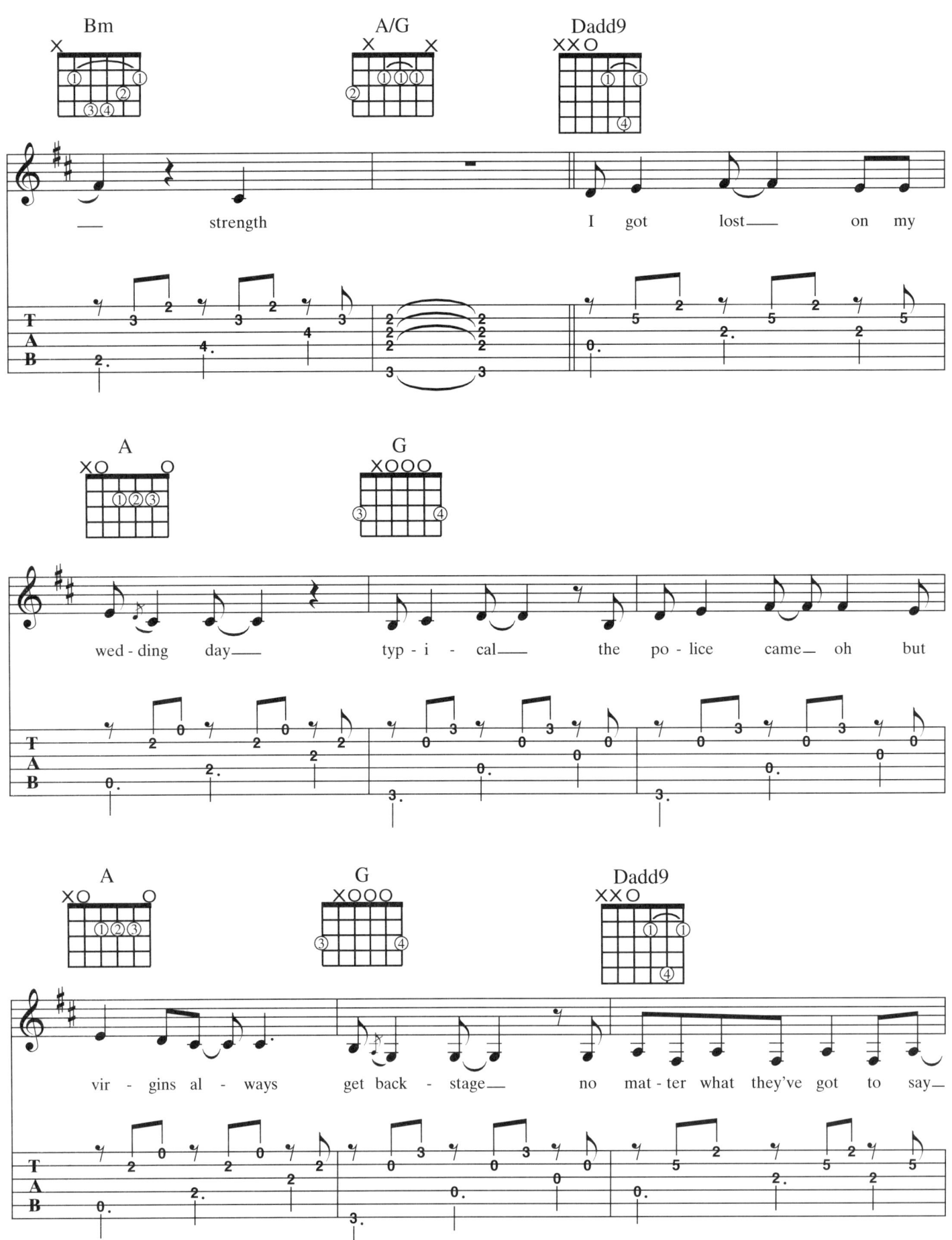

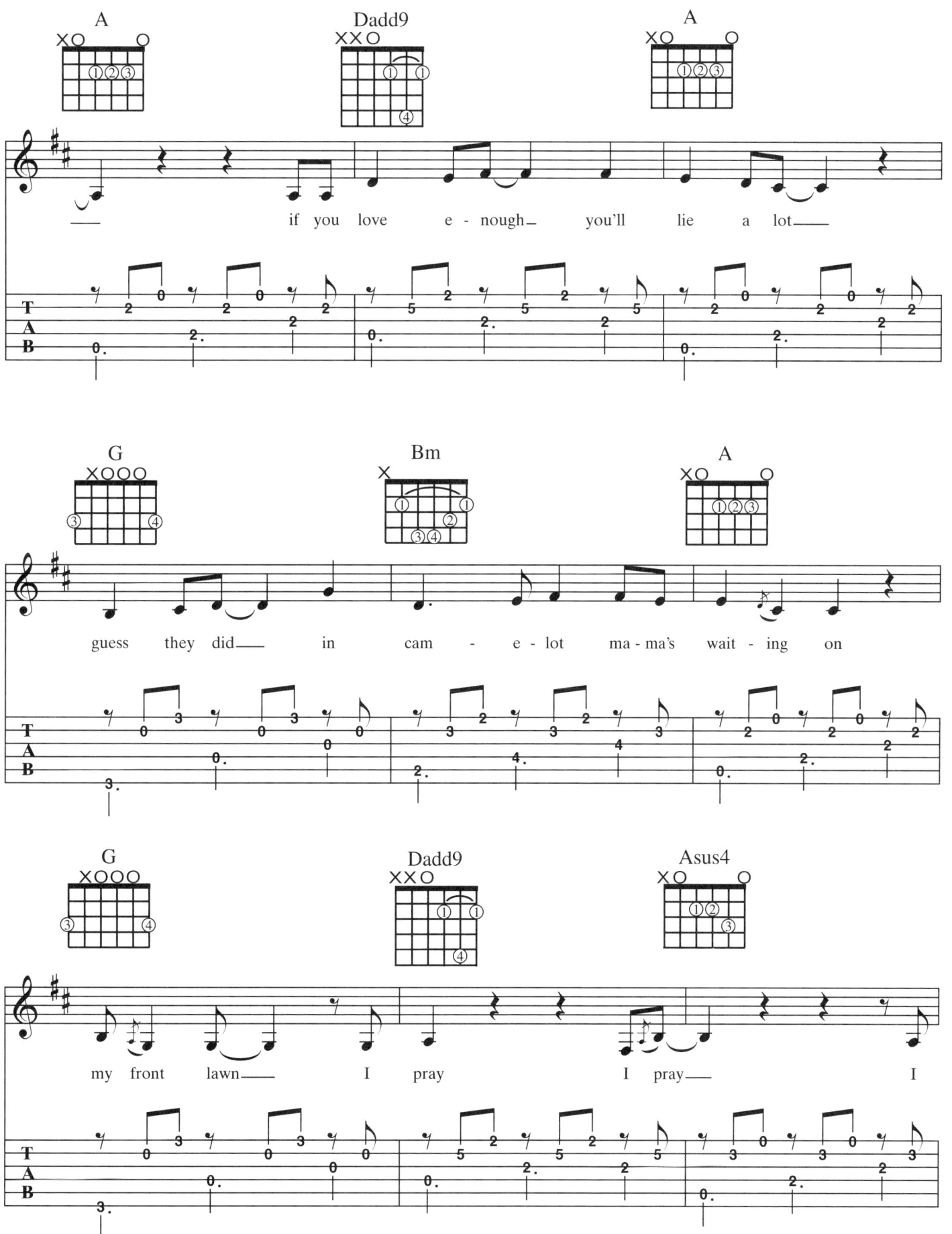

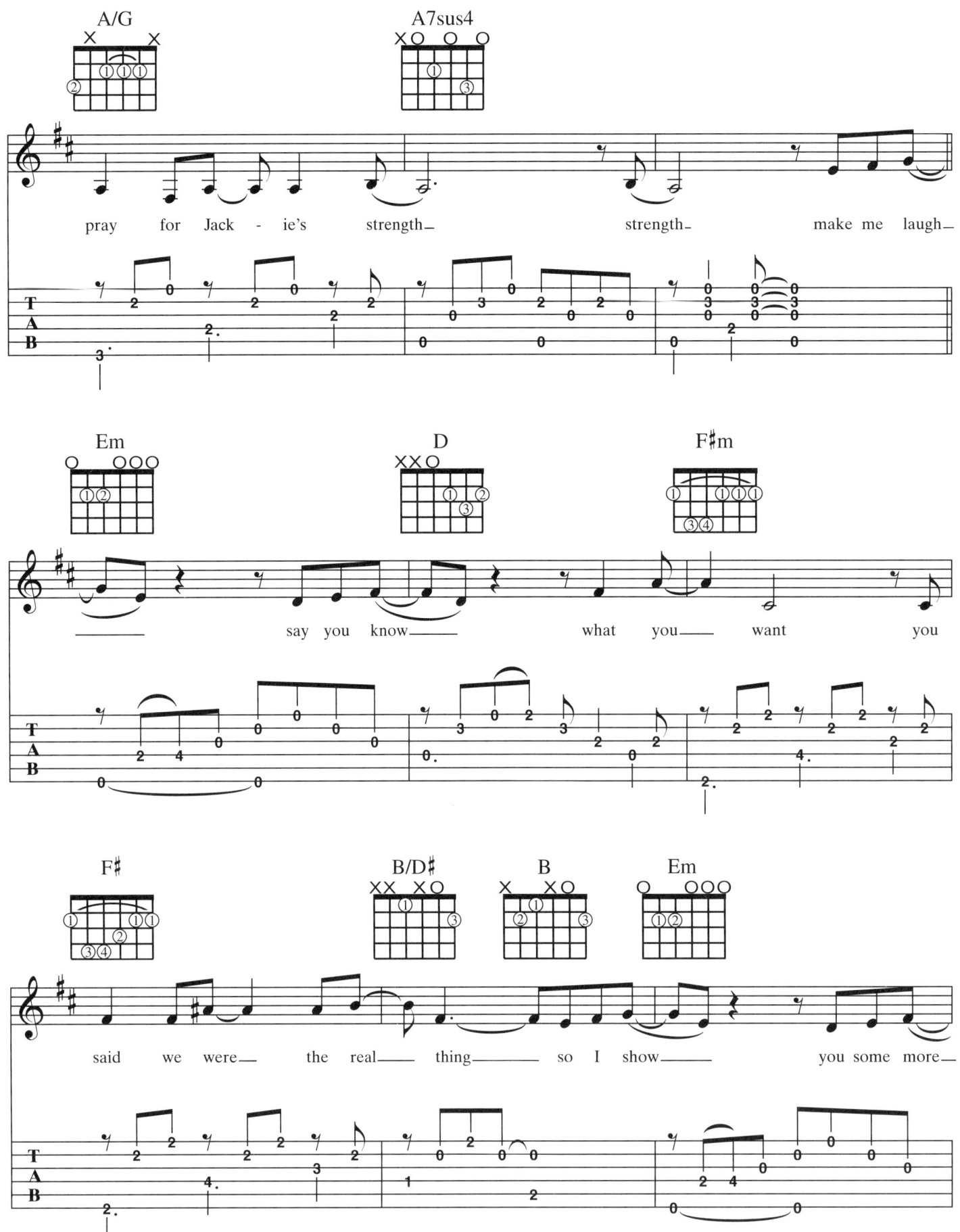

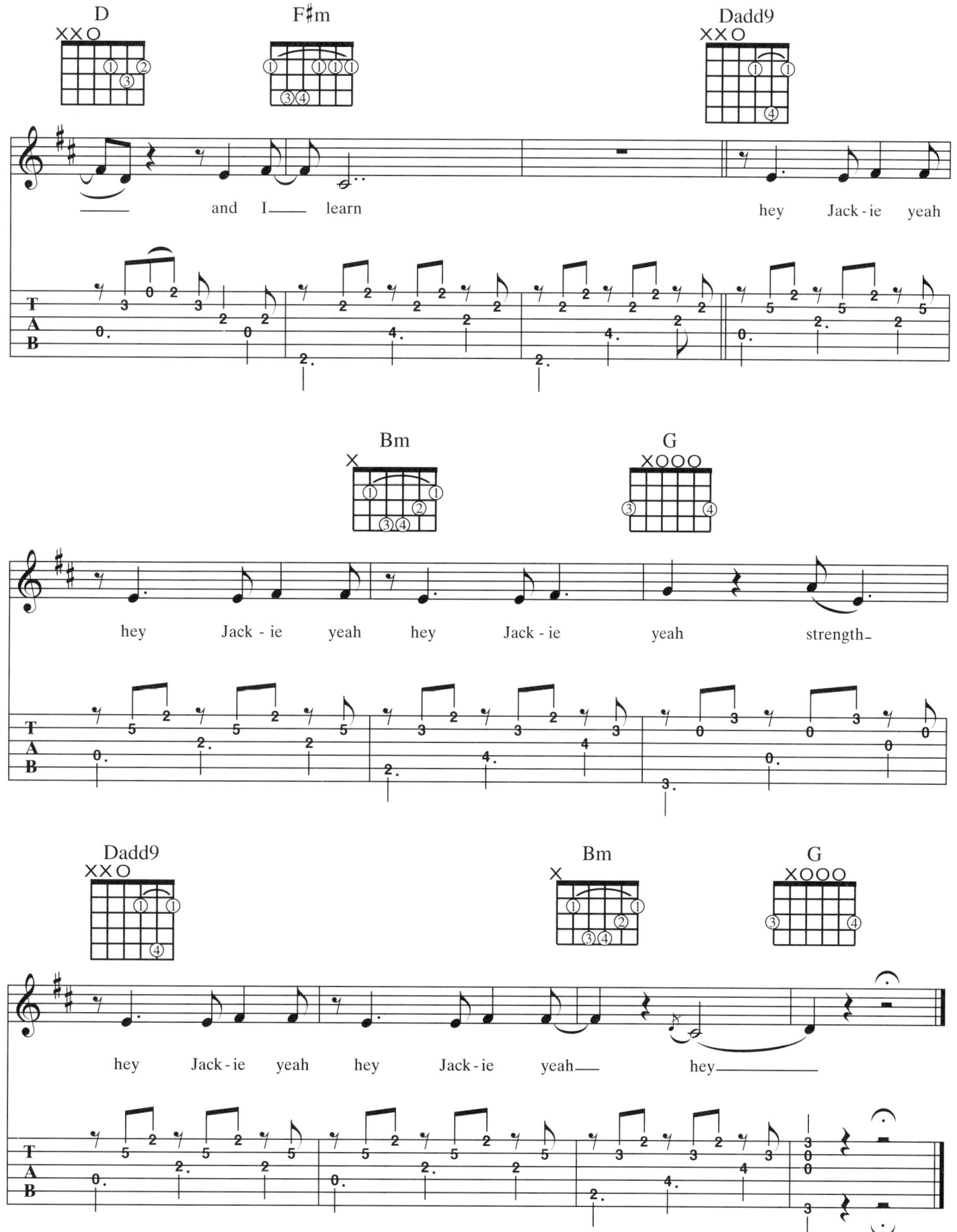

Spark

Words and Music by Tori Amos

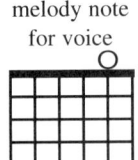
melody note for voice

Moderately

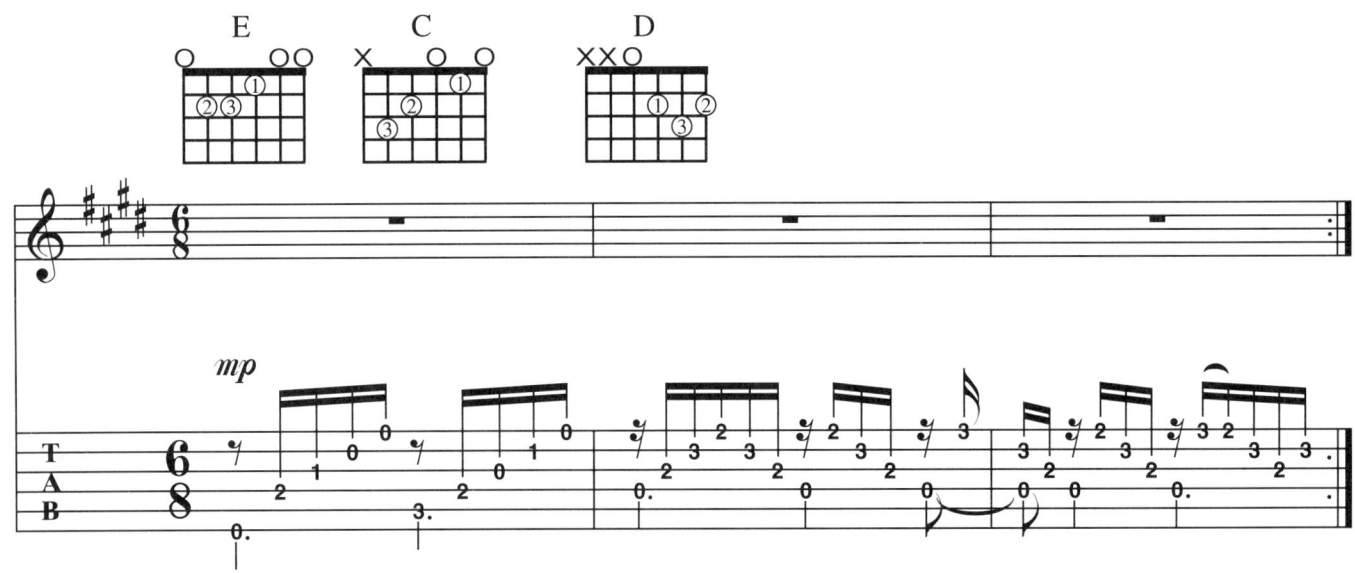

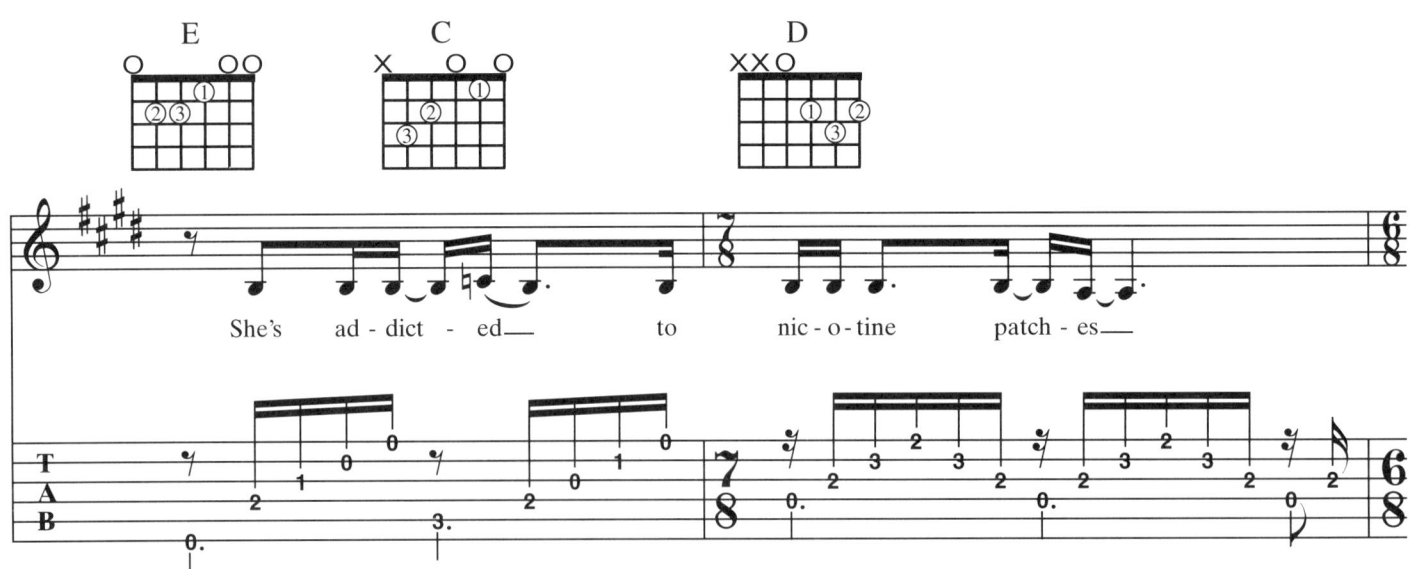

She's ad-dict-ed to nic-o-tine patch-es

Copyright © 1997 Sword and Stone Publishing Inc. (ASCAP)
International Copyright Secured. All Rights Reserved.

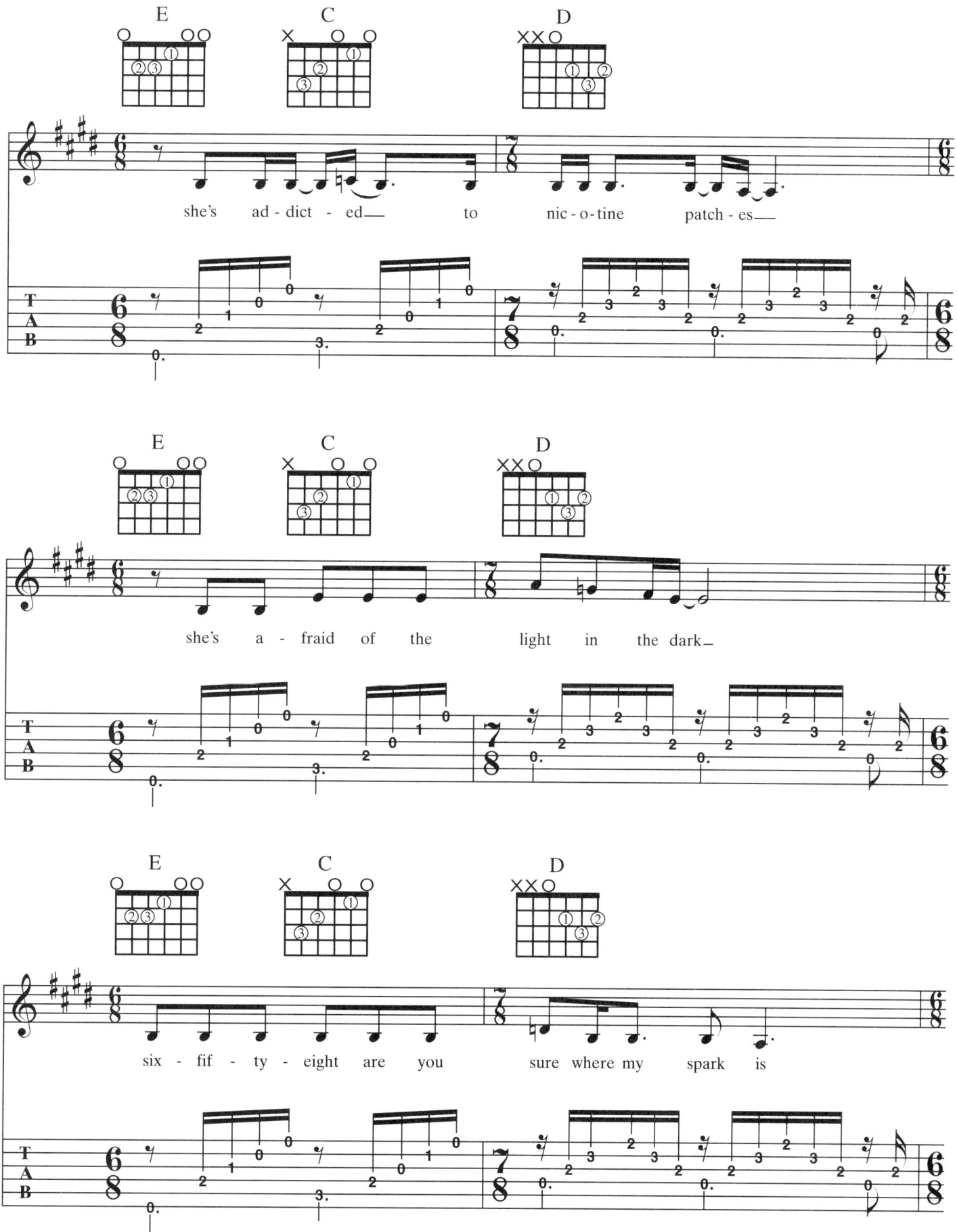

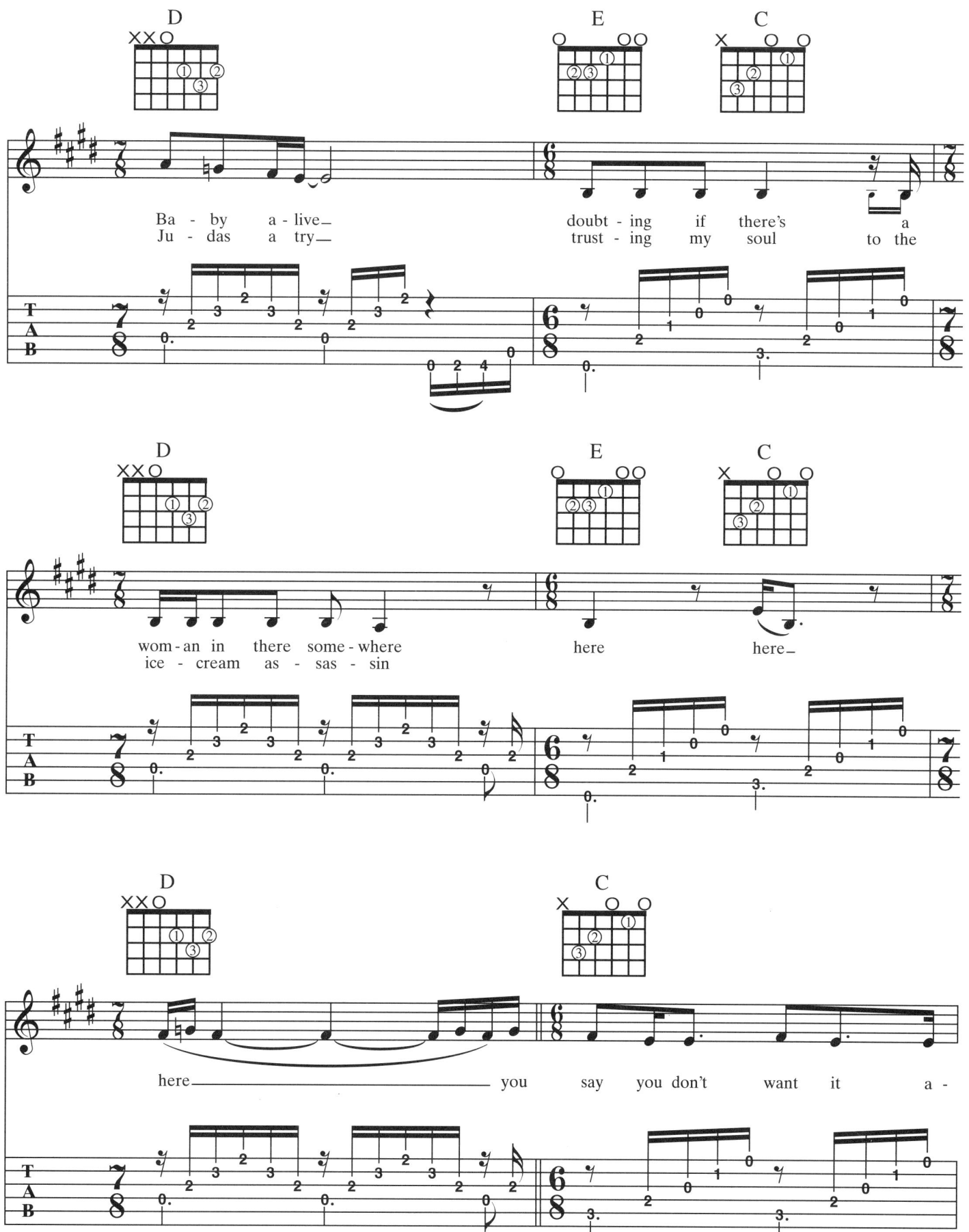

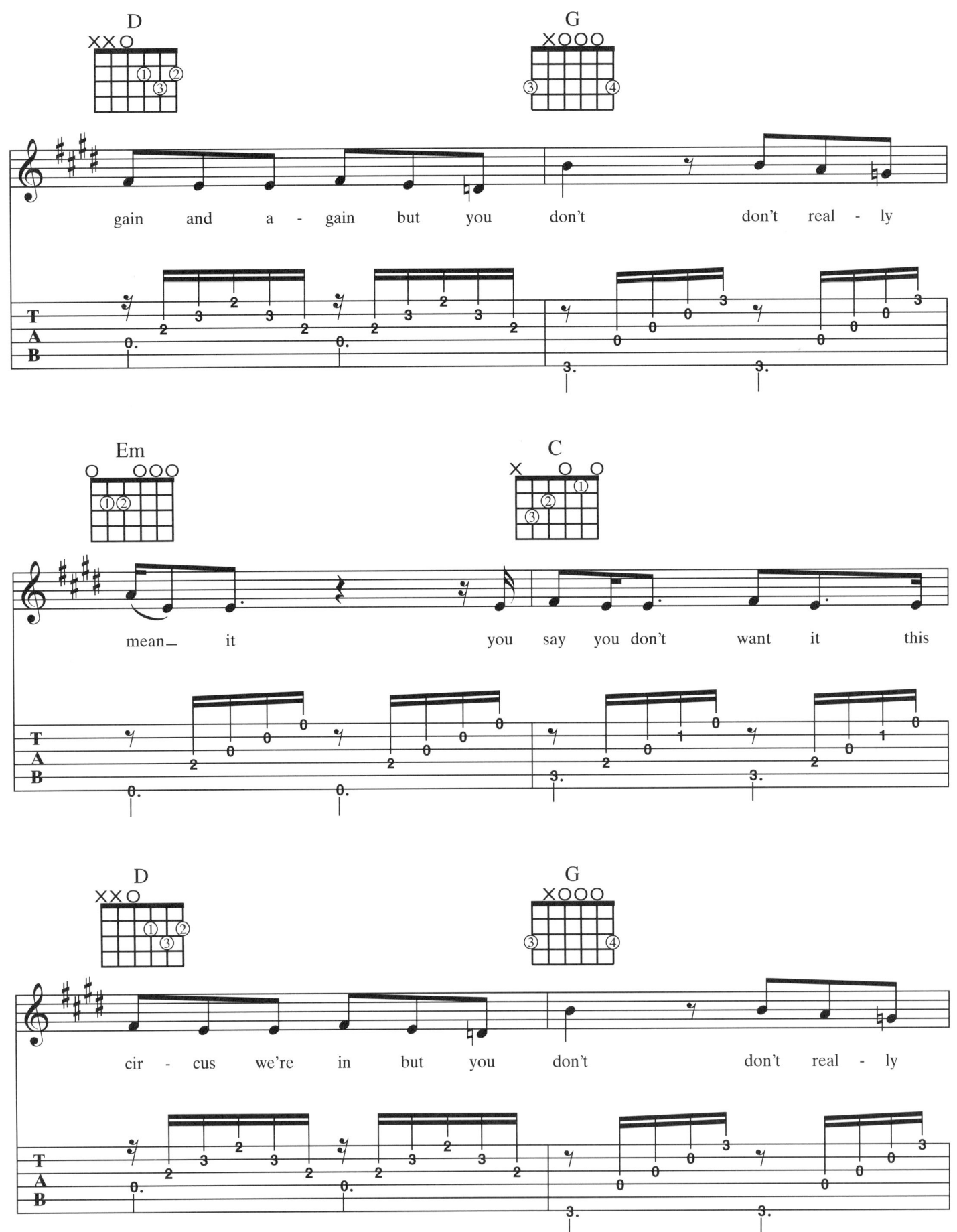

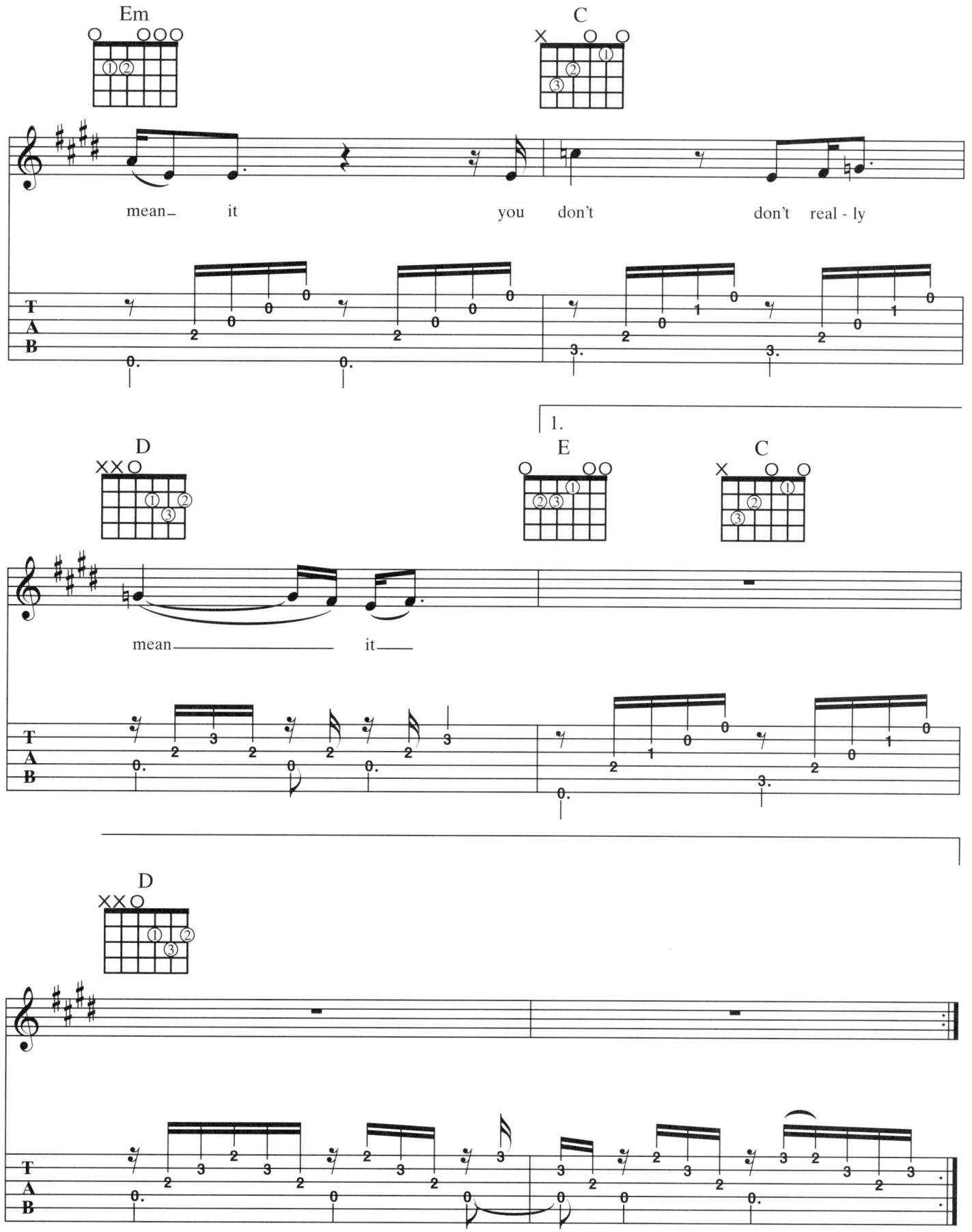

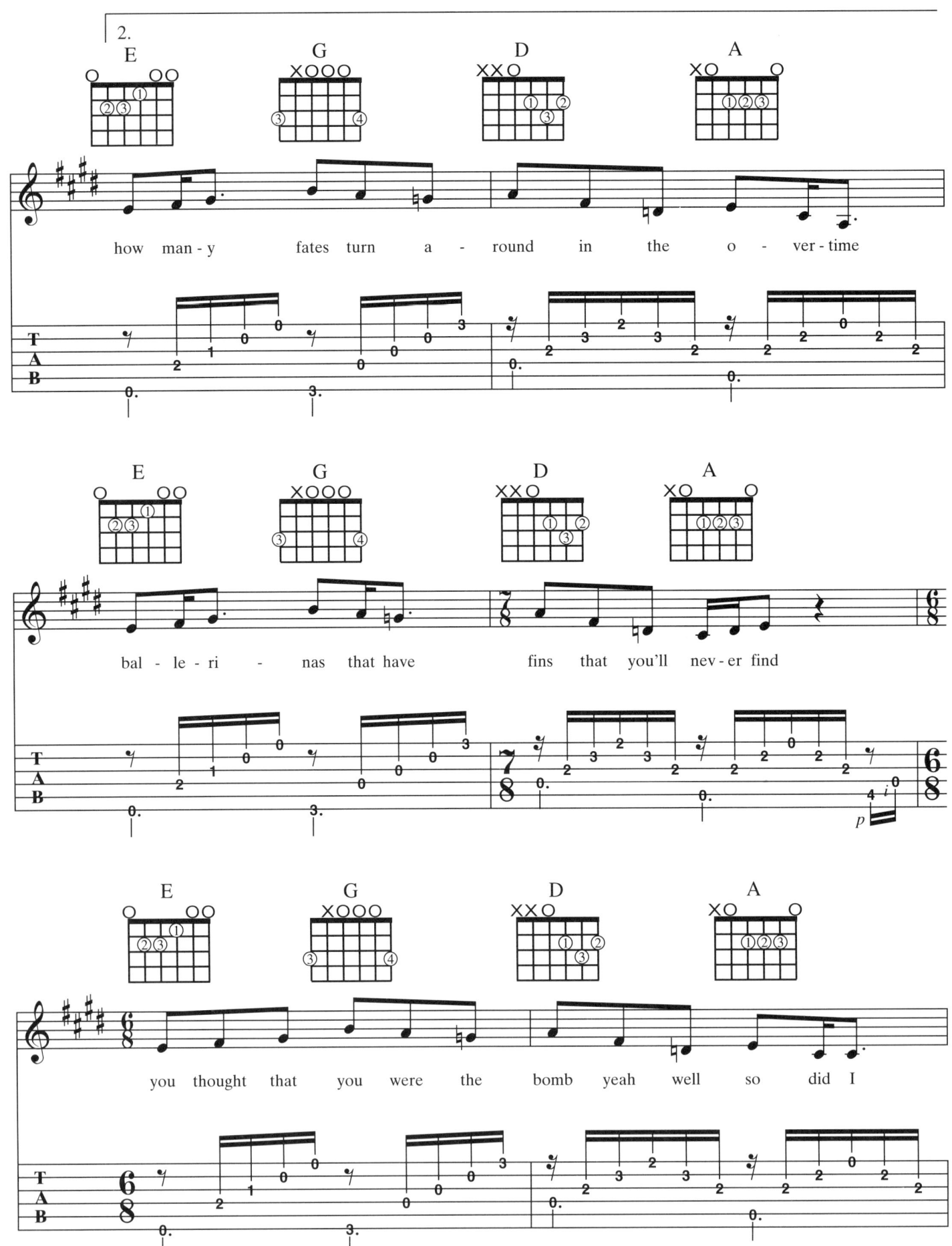

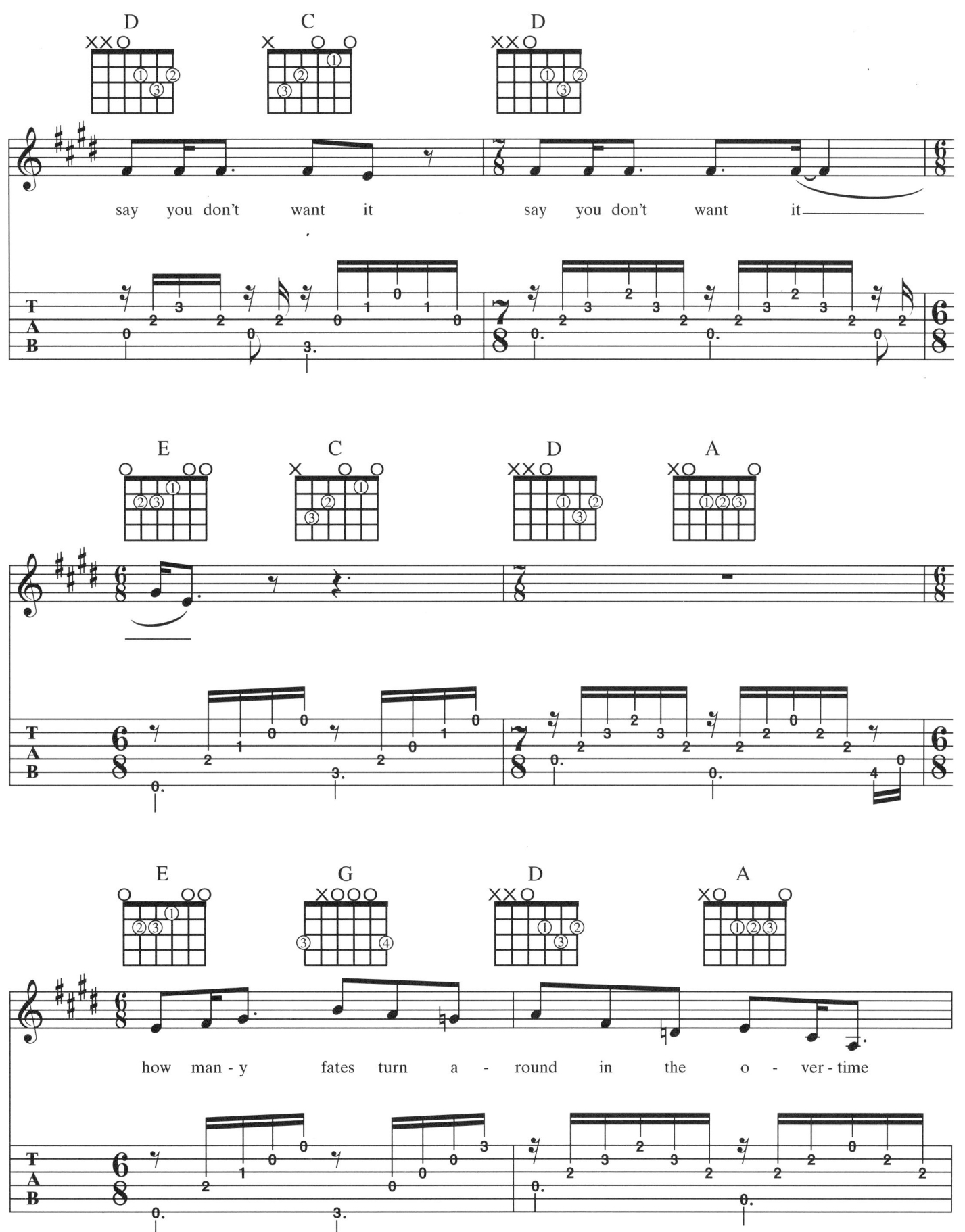

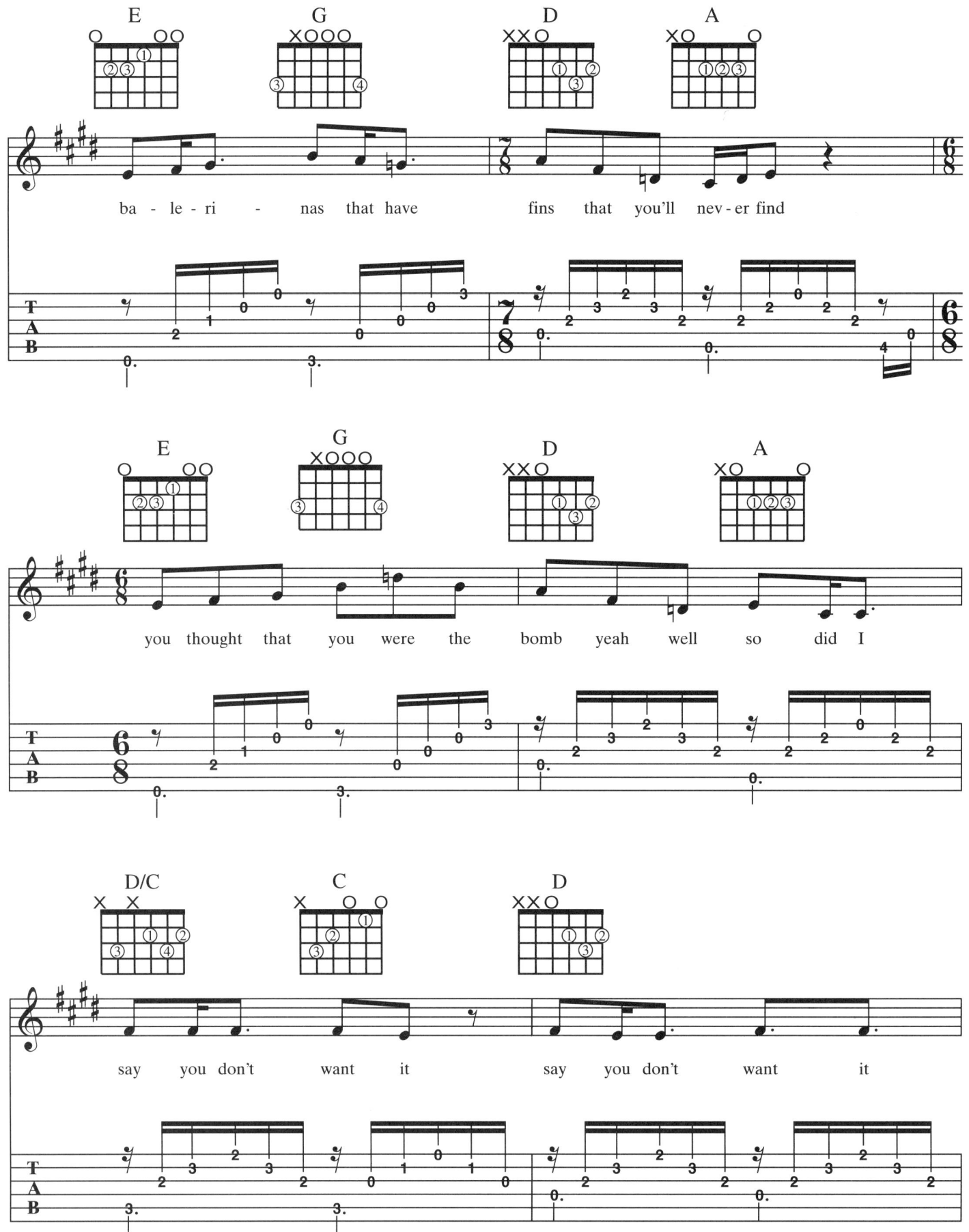

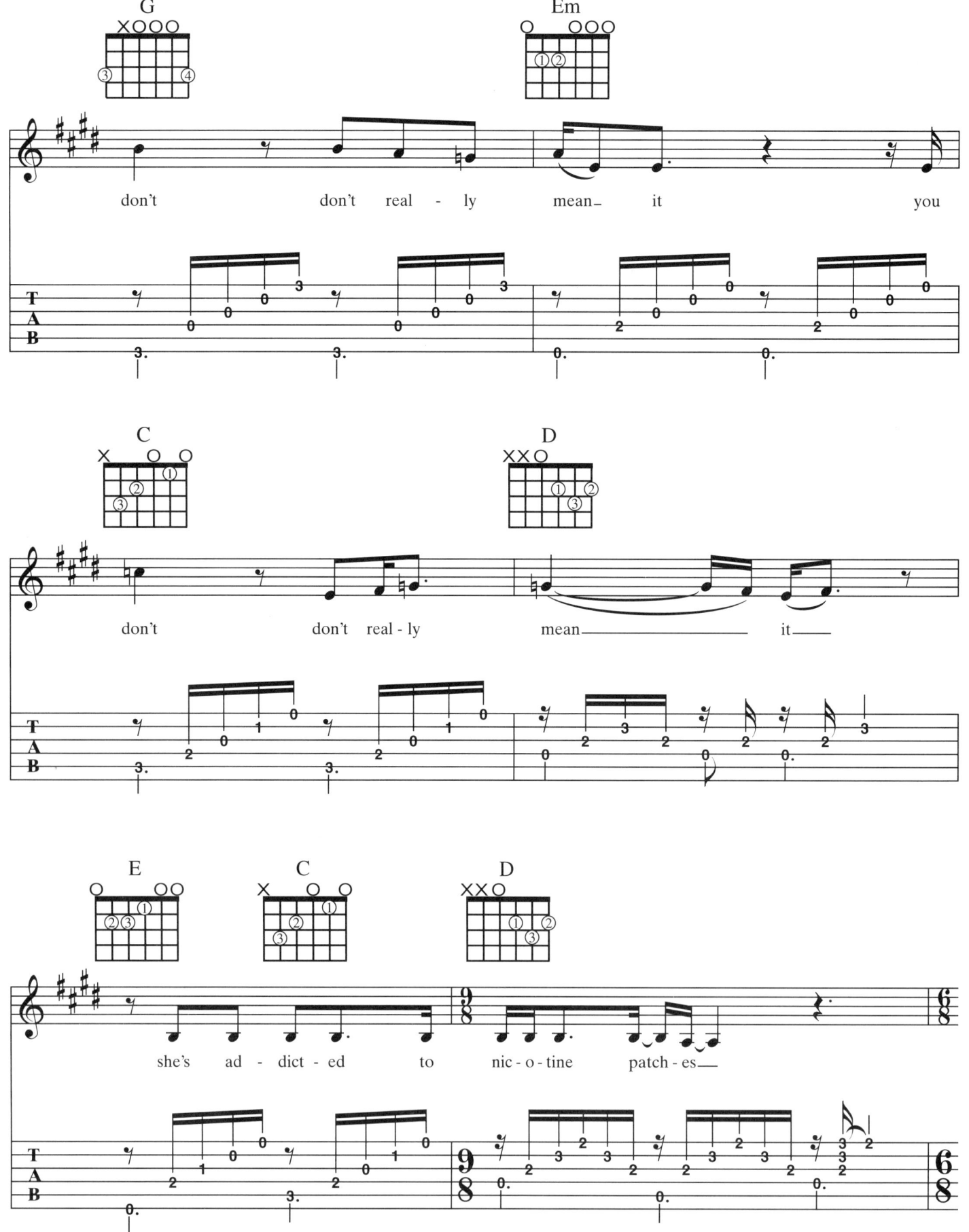

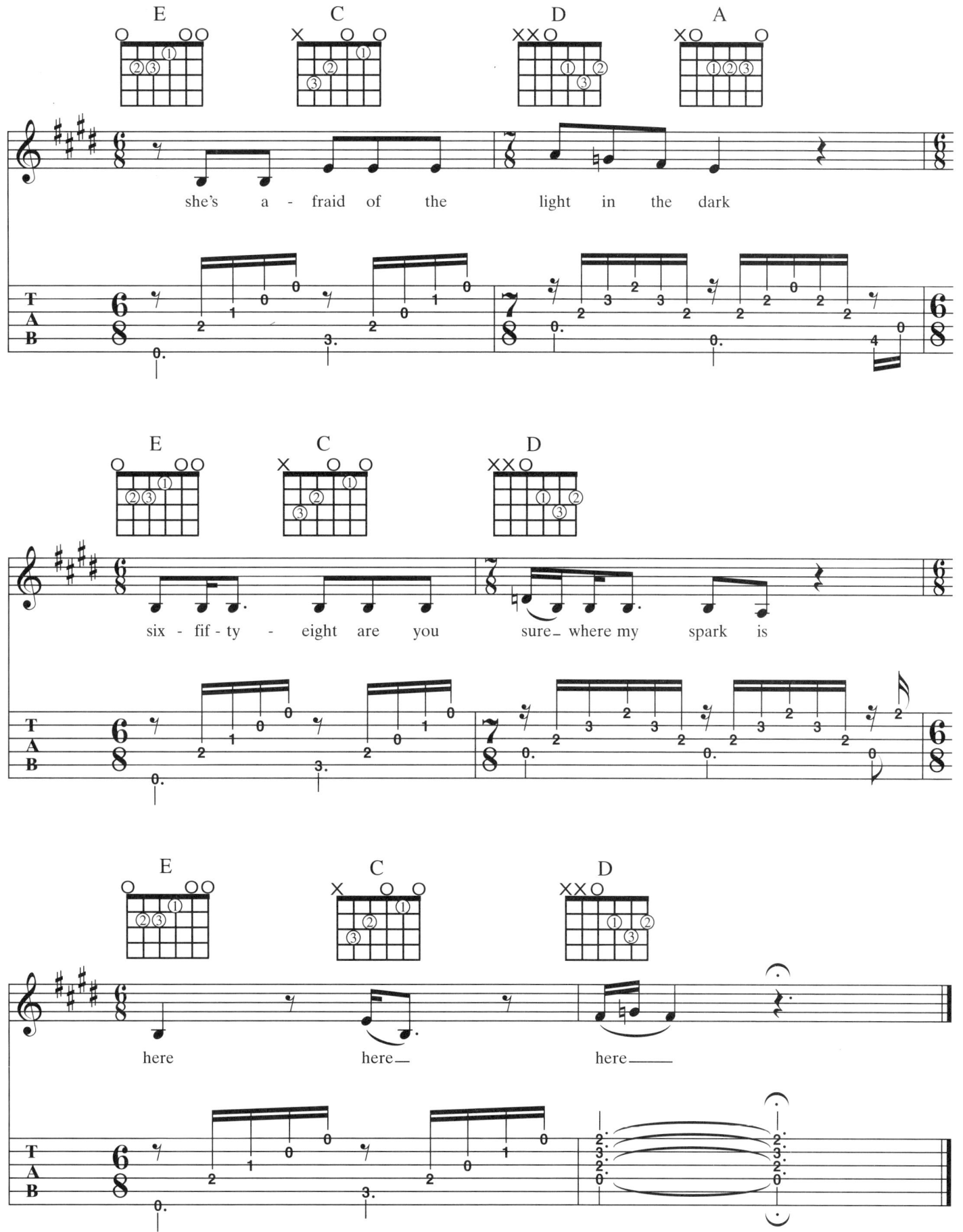

Black-Dove (January)
Words and Music by Tori Amos

melody note for voice

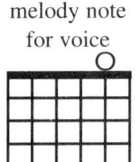

Moderately slow

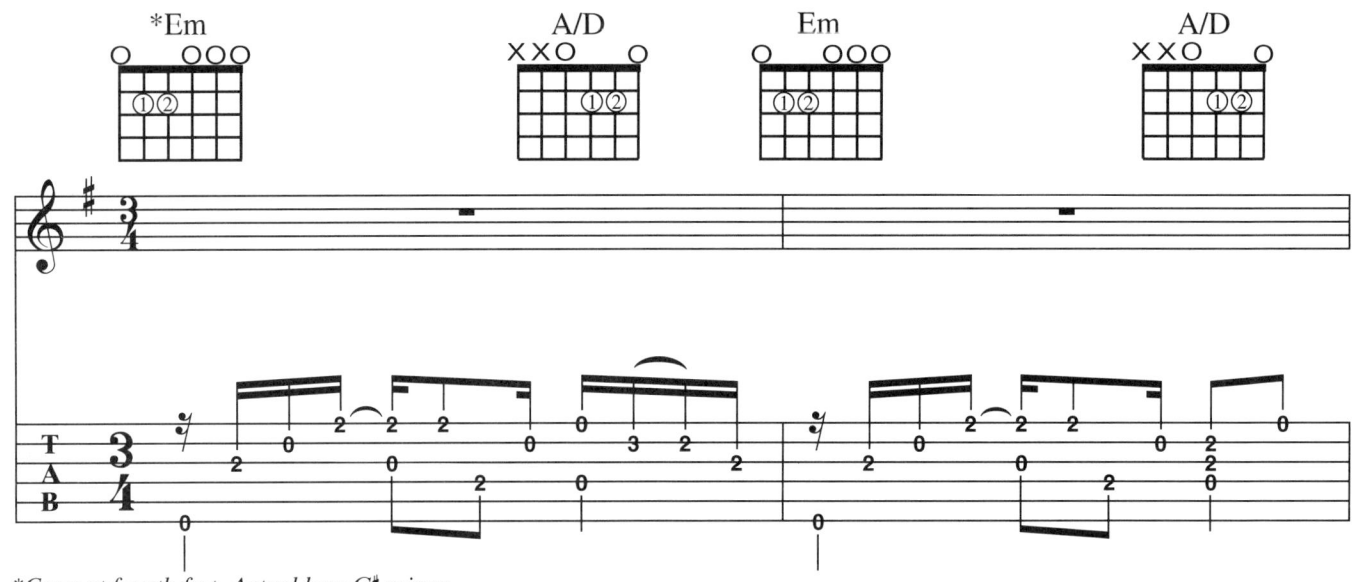

*Capo at fourth fret. Actual key: G# minor

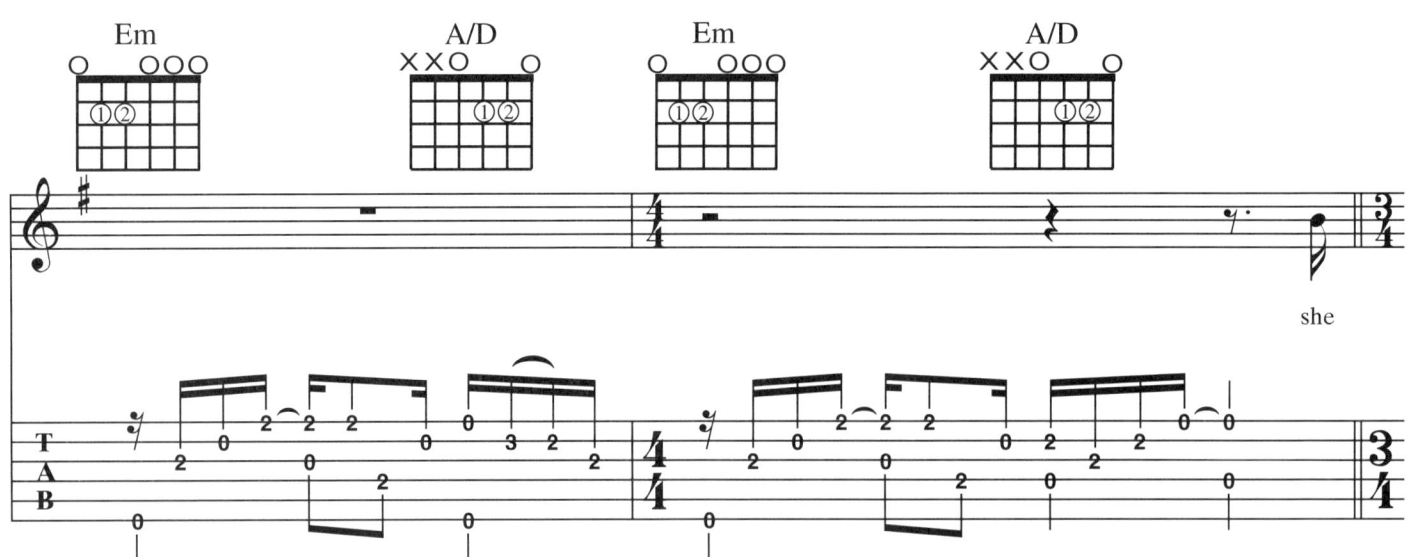

she

Copyright © 1997 Sword and Stone Publishing Inc. (ASCAP)
International Copyright Secured. All Rights Reserved.

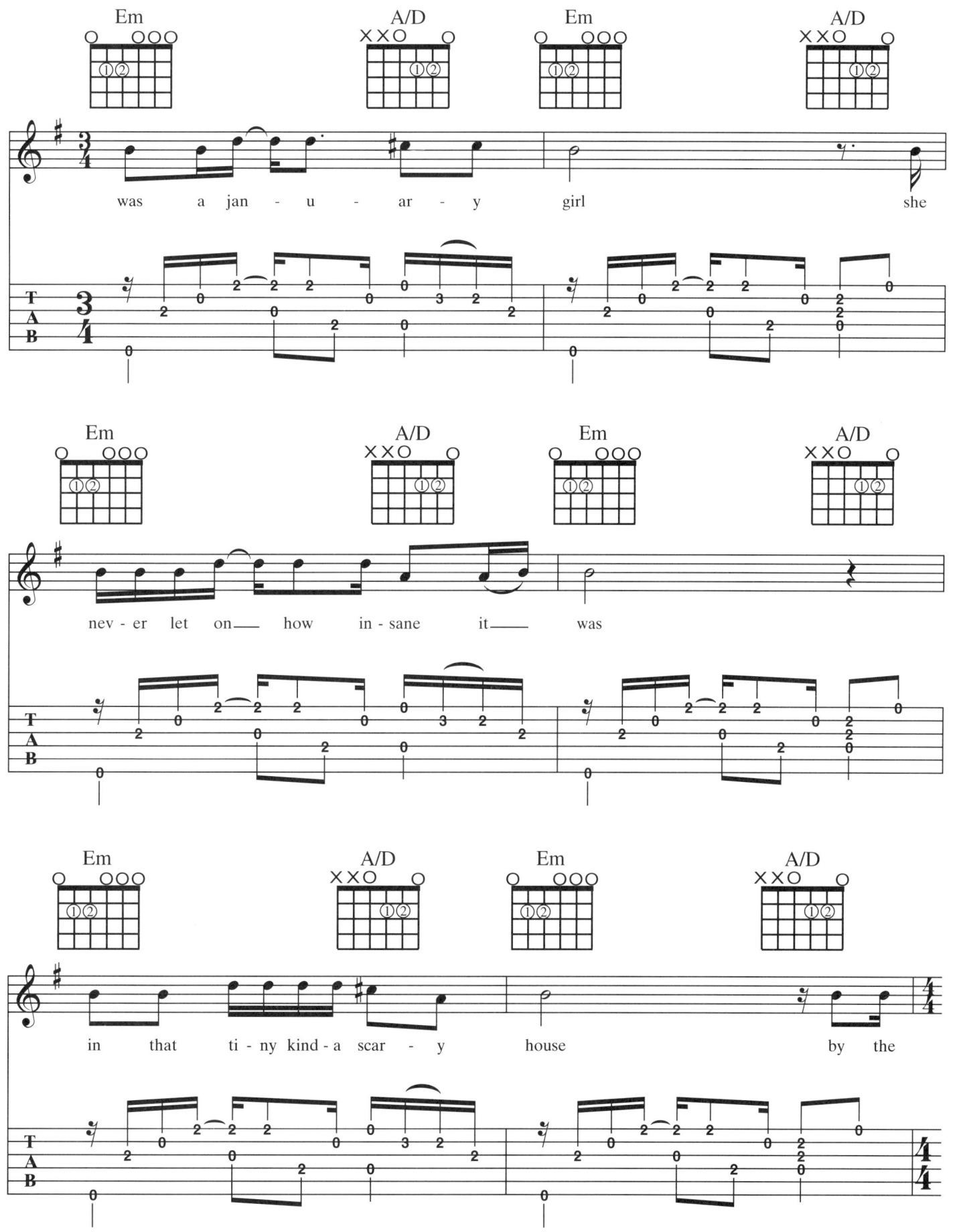

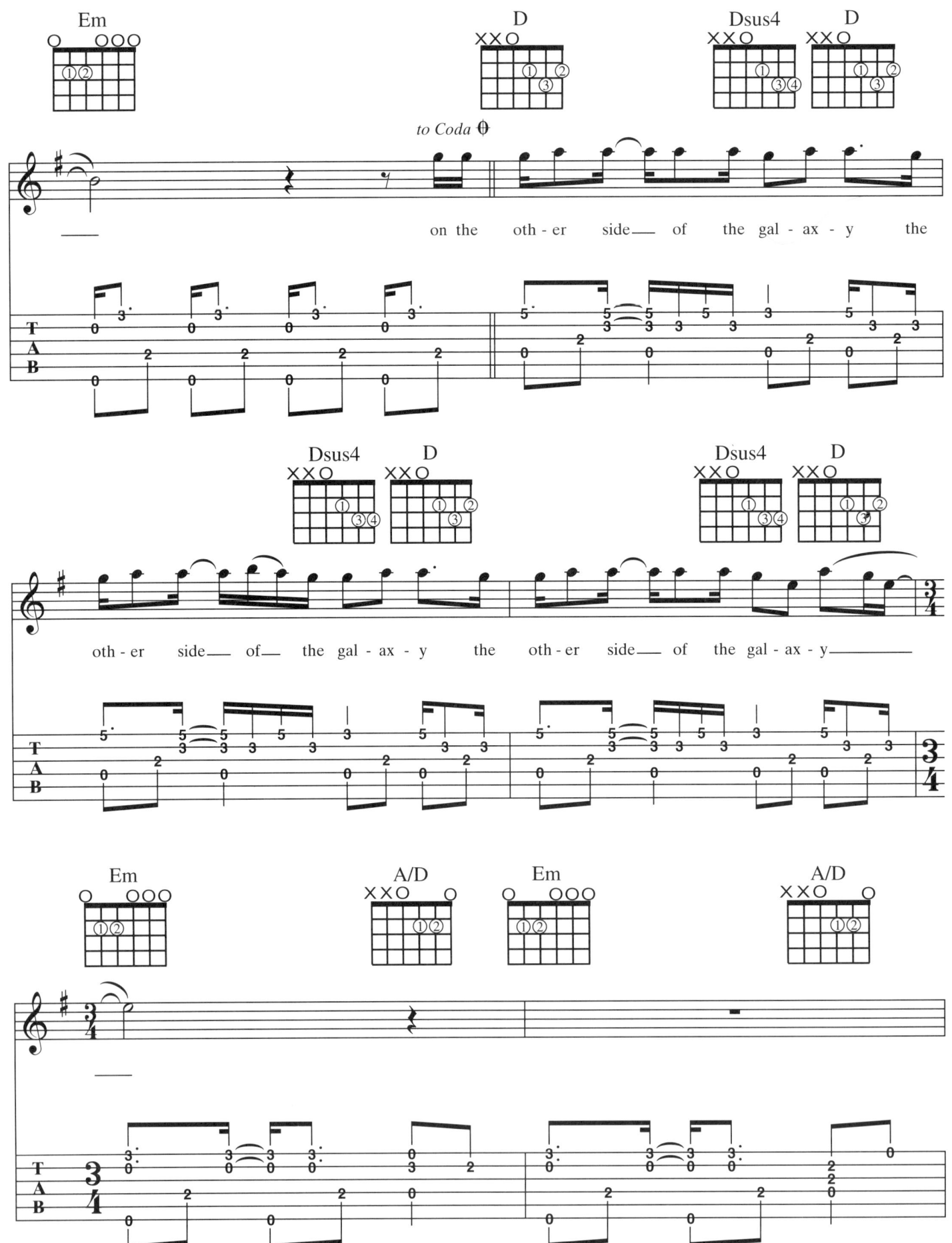

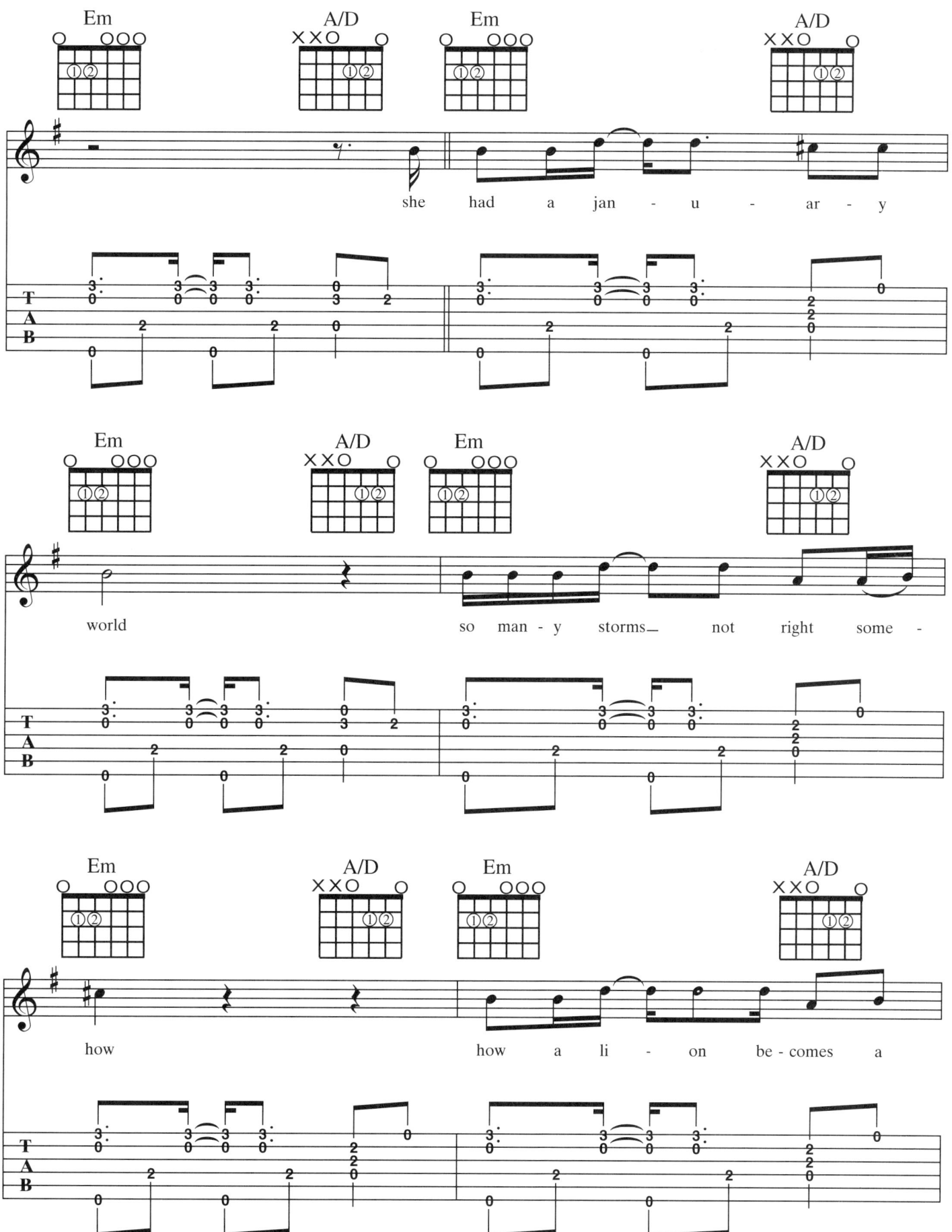

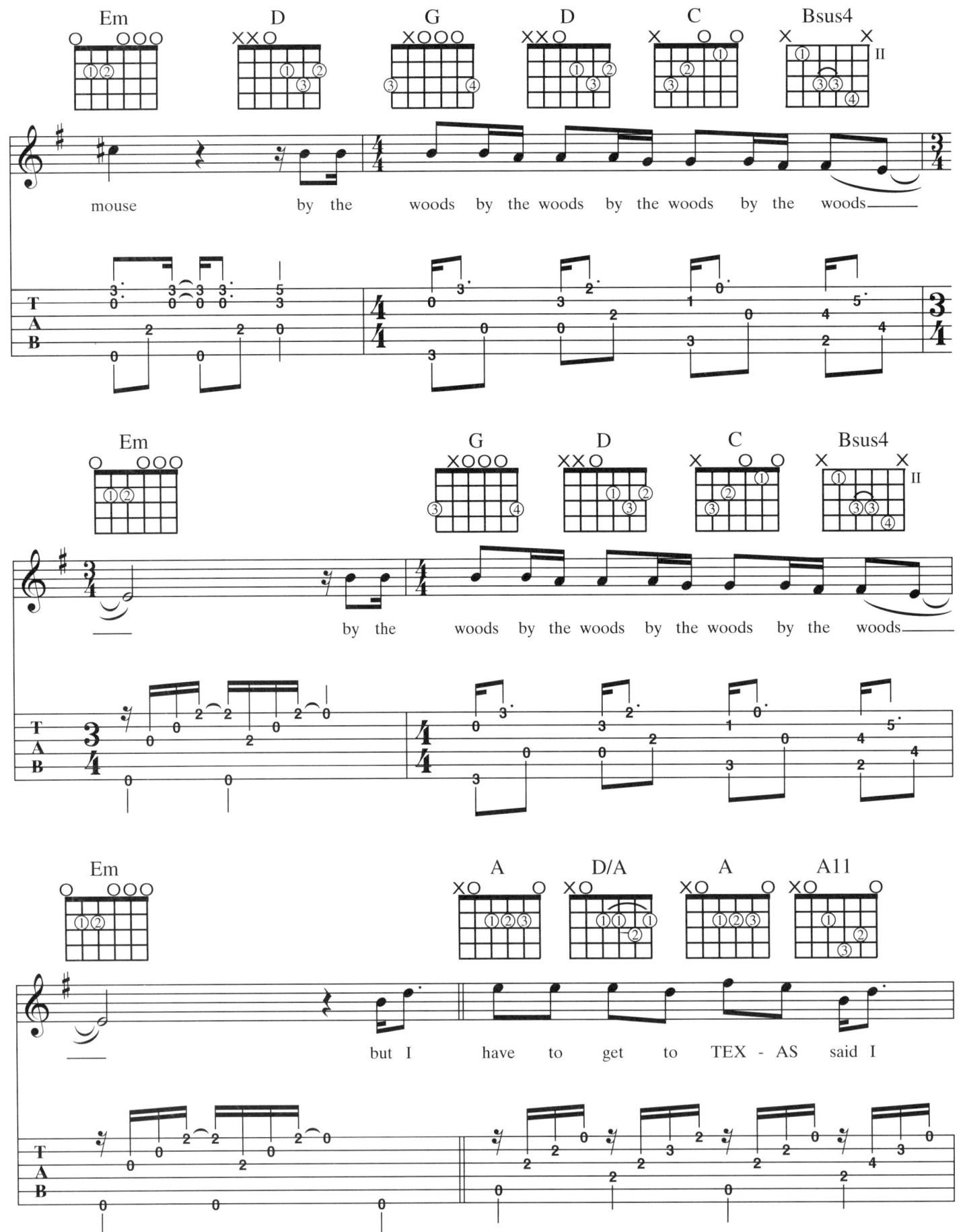

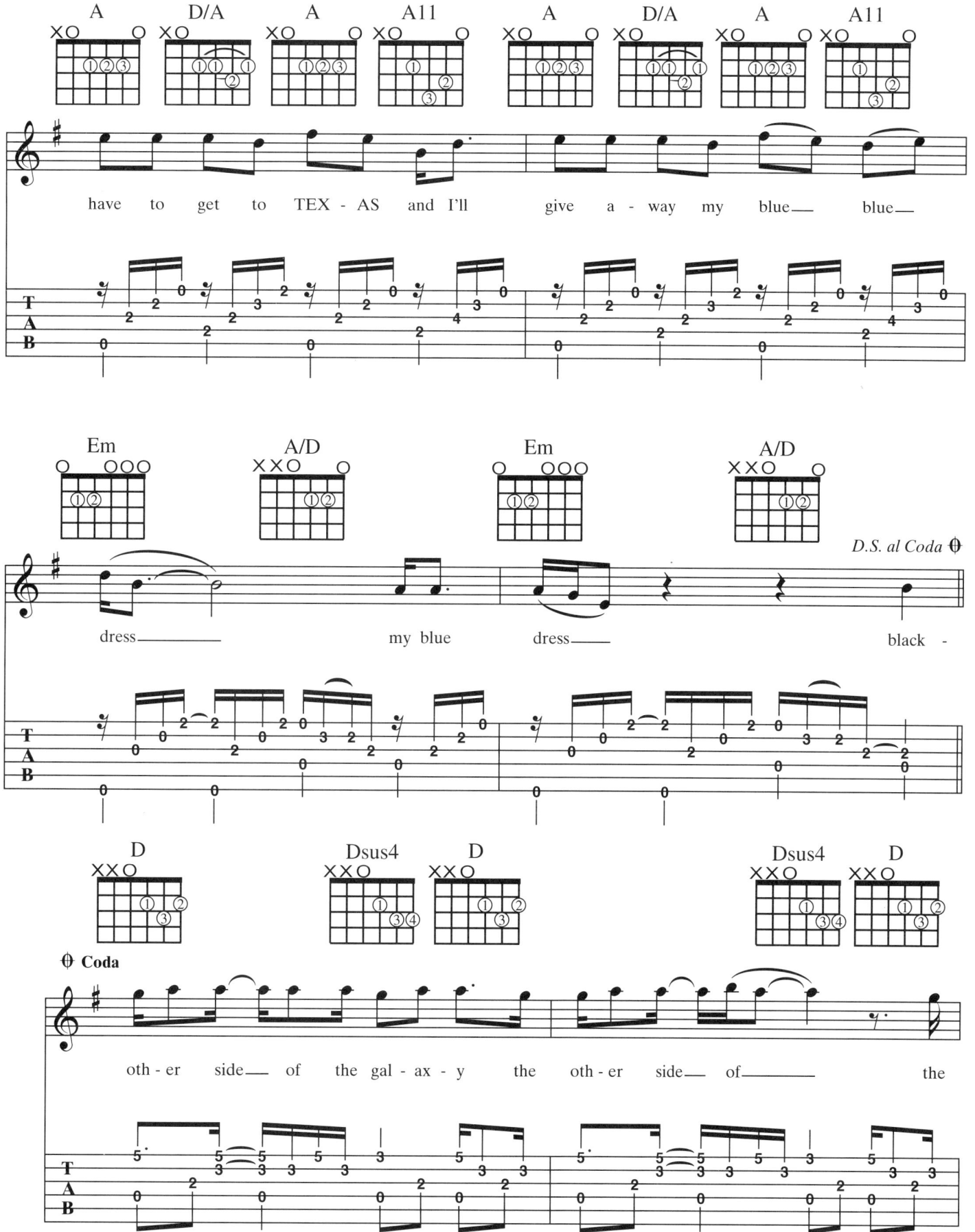

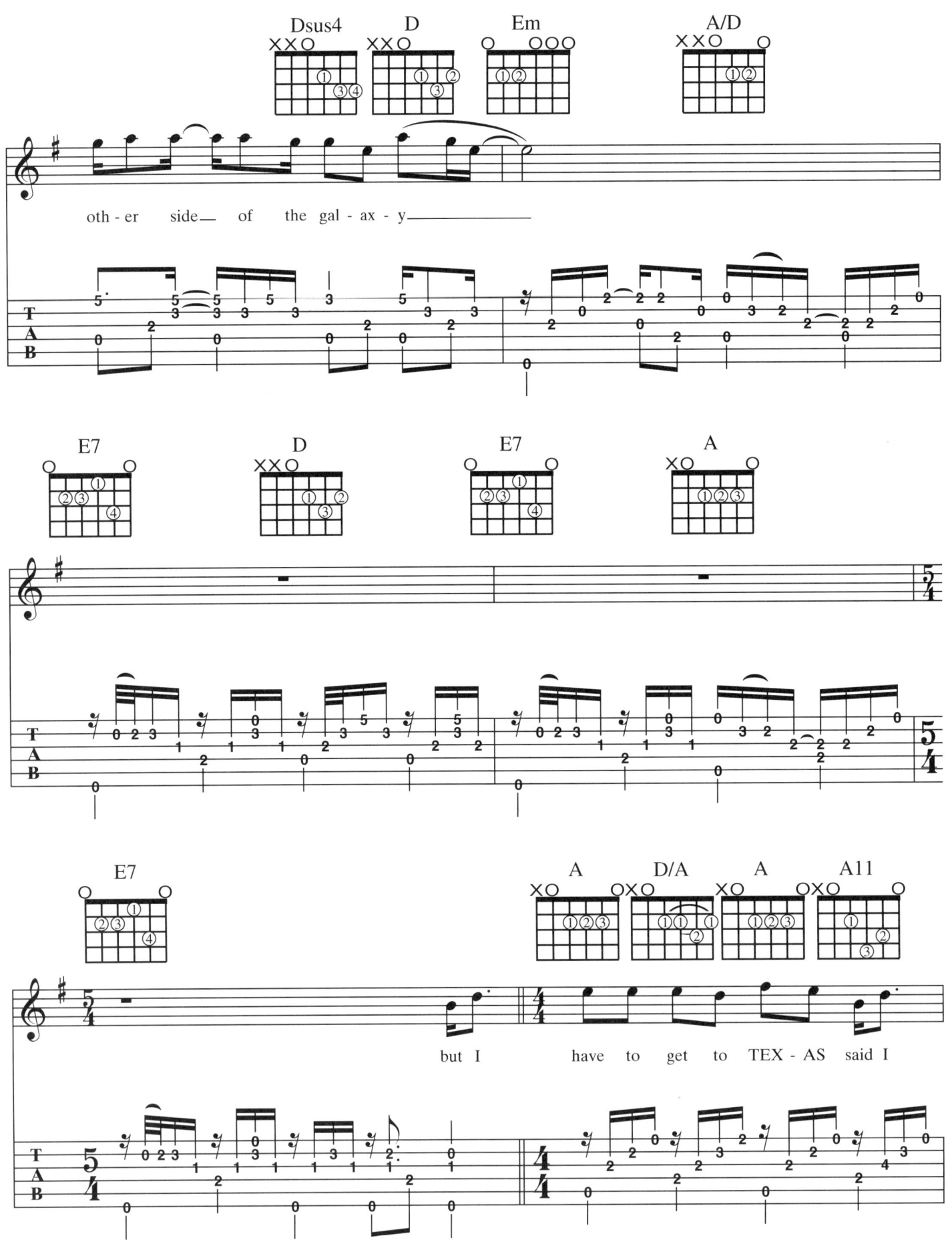

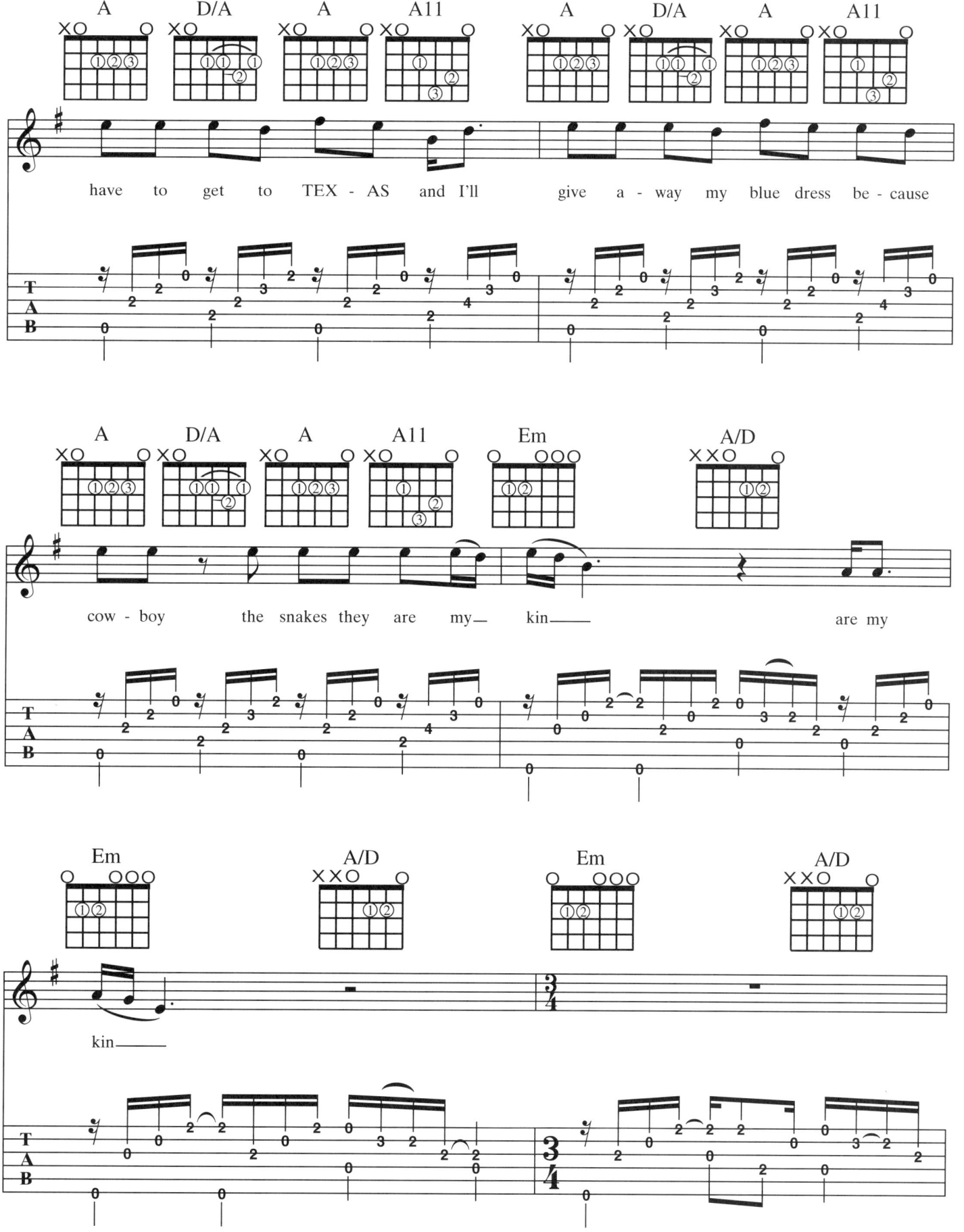

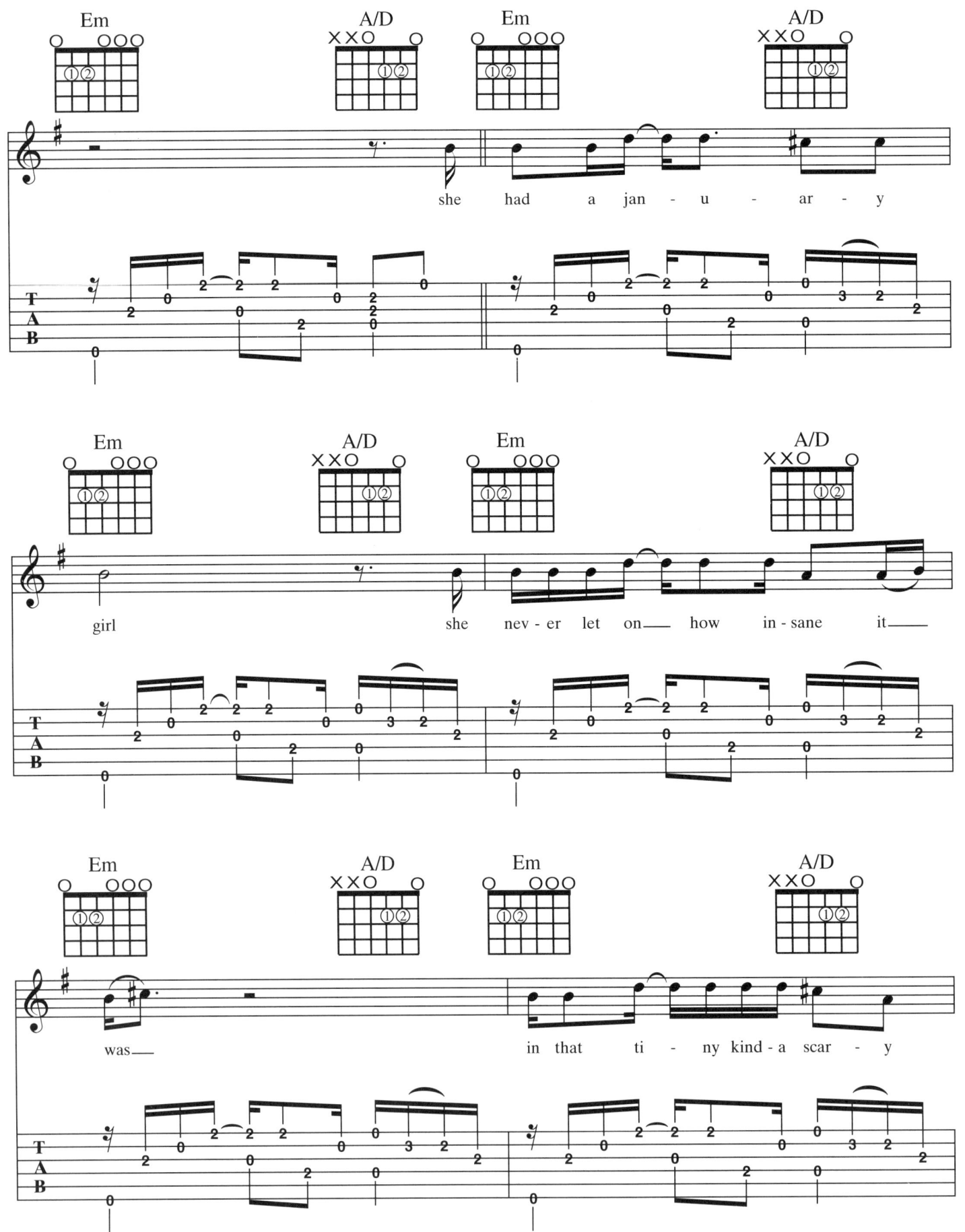

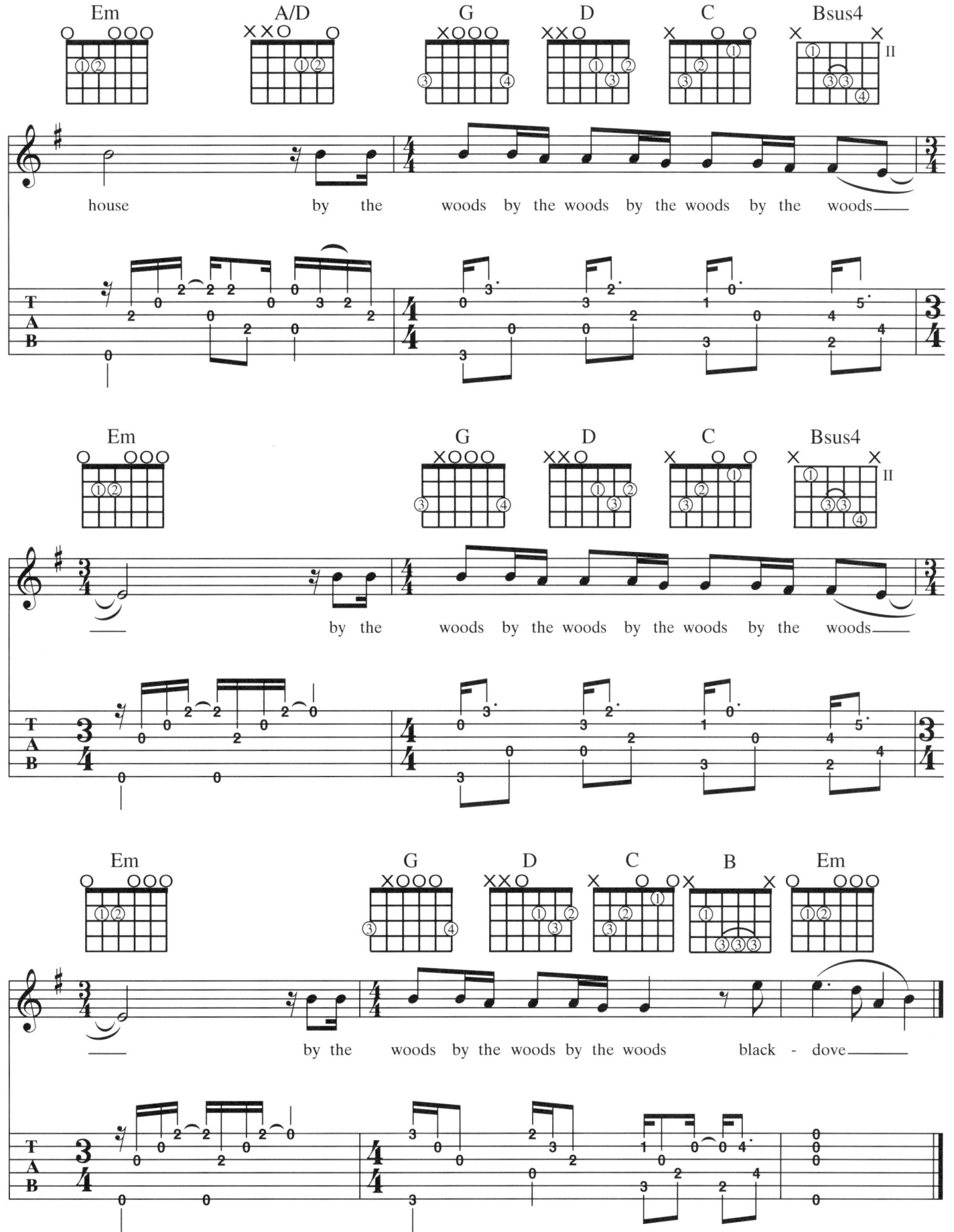

Talula
Words and Music by Tori Amos

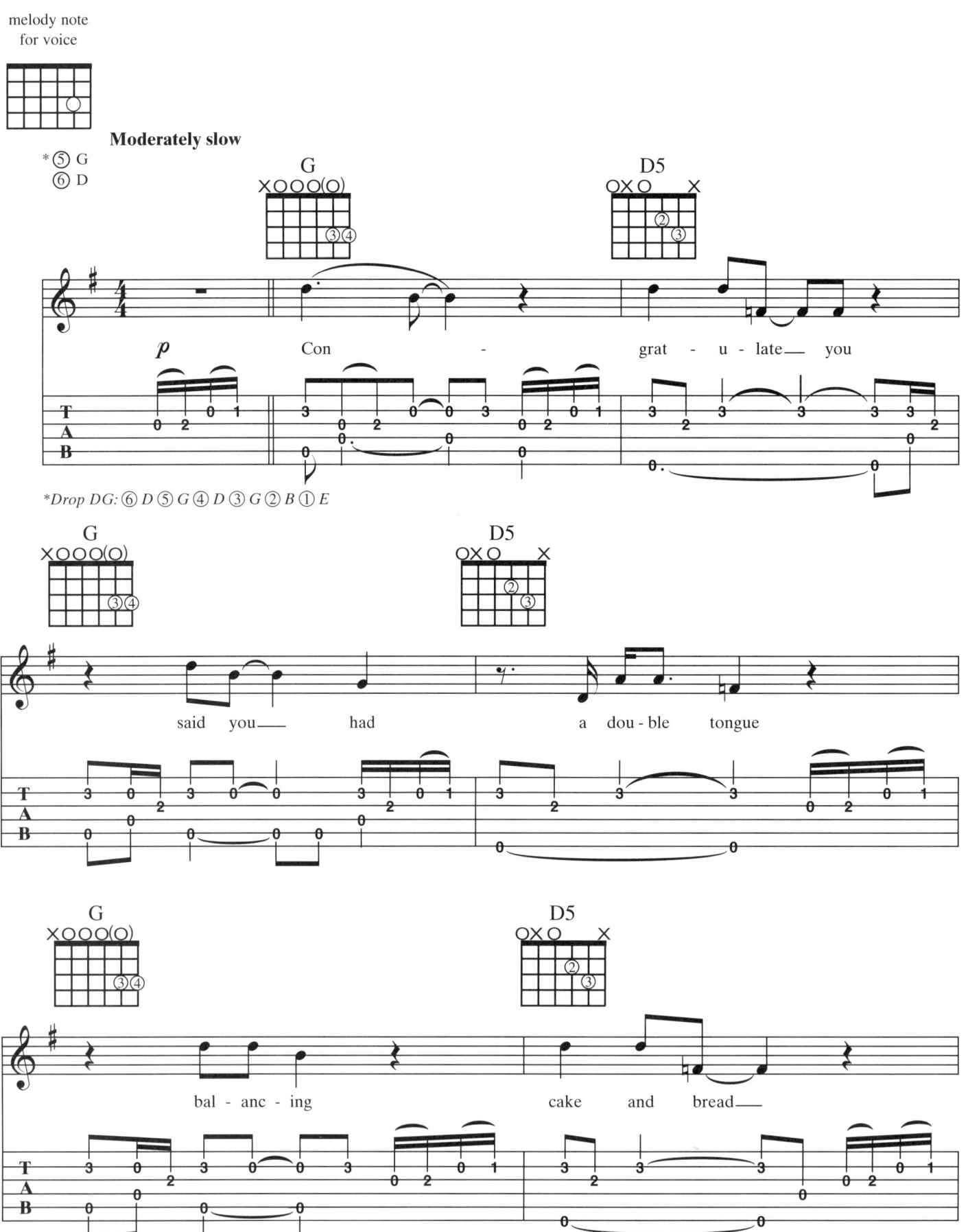

*Drop DG: ⑥ D ⑤ G ④ D ③ G ② B ① E

Copyright © 1995 Sword and Stone Publishing Inc. (ASCAP)
International Copyright Secured. All Rights Reserved.

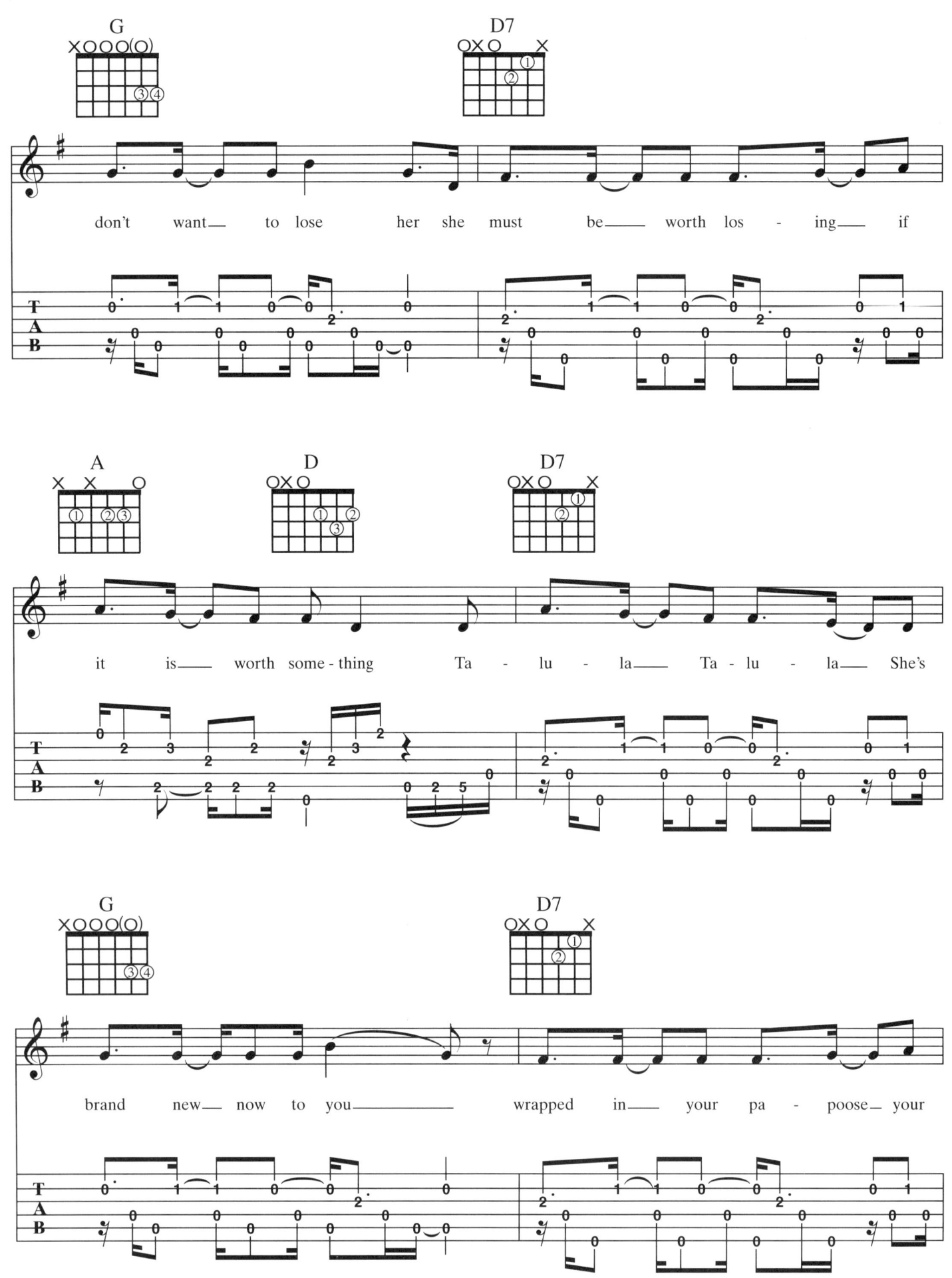

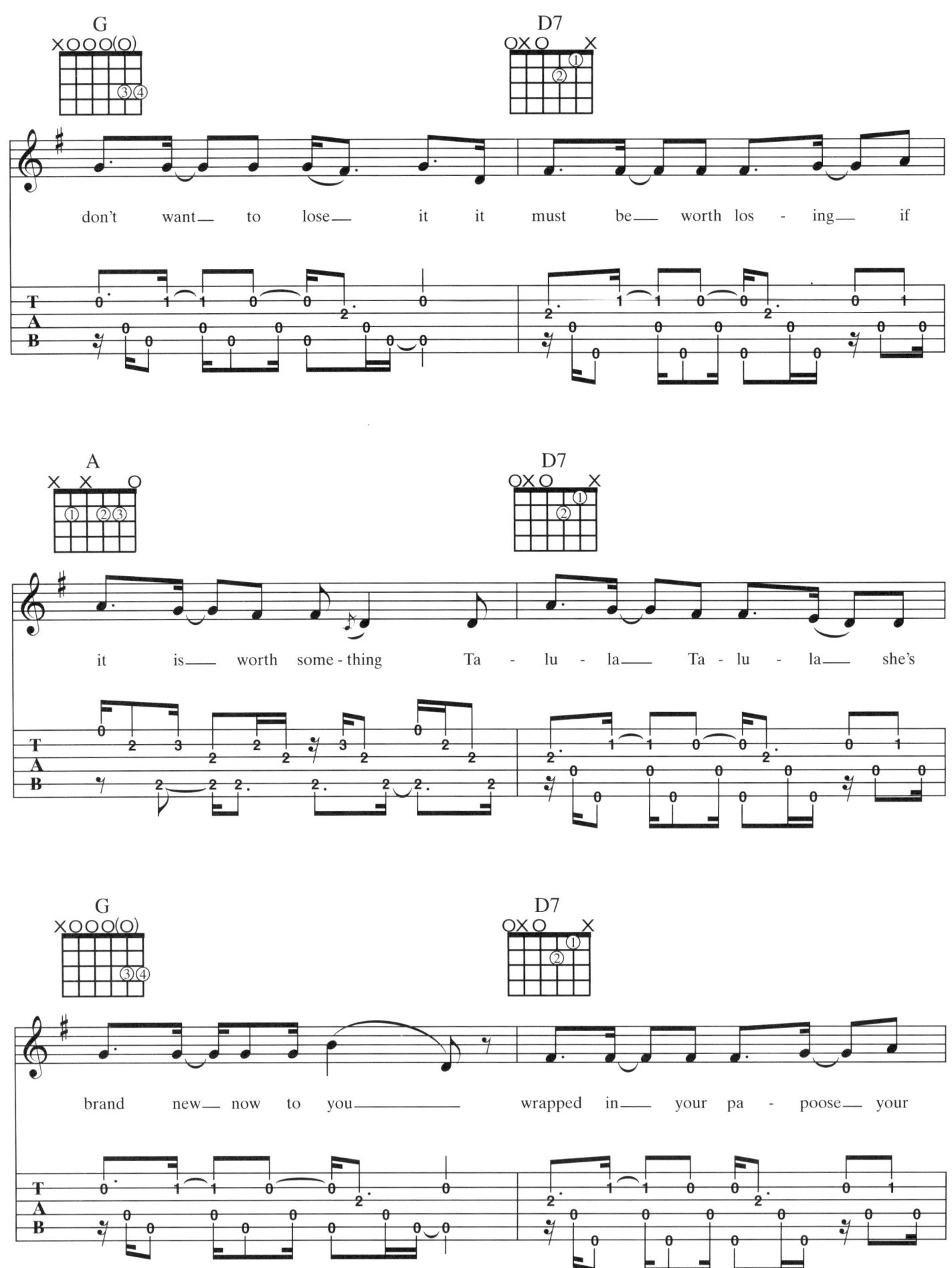

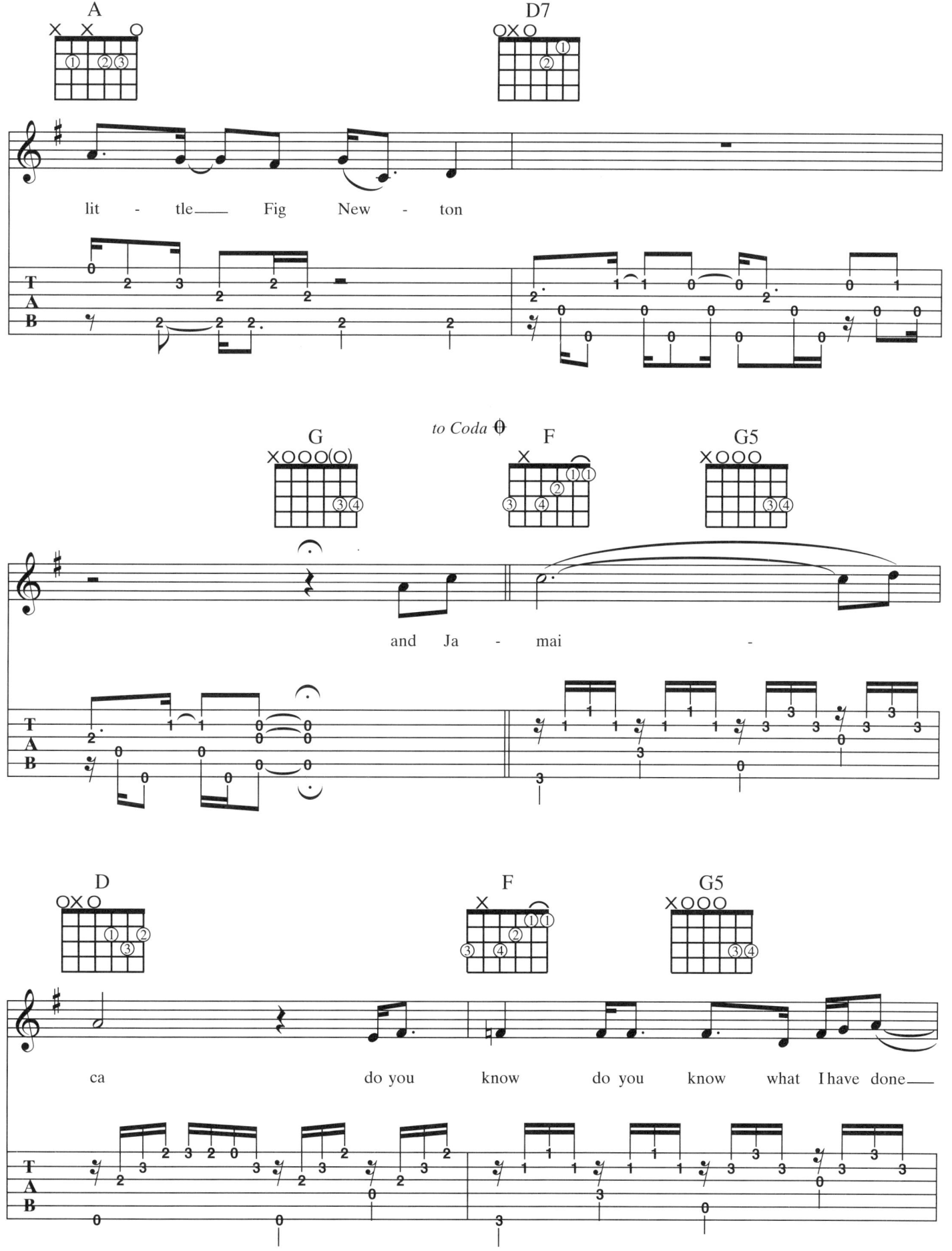

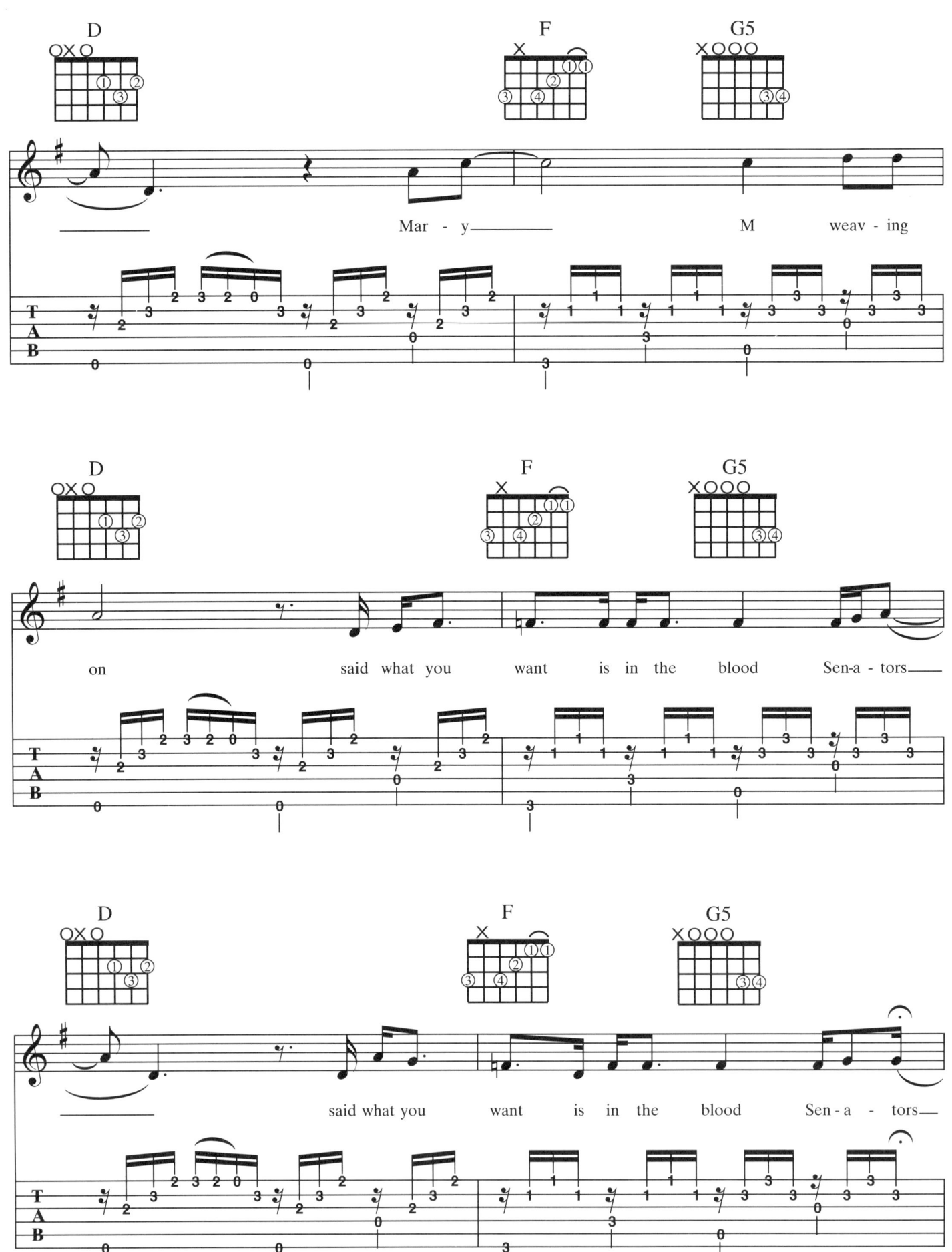

Winter

Words and Music by Tori Amos

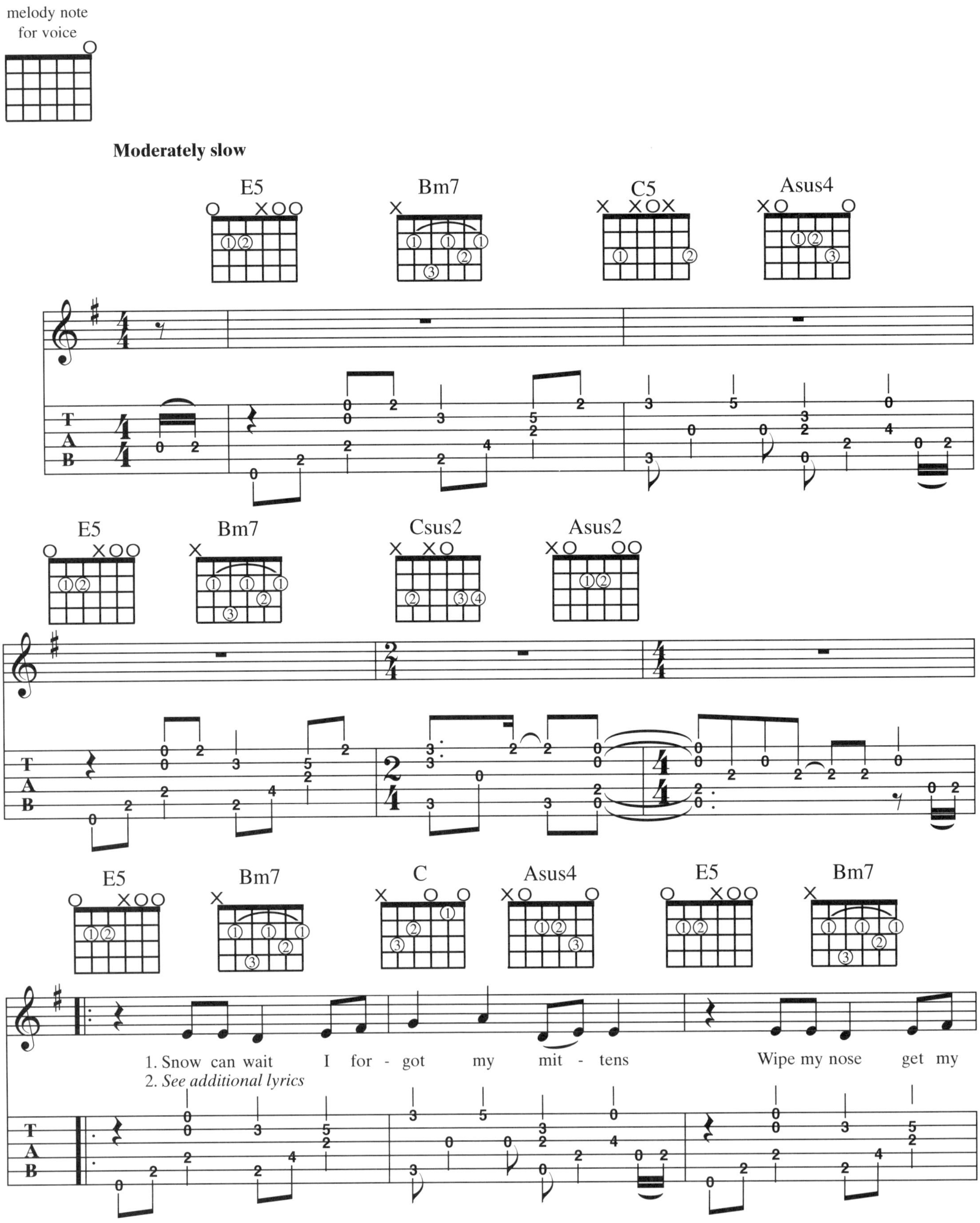

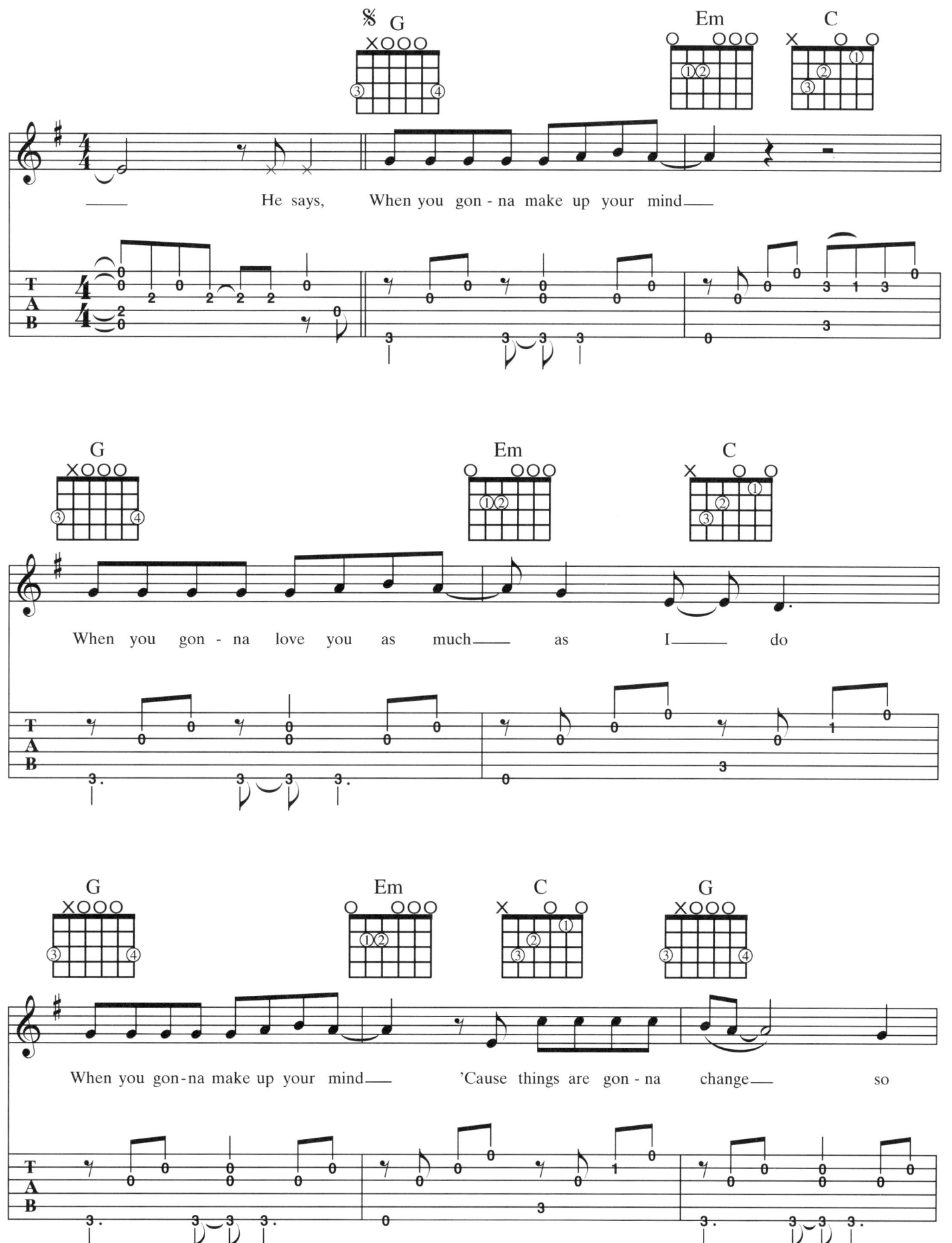

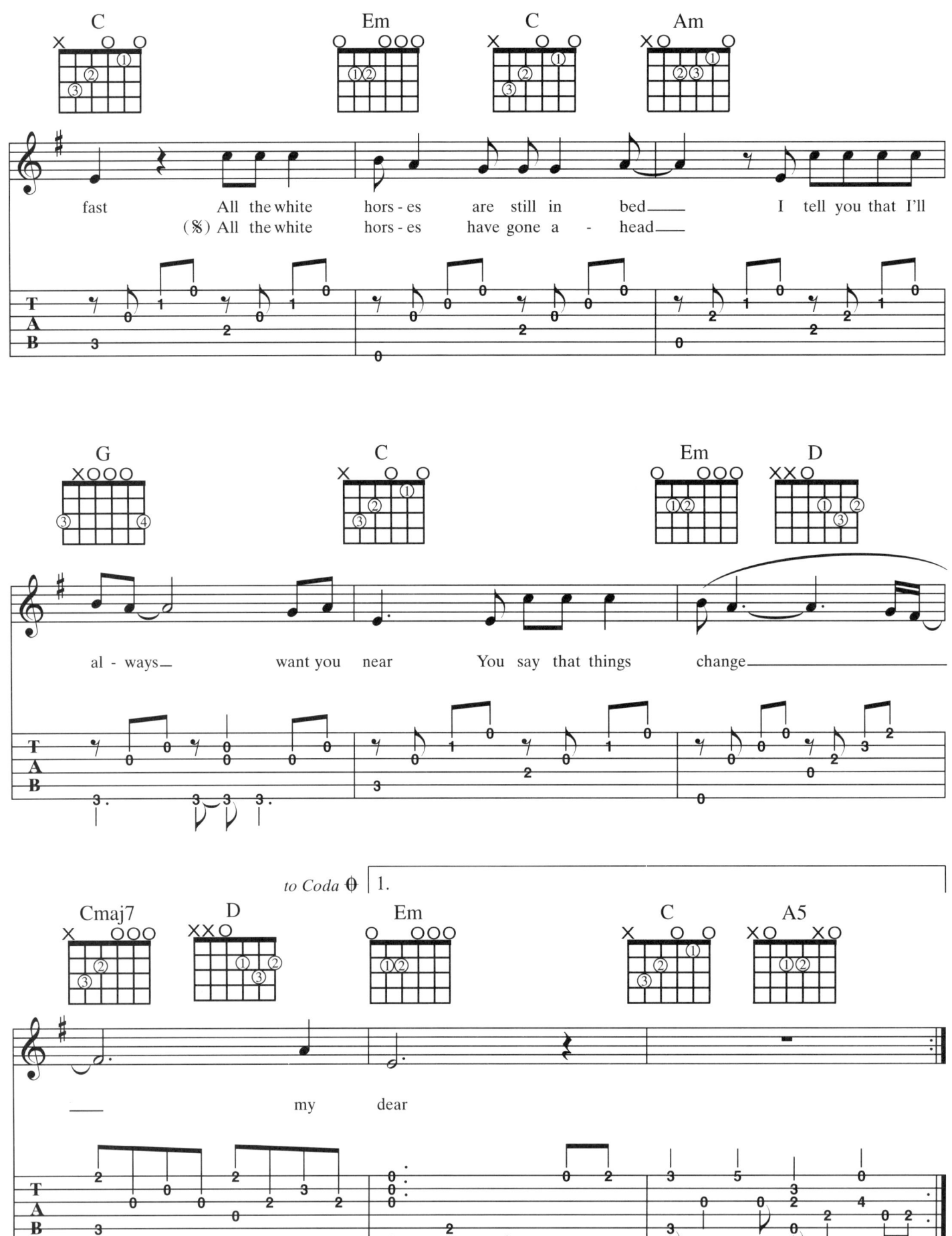

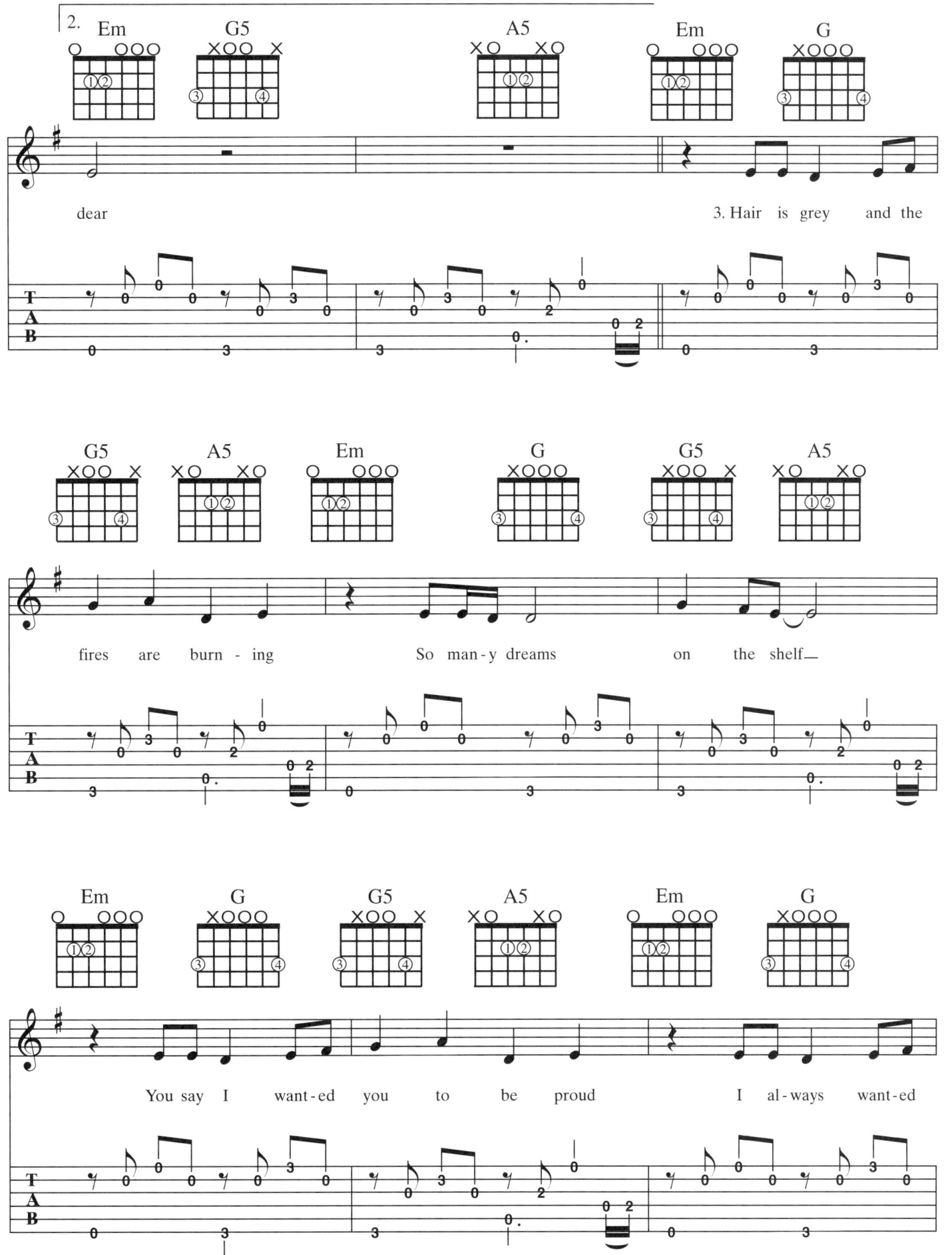

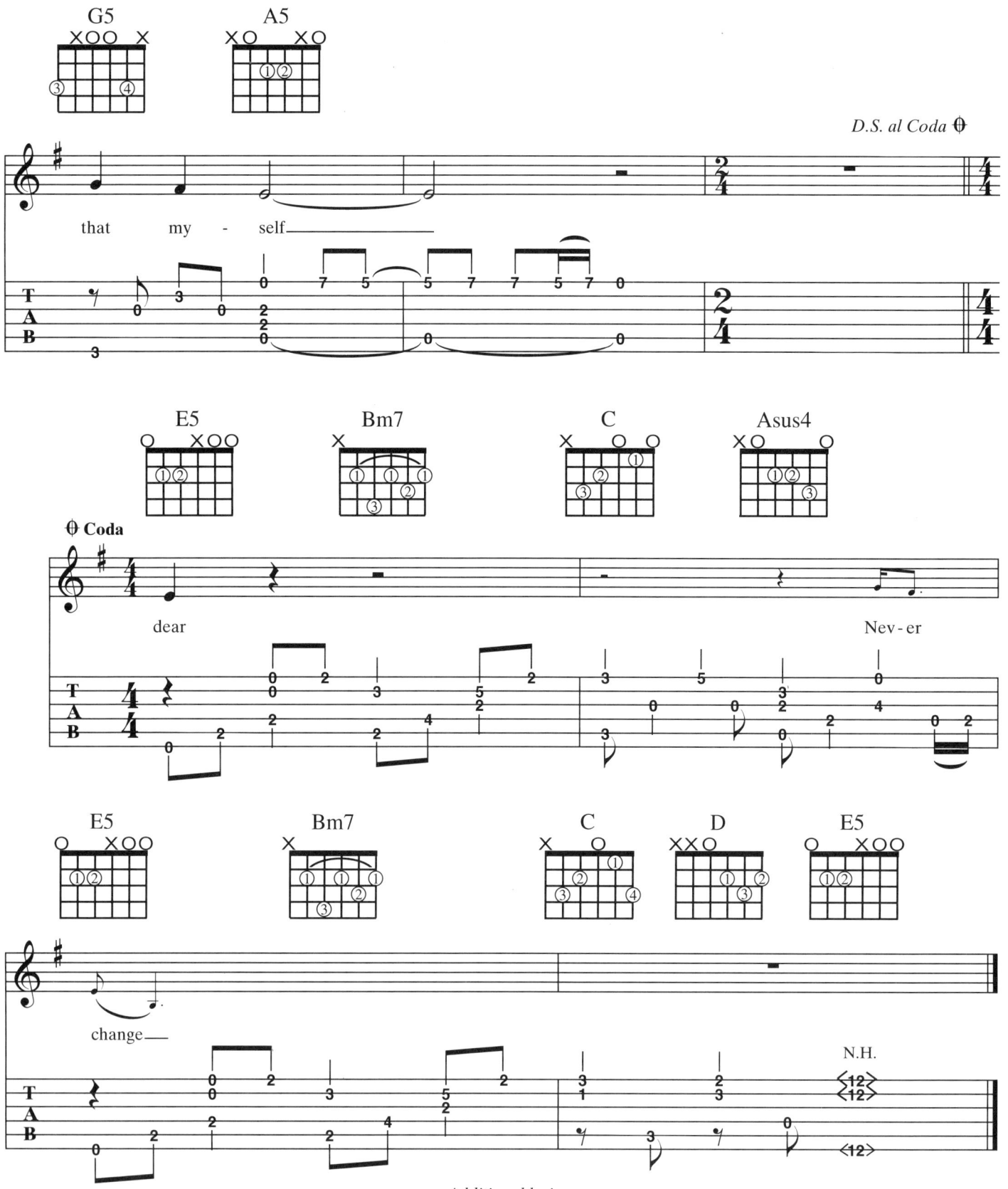

Additional lyrics

2. Boys get discovered as winter melts
   Flowers competing for the sun
   Years go by and I'm here still waiting
   Withering where some snowman was.

   Mirror mirror where's the crystal palace
   But I only can see myself
   Skating around the truth who I am
   But I know Dad the ice is getting thin.